D1400032

Tooth-Friendly Recipes, Table Manners and Tips for Dental Health
from the Alliance of the American Dental Association

Edited by Dinah Catey and Jan Miller

Foreword by James B. Bramson, D.D.S.

The Alliance of the American Dental Association is the organization of ADA-member
spouses committed to supporting the ADA through public oral health education,
legislative advocacy and the well being of the dental family.

Published by ICanPublish, North Manchester, Indiana
Bound by Heckman Bindery, Inc., North Manchester, Indiana
Printed by Modern Graphics, Inc., Peru, Indiana
Manufactured in the United States of America

10 9 8 7 6 5 4 3 2 1

Library of Congress Cataloging-in-Publication Data

Alliance of the American Dental Association
Dishing Up Smiles / Alliance of the American Dental Association

ISBN 0971148031

Library of Congress Control Number: 2004108545

table of contents

The nutritional analysis of recipes (excluding unknown items) has been computed using Deluxe MasterCook software.

foreword

foreword

As Executive Director of the American Dental Association, I am pleased to support the Alliance of the American Dental Association and its unique project, *DISHING UP SMILES*. In partnering with the ADA, the Alliance is dedicated to educating the American public about the importance of dental health.

The ADA has long recognized the important link between good oral health and healthy eating. Clearly, eating patterns, good food choices and proper nutrition are important factors for teeth and gums, but we know they are essential for overall health too. You cannot be healthy without good oral health.

Over seven out of every ten dentists are members of the American Dental Association. We're working hard as a professional organization to improve the public's oral health through education, service and research.

My congratulations to the Alliance of the ADA on this well-done publication — and Best Wishes to all its readers for a lifetime of good dental health!

James B. Bramson, D.D.S.
Executive Director
American Dental Association

introduction

The Alliance of the American Dental Association (AADA) is the national association of ADA-member spouses dedicated to raising public awareness of the importance of dental health. With active members from coast-to-coast, AADA promotes its message through involvement in a variety of educational programs in communities and schools across America.

In 2004, AADA is premiering its latest dental health education project, with publication of *DISHING UP SMILES* — Tooth-Friendly Recipes, Table Manners and Tips for Dental Health.

Within these pages, you will find special recipes from the kitchens of dental families across America, nutritional information for healthy eating, and facts about food and dental health — before and after receiving dental treatment. Dining etiquette from experts, dental health tips from the American Dental Association, and "educational" slogans from the children of America are also included.

The book is divided into nineteen sections — each sponsored by friends of dentistry committed to joining with the Alliance of the American Dental Association in advancing dental health in individuals of all ages.

We hope you will find *DISHING UP SMILES* not only pleasing to your palate — but also enlightening and entertaining!

abc
dental health tips

Dental Health Tips have been summarized from the American Dental Association Consumer Information website. Tips appear throughout the book.

For detailed tips to improve and maintain dental health, visit **www.ada.org**.

ADA Seal of Approval: Look for it!

Bacteria + bad brushing = bad breath.

Clean your tongue when you brush your teeth.

Dislodge food with dental floss—never with a sharp instrument.

Eat a balanced diet and limit between meal snacks.

Fluoride prevents tooth decay. Use products that contain it.

Guard your smile! Wear a mouthguard during contact sports.

Healthy smiles begin with eating healthy.

Infants' teeth can be harmed by letting babies fall asleep with a bottle of anything other than water.

Jaw or facial pain? Possible causes include toothache, sinus or TMD. A dentist can identify which one.

Knocked out tooth? Put it in milk and take it to the dentist quickly!

Lip or tongue bitten? Clean gently and apply a cold compress; if bleeding won't stop, go to the ER.

Maintain a healthy diet for optimum health.

Never put aspirin on an aching tooth. It can burn your gums.

Oral health habits are vital during puberty, menstruation, pregnancy and menopause.

Prevent plaque by brushing twice a day.

Questions about your oral health? Ask an ADA-member dentist.

Rinse with a mouthwash containing fluoride for added decay prevention.

Sores in the mouth lasting longer than two weeks need a dentist's attention.

Toothbrush replacement: Every 3 or 4 months—and more often for children.

Use only your own toothbrush!

Visit your dentist twice a year for cleanings and oral exams.

Wipe your baby's gums with clean gauze or cloth after each feeding. Start dental visits by age one or when the first tooth appears.

X-rays detect dental problems early—saving you time, money and unnecessary discomfort.

Your teeth will last a lifetime—if you take care of them!

Zzzz: Grind when you sleep? See a dentist for a nightguard.

breakfast & brunch

afternoon tea

appetizers & dips

soups & stews

salads

rice, pasta & sides

vegetables

tex-mex

poultry

dishing up smiles

Tooth-Friendly Recipes, Table Manners and Tips for Dental Health
from the Alliance of the American Dental Association

beef

pork

fish & seafood

goat

LOVE YOUR DENTIST

desserts

cookies, cakes & pies

chocolate

stop the pop!

dining check-u

breakfast & brunch

ingredients:

eating bread and butter

Bread, toast or rolls are offered at most meals. There are tricks to eating bread and ways to avoid using the wrong bread and butter (B&B) plate.

- Individual B&B plates are always on the left of the dinner plate.

- An individual butter knife is usually set at the top or on the right of the B&B plate, with the blade facing inward. If a butter knife is not offered, use a dinner knife and rest it across the top of the B&B plate during use.

- If a common butter is passed, take a small portion and place it on your B&B plate.

- If B&B plates are not offered, place the bread at the edge of your salad or dinner plate.

- Break and butter bread and rolls one bite at a time over your B&B plate—not in mid air.

- Breaking and buttering *one bite at a time* also applies to toast. When pre-buttered toast is served, break in bite-size pieces to spread jam.

- Eggs are commonly served at breakfast. Refrain from dipping toast in a soft yolk when eating out. Use your bread as a pusher.

- Crispy bacon can be picked up with your fingers; otherwise, use a knife and fork.

- In passing rolls, bread or other food items, always pass to the right. If you are the one who starts the passing, refrain from taking your portion until it comes back around.

buttery sweet french toast

Susan Barsness, IL

serves 12

6	eggs
1/2	cup half and half
2	tablespoons sugar
1	teaspoon ground cinnamon
5	tablespoons orange juice — no pulp
1	tablespoon vanilla — pure
2	tablespoons lemon juice
4	tablespoons butter
12	slices bread

Per Serving: 162 Calories; 8g Fat (45.7% calories from fat); 5g Protein; 17g Carbohydrate; 1g Dietary Fiber; 108mg Cholesterol; 206mg Sodium.

Exchanges: 1 Grain(Starch); 1/2 Lean Meat; 0 Fruit; 0 Non-Fat Milk; 1 1/2 Fat; 0 Other Carbohydrates.

In a large bowl, **whisk** together all ingredients except butter.

Dip 1 slice bread into egg mix being sure to coat both sides.

Melt butter on griddle, careful not to burn butter.

Place bread on griddle, **flip** after one minute, repeat.

Total cooking time is 3-4 minutes or until bread is golden brown on both sides.

Repeat with each slice of bread. May need to **add** more butter to griddle.

To **serve** all at the same time, **place** on platter in warm oven until ready to use.

For special treat, cover with warm maple syrup and sprinkle powdered syrup on top.

"So good the kids cannot get enough!" quotes

"do you brush good, floss twice a day? You should, to help stop tooth decay"

Kevin, Grade 4

cheese and ham quiche
Jackie Davis, IN

serves 8

1	pie crust (9 inch) — unbaked
1	cup cooked ham — diced
8	ounces shredded sharp cheddar cheese
2	teaspoons dried onion — minced
2	eggs
1	cup half and half
1/2	teaspoon salt
1/8	teaspoon pepper

Per Serving: 302 Calories; 22g Fat (65.1% calories from fat); 14g Protein; 13g Carbohydrate; 1g Dietary Fiber; 97mg Cholesterol; 703mg Sodium.

Exchanges: 1/2 Grain(Starch); 1 1/2 Lean Meat; 0 Vegetable; 0 Non-Fat Milk; 3 1/2 Fat.

Preheat oven to 400 degrees.

Bake unfilled pie shell.

Mix ham, cheese and onion and **place** in pie shell.

In a small bowl, **whisk** eggs, half and half, salt and pepper. **Pour** into pie shell.

Cover edges of pie shell with foil, bake 400 degrees, 35-40 minutes or until knife inserted in center comes out clean.

Let **stand** 10 minutes before cutting. **Serve.**

May freeze up to three months.

4

cinnamon coffee cake

Debbie Brown, IL

serves 16

topping

1/3	cup brown sugar
1/4	cup granulated sugar
1	teaspoon cinnamon
1	cup nuts — chopped
	sweet chocolate square — shaved

coffee cake

1/2	cup butter
1	cup granulated sugar
2	eggs
1	teaspoon vanilla
2	cups flour
1	teaspoon baking powder
1	teaspoon baking soda
1/2	teaspoon salt
1	cup sour cream

Per Serving: 275 Calories; 14g Fat (46.4% calories from fat); 4g Protein; 33g Carbohydrate; 1g Dietary Fiber; 45mg Cholesterol; 252mg Sodium.

Exchanges: 1 Grain(Starch); 1/2 Lean Meat; 0 Vegetable; 0 Non-Fat Milk; 2 1/2 Fat; 1 Other Carbohydrate.

Preheat oven to 350 degrees. **Grease** bundt or springform pan.

topping

In a small bowl, **mix** first 4 ingredients. **Set aside.**

coffee cake

In mixing bowl, **cream** butter and 1 cup granulated sugar.

Add eggs and vanilla.

In another bowl, **combine** dry ingredients. **Add** to egg mixture alternately with sour cream.

Place 1/2 batter in prepared bundt or springform pan.

Sprinkle with 1/2 topping mix.

Add rest of batter.

Sprinkle with rest of topping mix.

Bake 350, 35-40 minutes or until tests done.

Cool completely. **Garnish** with shaved chocolate before serving.

In the Middle Ages, before individual plates were used at the table, an aged slice of bread approximately six inches in diameter was used as a plate. The slice was called a trencher, from the French word trancher meaning, "to slice." Bread could also be used for a napkin or a spoon.

tidbits

cottage cheese raisin breakfast pie

Jan Miller, IN

serves 8

1	pound cottage cheese — small curd
3/4	cup granulated sugar
1/4	cup butter — melted
2	eggs
1	dash salt
2	tablespoons flour
1/2	cup raisins
1	pie crust (9 inch) — unbaked
	cinnamon

Preheat oven to 350 degrees.

In mixing bowl, **combine** first 6 ingredients. **Blend** well.

Stir in raisins.

Pour raisin mix into unbaked pastry shell.

Sprinkle with cinnamon.

Bake 350 degrees, 1 hour.

Per Serving: 325 Calories; 14g Fat (38.4% calories from fat); 11g Protein; 40g Carbohydrate; 1g Dietary Fiber; 67mg Cholesterol; 483mg Sodium.

Exchanges: 1 Grain(Starch); 1 1/2 Lean Meat; 1/2 Fruit; 2 1/2 Fat; 1 1/2 Other Carbohydrates.

"Pie for breakfast? Absolutely! Warm from the oven, this pie was a special treat at my grandmother's breakfast table during summer visits to Baltimore, Maryland."

"sugars in pop and candy don't make your teeth look dandy"

Anna Helene, Grade 2

"be smart
make your teeth
a work of art"

Brandi

festive french toast

Sue Ryser, UT

serves 10

3	tart apples — peeled, cored, thinly sliced
1	cup brown sugar
1/2	cup butter — melted
2 1/2	teaspoons cinnamon — divided
1/2	cup dried cranberries — or raisins
1	loaf french bread — cut into 1 inch slices
6	large eggs
1 1/2	cups milk
1	tablespoon vanilla

Per Serving: 346 Calories; 14g Fat (37.6% calories from fat);
9g Protein; 45g Carbohydrate; 2g Dietary Fiber; 142mg Cholesterol;
428mg Sodium.

Exchanges: 1 1/2 Grain(Starch); 1/2 Lean Meat; 1/2 Fruit;
0 Non-Fat Milk; 2 1/2 Fat; 1 Other Carbohydrates.

In 9x13 baking pan, **toss** apples with brown sugar, butter,
1 teaspoon cinnamon and cranberries until evenly coated.

Spread mixture evenly on bottom of pan. **Place** bread slices on
top of apple mix.

In medium bowl, **mix** eggs, milk, vanilla and 1 1/2 teaspoon
cinnamon.

Slowly **pour** egg mix over bread, soaking bread completely. **Cover.**
Refrigerate 4-24 hours.

Bake, covered, 375 degrees, 40 minutes. Uncover, **bake** additional
5 minutes.

Remove from oven. **Serve** warm.

" Fast, Easy, Delicious " quotes

granola

Paula Owens, TX

serves 50

42	ounces regular oats
16	ounces wheat germ — raw
12	ounces oat bran — raw
2	pounds sunflower seeds — unsalted, shelled
16	ounces coconut
2	cups pecans — chopped
2	cups sliced almonds
1	pound brown sugar
1 1/2	tablespoons salt
3	teaspoons vanilla
1/3	pound sesame seeds
2	cups water
1	cup oil

Per Serving: 431 Calories; 27g Fat (52.3% calories from fat); 14g Protein; 41g Carbohydrate; 9g Dietary Fiber; 0mg Cholesterol; 201mg Sodium.

Exchanges: 2 Grain(Starch); 1 Lean Meat; 0 Fruit; 4 1/2 Fat; 1/2 Other Carbohydrates.

Preheat oven to 250 degrees.

In extra large bowl, **mix** all ingredients well.

Spread an even, thin layer in a shallow pan.

Bake 250 degrees, 2 1/2 hours, stirring every 30 minutes. (May have to bake in batches.)

Store in airtight container.

" This favorite of family and friends can be used as a cereal adding fresh fruit, as a sprinkle for ice cream, eaten with cooked dried fruit or as a snack. "

"brush your teeth morning and night; keep your smile bright and white"

Samantha, Grade 3

"my dentist is my dad and my teeth are glad"

Sydney Age 7

ham and cheddar breakfast casserole

Paula Stahl, IN

serves 15

14	slices white bread — trimmed, buttered, cut in half
3	cups ham — diced
1	pound shredded cheddar cheese — divided
1/3	cup green pepper — minced, divided
5	eggs
2 2/3	cups milk
1/2	teaspoon paprika

Per Serving: 283 Calories; 17g Fat (53.4% calories from fat); 17g Protein; 15g Carbohydrate; 1g Dietary Fiber; 116mg Cholesterol; 709mg Sodium.

Exchanges: 1/2 Grain(Starch); 2 Lean Meat; 0 Vegetable; 0 Non-Fat Milk; 2 Fat.

Spray 9x13 baking dish.

Arrange half the cut bread slices on bottom of dish.

Layer all the ham, half the cheese and half the green pepper. **Repeat** bread, cheese and green pepper layers.

In mixing bowl, **combine** eggs and milk. **Mix** well. **Pour** over layers. **Sprinkle** with paprika.

Cover. Refrigerate overnight.

Bake 350 degrees, 45-50 minutes.

Serve hot.

" Delicious family favorite passed down from grandmother. Love to use this for holiday mornings and for overnight guests. "

hugo's breakfast crepes

Dr. Hugo Bertagni, IL

serves 12

crepes

6	eggs — beaten
1	cup milk
1	teaspoon vanilla
1	cup sugar — or substitute
1/2	stick butter — melted
1 1/2	cups flour, sifted

cottage cheese filling

16	ounces cottage cheese
1/2	cup sugar or sugar substitute
2	teaspoons vanilla

sour cream topping

16	ounces sour cream
1/2	cup sugar or sugar substitute
2	teaspoons vanilla

Per Serving: 381 Calories; 16g Fat (36.6% calories from fat); 11g Protein; 49g Carbohydrate; trace Dietary Fiber; 127mg Cholesterol; 251mg Sodium.

Exchanges: 1/2 Grain(Starch); 1 Lean Meat; 0 Non-Fat Milk; 2 1/2 Fat; 2 Other Carbohydrates.

crepes

Mix first 5 ingredients.

Continue stirring, **add** flour until mixture is runny pancake texture.

Heat crepe pan.

Pour egg mix in center of pan and roll to cover bottom.

Turn once. **Cook** to light golden color on both sides.

Remove from pan. **Stack** on plate. **Cover** with cloth to keep warm.

When ready to serve, **place** fresh fruit and/or preserves in center, top with cottage cheese mix. **Fold**.

Top with sour cream mixture.

cottage cheese filling

Mix all ingredients together, adding more sugar, if desired.

sour cream topping

Mix all ingredients together adding more sugar, if desired.

" When the kids were all home, I made these every Sunday morning as a special treat. "

sausage biscuits

Karla Daubenspeck, FL

serves 12 • yields 24 biscuits

2 1/2   cups baking mix

2   pounds sausage, seasoned, cooked and drained

1/2   pound grated sharp cheddar cheese

1/2   cup water — (may add up to 3 tablespoons more)

Per Serving: 492 Calories; 40g Fat (73.8% calories from fat); 15g Protein; 17g Carbohydrate; 1g Dietary Fiber; 71mg Cholesterol; 914mg Sodium.

Exchanges: 1 Grain(Starch); 2 Lean Meat; 7 Fat.

Preheat oven to 400 degrees.

In large mixing bowl, **combine** all ingredients lightly, just until evenly mixed.

Drop by tablespoon on cookie sheet.

Bake 400 degrees, 10 minutes or until lightly browned.

Best if served warm.

"Originated by my mother, Helen Yates. A creative appetizer or side dish with eggs or fruit. Excellent for brunch."

spanish eggs

Sue Ryser, UT

serves 16

16   eggs — beaten

2   cups shredded mozzarella cheese

2   cups shredded cheddar cheese

8   ounces ham — cubed (or meat of your choice)

1/2   teaspoon onion salt

1/2   teaspoon garlic salt

2   cups milk

Per Serving: 212 Calories; 15g Fat (64.7% calories from fat); 16g Protein; 3g Carbohydrate; trace Dietary Fiber; 227mg Cholesterol; 518mg Sodium.

Exchanges: 2 Lean Meat; 0 Non-Fat Milk; 2 Fat; 0 Other Carbohydrates.

Nutritional analysis does not include toppings.

Preheat oven to 325 degrees. **Grease** 9x13 baking pan.

Mix all ingredients. **Pour** into prepared pan.

Bake 325, 40 - 45 minutes or until egg mixture is set.

Cut into squares. **Serve** warm.

Top with salsa, green peppers, green onions, guacamole and/or sour cream.

"A great breakfast or brunch casserole. Can be kept in refrigerator until ready to bake."

importance of baby teeth

Children need strong, healthy teeth to chew their food, speak properly and have an attractive smile. Baby teeth also keep a space in the jaw for the adult teeth. If a baby tooth is lost too early, the teeth beside it may drift into the empty space. When it is time for the adult teeth to come in, there may not be enough room—making the teeth crooked or crowded.

To help keep your child's baby teeth in place:

- Never allow your child to fall asleep with a bottle containing milk, formula, fruit juice or sweetened liquids, which can lead to decay.
- Wipe your baby's gums with a clean gauze pad after each feeding.
- Begin brushing your child's teeth when the first tooth erupts. Clean and massage gums in areas that remain toothless.
- If your local water supply does not contain fluoride, ask your dentist how your child should get it.
- Start regular dental visits by your child's first birthday. If you think your child has dental problems, take the child to the dentist as soon as possible.

"keep your teeth clean so they won't turn green"

Courtney, Age 6

afternoon tea

ingredients:

history of afternoon tea

The Seventh Duchess of Bedford, Anna, is given credit for initiating the ritual of Afternoon Tea. Because of the long hours between lunch and the evening meal, she suffered from afternoon "sinking spells". She remedied them with a tray of tea, bread and butter, and cake. Anna enjoyed the new habit so much she began inviting friends, and soon tea progressed from a simple "drink with jam and bread" to a full-blown social event among the aristocracy. Today, tea is the second most consumed beverage in the world; only water surpasses it.

there are several different forms of "tea"

- **Afternoon Tea** — is usually served between 3:00 and 5:00 p.m., but the hours are often stretched slightly in either direction. Along with choice of tea, it includes three distinct courses—tiny sandwiches first to blunt the appetite; then scones, and finally pastries.

- **Royal Tea** — The addition of champagne or sherry to the three courses giving it the distinction of royal.

- **High Tea** — is a simple but hearty sit-down meal. The menu often includes meat pies, Welsh rarebit, sausage, cold meats, breads, cheese, jam, butter, relishes, desserts, fruits and tea. High Tea is not a sophisticated or dainty event. It originated during the Industrial Revolution as the main meal of the day for workers who returned home very hungry after a long, hard day in the fields, shops, factories and mines. The food is placed on the table family style, and dishes are passed from guest to guest. Today, High Tea may also be offered in the form of a buffet supper, and alcohol may also be served.

all tea comes from the camellia sinensis plant

There are several types of tea:

- **Black** tea is fermented and requires steeping at least 3 minutes. Very few black teas require more than six minutes. Black tea may be taken with milk, sugar or lemon.

- **Oolong** tea is semi-fermented and usually requires 7 minutes to steep. Oolong teas are taken plain.

- **Green** tea is not fermented and requires only about 1 to 2 minutes to steep. Green teas are also taken plain.

- **Flavored** teas are produced by blending black tea with natural ingredients, such as mint leaves.

- **Finished** teas may also be sprayed with authentic or artificial essences.

- **Herb** and **floral** teas are not produced from the tea plant, Camellia Sinensis, but are blends of other herbs and flowers that are often processed, flavored and packaged. Unless they are blended with black tea, herbal concoctions do not contain caffeine.

bacteria + bad brushing = bad breath.

how to brew the perfect pot of tea

The essential ingredients for making an excellent pot of tea include a ceramic, china, porcelain or glass teapot, good tea leaves, fresh water and timing. The water is an important component to a fine pot of tea. If your tap water contains additives, it is best to use filtered or bottled water when preparing tea.

- Run cold water from the faucet for at least one minute, and then fill the tea kettle with sufficient water to warm the teapot and make the tea.
- When the water is near boiling, pour some into the teapot and swirl it around to warm the pot.
- Measure a rounded teaspoon of loose tea for each cup of water the teapot holds. Add an extra teaspoon if a strong tea is preferred. You may place the tea directly in the pot or use a tea infuser or filter.
- If you put the leaves directly in the teapot, stir the liquid and strain or decant the steeped tea into another heated teapot. A bitter-tasting "stewy" tea will result from liquor left on the leaves for a long period of time.
- Steeping depends on the size of the leaf. Large leaves require longer steeping, and small leaves steep more quickly. Steep the tea a little less time than recommended by the manufacturer to avoid bitterness.
- Milk, sugar and lemon may be added to tea. Do not use cream as it will mask the flavor of the tea, and never use milk and lemon together, as it will curdle. Add the sugar before the lemon because the citric acid from the lemon will prevent the sugar from dissolving.

tea concentrate
Nancy Sweet, IN

6 cups boiling water

9 teaspoons loose tea or 9 tea bags

Per Serving: 0 Calories; 0g Fat (0.0% calories from fat); 0g Protein; 0g Carbohydrate; 0g Dietary Fiber; 0mg Cholesterol; 43mg Sodium.

Exchanges: .none

In tea kettle, **bring** fresh cold water to a rolling boil.

Pour over tea bags (or loose tea) in tea pot. Infuse black tea 3 - 5 minutes, adjusting for personal taste.

Avoid infusing longer than suggested as this will make tea bitter.

If stronger tea is desired, **add** another tea bag or more loose tea.

Add 6 cups hot water just before serving, (or half water to half concentrate).

how to make the perfect tea sandwich

- Use firm, thinly sliced bread. White, whole wheat, oatmeal, pumpernickel, sourdough, and rye are easy to find.

- Spread slices to the edge of the bread with softened unsalted butter to protect bread from soggy fillings.

- Arrange sandwiches, one layer deep, on cookie sheets; cover with waxed paper and a slightly damp dishtowel. Refrigerate until time to serve.

- When ready to serve, trim crusts with a serrated knife and cut into fingers or triangles.

- Plan on three to five assorted sandwiches per person.

"tooth decay is the price to pay so brush your teeth 3 times a day"

Andrew, Grade 4

open-face herbed cheese and tomato sandwiches

Nancy Sweet, IN

serves 12

4	ounces goat cheese — softened
1	clove garlic — minced
1/4	cup fresh basil leaves — minced
1	baguette — sour dough
12	slices Roma tomato — or chopped sun-dried tomatoes

In food processor, **combine** first 3 ingredients until well blended. (If cheese is too thick, add bit of cream or milk.)

Refrigerate in airtight container several hours to blend flavors.

Slice baguette into 1/2 - 3/4 inch slices. **Spread** each slice with cheese mixture.

Top each slice with tomato.

Serve.

Per Serving: 173 Calories; 5g Fat (25.1% calories from fat); 7g Protein; 26g Carbohydrate; 2g Dietary Fiber; 10mg Cholesterol; 274mg Sodium.

Exchanges: 1 1/2 Grain (Starch); 1/2 Lean Meat; 1 Vegetable; 1/2 Fat.

parsley and cucumber, prosciutto or salmon sandwiches

Nancy Sweet, IN

serves 12

1	cup fresh parsley — leaves
1/4	cup mayonnaise
1/4	cup cream cheese — softened
1/4	cup onions — chopped or scallions
1	tablespoon lemon juice
1	clove garlic — crushed
1/2	teaspoon salt
	dash white pepper
12	slices cucumber — prosciutto or salmon
12	slices pumpernickel bread — or cocktail whole wheat

In blender, **combine** first 8 ingredients until smooth. **Scrape** sides as needed.

Trim crust from bread.

Spread parsley mix on each slice of bread. **Top** with cucumber, prosciutto or salmon.

Serve sandwich opened or closed.

Per Serving: 173 Calories; 7g Fat (34.5% calories from fat); 5g Protein; 24g Carbohydrate; 5g Dietary Fiber; 7mg Cholesterol; 353mg Sodium.

Exchanges: 1 Grain (Starch); 0 Lean Meat; 2 Vegetable; 0 Fruit; 1 Fat.

peanut butter and jelly tea sandwiches

Karen Hickman, IN

serves 6

12	slices bread — thin sandwich
6	tablespoons peanut butter
6	tablespoons jelly — may use different flavors

Spread 1 tablespoon peanut butter on one slice bread.

Spread 1 tablespoon jelly on top of peanut butter.

Place second slice bread on top of jelly.

Remove crust. May cut into shapes using cookie cutter, if desired.

Repeat for each sandwich.

Per Serving: 281 Calories; 10g Fat (31.3% calories from fat) 8g Protein; 41g Carbohydrate; 2g Dietary Fiber; 1mg Cholesterol; 351mg Sodium.

Exchanges: 2 Grain (Starch); 1/2 Lean Meat; 2 Fat; 1 Other Carbohydrates.

" A nice addition if small children are invited to Tea. "

tea sandwiches
Sylvia Greer, TN

serves 8 • yields 8 sandwiches

8	slices white bread — crusts removed
8	ounces cream cheese — softened
1	small can crushed pineapple — drained

Per Serving: 184 Calories; 11g Fat (52.1% calories from fat)
4g Protein; 18g Carbohydrate; 1g Dietary Fiber; 31mg Cholesterol;
219mg Sodium.

Exchanges: 1 Grain(Starch); 1/2 Lean Meat; 1/2 Fruit; 2 Fat.

Cut bread slices into shapes with cookie cutters.

In food processor, **blend** cream cheese and pineapple.

Spread pineapple mix on bread.

Garnish top with pineapple. (Or olive or twist of sliced cucumber depending on ingredient mixed with cream cheese.)

Serve.

For variety, add small jar of sliced olives or thinly sliced fresh cucumbers instead of pineapple.

aunt ruth's scones
Ruth Vanick, PA "Sister M. Helen Regina, OSF"

serves 12

3	cups flour
1	cup sugar
1	tablespoon baking powder
1	teaspoon salt
1	teaspoon baking soda
1 1/2	cups raisins
2	eggs
2	cups sour cream — may use low-fat
2	tablespoons oil

Per Serving: 346 Calories; 11g Fat (29.1% calories from fat)
6g Protein; 57g Carbohydrate; 2g Dietary Fiber; 48mg Cholesterol;
437mg Sodium.

Exchanges: 1 1/2 Grain (Starch); 0 Lean Meat; 1 Fruit; 0 Non-Fat
Milk; 2 Fat; 1 Other Carbohydrates.

Preheat oven to 350 degrees. Grease cupcake tin.

In large bowl, **combine** first 6 ingredients.

Add remaining ingredients. **Mix** well. **Pour** into prepared cupcake tins.

Bake 350 degrees, 20 minutes or until test done.

Cool on rack. **Serve** warm or cold.

currant scones

Karen Hickman, IN

serves 12

2	cups flour
1/3	cup sugar
1	tablespoon baking powder
1/2	teaspoon salt
6	tablespoons butter — cold, unsalted
1/2	cup currants
1	large egg
1/2	cup heavy cream — plus, 3 tablespoons
3	tablespoons sugar

Per Serving: 217 Calories; 10g Fat (40.7% calories from fat)
3g Protein; 30g Carbohydrate; 1g Dietary Fiber; 45mg Cholesterol;
279mg Sodium.

Exchanges: 1 Grain (Starch); 0 Lean Meat; 1/2 Fruit; 0 Non-Fat
Milk; 2 Fat; 1/2 Other Carbohydrates.

Preheat oven to 425 degrees.

In large bowl, **whisk** together first 4 ingredients.

Add butter. **Blend** with pastry blender to size of coarse crumbs.
(Do not allow butter to melt or soften to form a paste.)

Stir in currants.

In small bowl, **whisk** egg and 1/2 cup cream. **Add** to currant mix.

Stir with wooden spoon until dry ingredients are moist.

Form dough into ball. **Knead** gently against sides of bowl until
sides are clean.

On lightly floured surface, **pat** dough to approximately 8 inches in
diameter x 3/4 inch thick. **Cut** into 12 small wedges.

Place on ungreased baking sheet. **Brush** tops with remaining
cream, **sprinkle** with remaining sugar.

Bake 425 degrees, 12-15 minutes.

Cool on rack.

Serve warm or cold.

"brush your teeth day and night so they will be very bright"

Braxton, Grade 3

shortbread

serves 20

Karen Hickman, IN

3/4   cup granulated sugar — divided

1   cup softened butter

2   cups flour

Per Serving: 156 Calories; 9g Fat (53.2% calories from fat)
1g Protein; 17g Carbohydrate; trace Dietary Fiber; 25mg
Cholesterol; 94mg Sodium.

Exchanges: 1/2 Grain (Starch); 2 Fat; 1/2 Other Carbohydrates.

Preheat oven to 300 degrees.

In large bowl **combine** 1/2 cup sugar, butter and flour. Blend with pastry blender.

Pat into 9x13 baking pan.

Bake 300 degrees 30-40 minutes or until golden brown.

Remove from oven. Prick all over with fork. Sprinkle with 1/4 cup sugar while hot.

Cut into squares. Serve.

pineapple bread

serves 24 • yields 2 loaves

Shirley Walsh, LA

1/2   cup margarine

1   cup sugar

2   eggs

2   cups all-purpose flour

2   teaspoons baking powder

1/2   teaspoon salt

8   ounces crushed pineapple in juice

1   teaspoon vanilla

Per Serving: 116 Calories; 4g Fat (32.9% calories from fat);
2g Protein; 18g Carbohydrate; trace Dietary Fiber; 16mg
Cholesterol; 134mg Sodium.

Exchanges: 1/2 Grain(Starch); 0 Lean Meat; 0 Fruit; 1 Fat;
1/2 Other Carbohydrates.

Preheat oven to 350 degrees. **Grease** two 9 inch loaf pans.

In large bowl, **cream** margarine.

Gradually **add** sugar, **beating** well.

Add eggs, one at a time, **beating** well after each addition.

In another bowl, **combine** flour, baking powder and salt.

Add flour mix to creamed mixture alternately with pineapple, **mixing** well.

Stir in vanilla.

Divide equally into loaf pans.

Bake 350 degrees, 55 minutes or until tests done.

Cool 15 minutes in pan, then **turn out** onto cooling rack and cool completely.

banana bread

Nancy Colantino, IL

serves 12 • yields one loaf

1/4	cup butter — or margarine
1/2	cup brown sugar
1	egg — beaten
1	cup oatmeal — uncooked, or bran cereal
1 1/2	cups bananas — (about 4-5) ripe, mashed
1	teaspoon vanilla
1 1/2	cups flour — white, whole wheat or combination
2	teaspoons baking powder
1/2	teaspoon baking soda
1/2	cup nuts — chopped

Per Serving: 209 Calories; 8g Fat (34.5% calories from fat) 4g Protein; 31g Carbohydrate; 2g Dietary Fiber; 26mg Cholesterol; 181mg Sodium.

Exchanges: 1 Grain (Starch); 0 Lean Meat; 1 1/2 Fat; 1/2 Other Carbohydrates.

Preheat oven to 350 degrees. **Grease** 8 or 9 inch loaf pan.

In electric mixer, **cream** butter and sugar until light.

Add egg. **Mix.**

Add cereal, bananas and vanilla. **Stir.**

In a bowl, **combine** the remaining ingredients. **Add** to banana mix, stirring only to moisten the flour.

Pour into prepared pan.

Bake 350 degrees, one hour, or until bread tests done.

" Aimed at low-sugar and low-fat, but still tastes great! "

"don't eat candy, or your teeth won't be dandy"

Angel, Age 8

"brush 4 times a day keep the holes away"

Chris, Age 9

cream cheese biscuits
Karen Hickman, IN

serves 24

6	ounces cream cheese — softened
1	stick butter — softened
1/8	teaspoon salt
1	cup flour

Per Serving: 78 Calories; 6g Fat (73.0% calories from fat)
1g Protein; 4g Carbohydrate; trace Dietary Fiber; 18mg Cholesterol;
71mg Sodium.

Exchanges: 1/2 Grain (Starch); 0 Lean Meat; 1 Fat.

In large mixing bowl, using electric mixer, **combine** first 2 ingredients.

Add last 2 ingredients, use mixer until dry ingredients are moist. Then **work** with hands until dough forms.

Cover with plastic wrap. **Refrigerate** at least 1 hour.

Preheat oven to 400 degrees.

Roll dough on floured surface to 1/4 inch thick. **Cut** with small biscuit cutter. Place on baking sheet.

Bake 400 degrees 15 minutes or until golden brown.

Cool on rack. **Serve**.

Variation: Put thumbprint in center and fill with favorite jam or jelly before baking.

gift of the magi bread
Melodi Duwell, SC

serves 36

2	cups granulated sugar
1	cup margarine
4	eggs
2	teaspoons vanilla
4	cups flour
2	teaspoons baking soda
1	teaspoon salt
2	cups mashed bananas — (about 4 large), ripe
1	cup maraschino cherries — drained and chopped
2	cups mandarin oranges — drained and chopped
2	cups coconut
8	ounces dates — chopped and pitted
1 1/2	cups nuts — coarsely chopped, optional

Per Serving: 239 Calories; 11g Fat (38.7% calories from fat); 4g Protein; 34g Carbohydrate; 2g Dietary Fiber; 21mg Cholesterol; 200mg Sodium.

Exchanges: 1 Grain (Starch); 0 Lean Meat; 1/2 Fruit; 2 Fat; 1 Other Carbohydrates.

Preheat oven to 350 degrees.

Prepare pans with cooking spray or paper muffin cups.

Cream sugar, margarine and eggs with electric mixer, until fluffy.

Add vanilla.

Add half dry ingredients, then half bananas to creamed mixture.

Repeat.

Stir in fruits and nuts.

Spoon into prepared pans.

Bake 350 degrees, until toothpick inserted in middle comes out clean.

Makes:
3 eight-inch loaves — *Bake 1 hour 15 minutes.*
10 mini-loaves — *Bake 30 - 45 minutes.*
3 dozen regular sized muffins — *Bake 20-22 minutes.*
5 trays mini-muffins — *Bake 12 - 15 minutes.*

No etiquette book offers instruction on extending the pinkie finger when holding a teacup. The crooked, extended pinkie dates back to the 11th Century Crusades and the courtly etiquette of knighthood. Since ancient Rome, a cultured person ate with three fingers, a commoner with five – thus the birth of the raised pinkie as a sign of elitism.

tidbits

health benefits of drinking tea

- One study found that tea increases the body's defenses against infection and contains a substance that may be turned into a drug to protect against disease.

- A study of green tea found that when people drank it with every meal, they burned 50 to 70 calories more per day.

- Gargling with green tea can help fight bad breath. It was found that the polyphenols in green tea were effective at neutralizing bacteria and odor-causing compounds better than mints or gum.

"brushing at least twice a day makes all those cavities go away"

Tanea, Grade 1

appetizers & dips

ingredients:

eating appetizers

Appetizers are served at many different events, and it is often a challenge to socialize while juggling a drink and food.

- Do one thing at a time; avoid having both hands full.

- Use the left hand to hold a drink — keeping the right hand dry to greet people and shake hands.

- Eat a little something before an event to curb your hunger.

- Don't double dip crudités or crackers in a common dip.

- Buffet tables are generally visited many times. Never overload your plate and get a clean one each time you return.

- Never put soiled dishes on the food tables at a buffet.

"cavities are really bad! they make me feel very sad. so brush and floss every day to keep the sugarbugs far away"

Brett, Grade 2

artichoke pizza

Chris and Dr. Jeff Socher, IL

serves 12

1	teaspoon light olive oil
1	pizza crust
8	ounces fontina cheese — grated
1	can artichoke hearts — rinsed, drained, sliced (not marinated)
1/4	pound prosciutto — chopped
6	ounces gorgonzola cheese — crumbled
1/2	cup walnut — pieces

Per Serving: 290 Calories; 16g Fat (49.5% calories from fat); 15g Protein; 22g Carbohydrate; 1g Dietary Fiber; 41mg Cholesterol; 885mg Sodium.

Exchanges: 1 1/2 Grain(Starch); 1 1/2 Lean Meat; 0 Vegetable; 2 Fat; 0 Other Carbohydrates.

Preheat oven to 350 degrees.

Place crust on pizza pan and **spread** with light olive oil.

Sprinkle on fontina cheese.

Arrange artichoke hearts on cheese.

Top with prosciutto, gorgonzola and walnuts.

Bake 350 degrees, 15-20 minutes or until cheese melts.

Cut into serving pieces. **Serve** slightly warm or at room temperature.

clean your tongue
when you brush your teeth.

"eating, smiling and talking,
my dentist will say,
is made possible by brushing
and flossing 3 times a day"

Brandon, Grade 2

bruschetta
Lori Daby, CA

serves 6

2	medium tomatoes — diced
2	tablespoons fresh basil — finely chopped
1	clove garlic — minced
1/2	baguette — cut in 1/2" thick slices
1	tablespoon extra virgin olive oil
1/2	teaspoon salt
1/4	teaspoon pepper

Per Serving: 133 Calories; 4g Fat (23.7% calories from fat); 4g Protein; 22g Carbohydrate; 2g Dietary Fiber; 0mg Cholesterol; 412mg Sodium.

Exchanges: 1 1/2 Grain(Starch); 1/2 Vegetable; 1/2 Fat.

In broiler, **toast** baguette slices until golden brown. (**Place** about 2 inches under broiler.)

Remove from oven, brush each slice with olive oil.

In mixing bowl, **combine** tomatoes and spices together.

Spoon tomato mix on toast.

Serve.

"Great as an appetizer or served with a pasta dish.
Topping can be made ahead but drain before serving."

cheese souffle appetizer

Jan Bleeke, IN

serves 8

1	cup shredded swiss cheese
1	cup mayonnaise
1	cup onion — finely chopped

Per Serving: 258 Calories; 27g Fat (90.1% calories from fat);
5g Protein; 2g Carbohydrate; trace Dietary Fiber; 23mg Cholesterol;
194mg Sodium.

Exchanges: 1/2 Lean Meat; 1/2 Vegetable; 2 1/2 Fat.

Preheat oven to 350 degrees.

In mixing bowl, **combine** all ingredients. **Mix** well.

Pour into souffle dish.

Bake 350 degrees, 30 minutes.

Serve with your favorite crackers.

crab dip

Jean Wiley, IN

serves 6

1/2	cup green onions — chopped
8	ounces cream cheese
1/2	cup mayonnaise
1	teaspoon prepared horseradish
1	cup crab meat

Per Serving: 289 Calories; 29g Fat (87.3% calories from fat);
8g Protein; 2g Carbohydrate; trace Dietary Fiber; 68mg Cholesterol;
295mg Sodium.

Exchanges: 1 Lean Meat; 0 Vegetable; 3 1/2 Fat; 0 Other
Carbohydrates.

In mixing bowl, **combine** all ingredients, adding crab last.

Mix well.

Pour into serving bowl. **Refrigerate** until ready to serve.

Serve with potato chips.

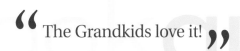

"The Grandkids love it!" quotes

"candy dandy will give your teeth a fright; unless your brush them bright each night"

Walker, Age 7

crab meat appetizers

Lady Claire Studstill, AL

serves 20 • yields 48

3/4	stick margarine — softened
1	jar sharp cheddar cheese spread
1	tablespoon mayonnaise
1	teaspoon garlic powder
1	can crab meat — drained
6	English muffins — split

Per Serving: 83 Calories; 4g Fat (47.8% calories from fat); 3g Protein; 8g Carbohydrate; trace Dietary Fiber; 6mg Cholesterol; 146mg Sodium.

Exchanges: 1/2 Grain(Starch); 0 Lean Meat; 1 Fat.

Preheat oven to 350 degrees.

Combine margarine, cheese spread, mayonnaise, and garlic powder in microwavable bowl. **Heat** until melted.

Add crab meat, **blend** thoroughly.

Top English muffins with crab mixture.

Bake 350 degrees, 15 minutes or until lightly browned.

Cut into fourths with pizza cutter.

May be frozen.

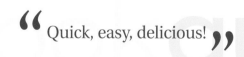

" Quick, easy, delicious! " quotes

deviled mushrooms

Doris Waldschmidt, IL

serves 8 • yields 16 mushroom caps

1	small onion — minced
2	tablespoons butter
3	slices white bread — lightly toasted, crumbled
1/4	teaspoon pepper
1	teaspoon garlic salt
1/2	cup beef broth
2	teaspoons soy sauce
1	pound mushroom caps — cleaned

Per Serving: 75 Calories; 3g Fat (39.6% calories from fat); 3g Protein; 9g Carbohydrate; 1g Dietary Fiber; 8mg Cholesterol; 504mg Sodium.

Exchanges: 1/2 Grain(Starch); 0 Lean Meat; 1 Vegetable; 1/2 Fat; 0 Other Carbohydrates.

Preheat oven to 325 degrees. (Some ovens may require 350 degrees.) Generously **butter** a shallow baking pan.

In skillet, **melt** butter. **Saute** onion in melted butter, 5 minutes.

Remove from heat, **add** bread, seasonings, broth and soy sauce.

Fill each mushroom with onion mixture, making mounds.

Place in prepared pan.

Bake 325-350 degrees, 10-15 minutes.

These can be prepared the day before and baked just prior to serving.

"if you like to look fine, you should make your teeth shine"

Destini, Grade 4

fabulous shrimp dip

Debbie Brown, IL

serves 12

12	ounces cream cheese — softened at room temperature
2	stalks celery — diced
1	small onion — diced
5	tablespoons chili sauce — increase to taste
2	dashes ketchup — increase to taste
1	tablespoon worcestershire sauce
1	bag frozen small shrimp — thawed and drained, or one can medium shrimp, drained
	garlic salt — to taste
	lemon juice — to taste

In mixing bowl, **combine** cream cheese, celery and onion.

Add chili sauce, ketchup and worcestershire sauce. **Mix** thoroughly.

Fold in shrimp.

Add garlic salt and lemon juice, to taste.

Refrigerate.

Serve with crackers.

Per Serving: 106 Calories; 10g Fat (82.5% calories from fat); 2g Protein; 2g Carbohydrate; trace Dietary Fiber; 31mg Cholesterol; 105mg Sodium.

Exchanges: 1/2 Lean Meat; 0 Vegetable; 2 Fat; 0 Other Carbohydrates.

hanky pankies

Diane Obenauer, OH

serves 24

2	pounds sausage — for more flavor, use one pound regular and one pound hot
1/2	teaspoon garlic salt
1	tablespoon worcestershire sauce
1	teaspoon dry mustard
1	teaspoon oregano
1	pound processed American cheese — cubed

Brown sausage in large skillet, over medium high heat. **Drain.**

Add spices. **Stir** in cheese until melted.

Place on rye or pumpernickel party rounds.

Freeze on cookie sheets.

Bake from FROZEN state, 375 degrees, 10 - 12 minutes or until bubbly.

(Must bake from frozen state or cheese will run everywhere.)

Serve.

May be frozen several months in airtight plastic container or cookie tins.

Per Serving: 230 Calories; 21g Fat (83.4% calories from fat); 9g Protein; 1g Carbohydrate; trace Dietary Fiber; 44mg Cholesterol; 572mg Sodium.

Exchanges: 0 Grain(Starch); 1 Lean Meat; 3 1/2 Fat; 0 Other Carbohydrates.

" My boys and their friends, as well as our friends, just LOVE these! "

hummus

Chris Slyby, IN

serves 12

2	cups garbanzo beans, canned — drained
1/3	cup tahini — (ground sesame seeds), found in gourmet shops or health food stores
1/4	cup lemon juice
1	teaspoon salt
2	cloves garlic — optional
1	tablespoon olive oil
1	teaspoon fresh parsley — minced
	pita bread — cut in wedges, or crackers

In food processor, **blend** garbanzo beans, tahini, lemon juice, salt and garlic.

Pour hummus into serving bowl.

Drizzle oil over top of hummus and sprinkle with parsley.

Serve with pita wedges or crackers.

Per Serving: 60 Calories; 2g Fat (23.3% calories from fat); 2g Protein; 10g Carbohydrate; 2g Dietary Fiber; 0mg Cholesterol; 297mg Sodium.

Exchanges: 1/2 Grain(Starch); 0 Vegetable; 0 Fruit; 1/2 Fat.

> "We have a contest at our house to see who makes the best ! "

jezebel sauce

Carol Cooke, MO

serves 20 • yields 4 cups

1	tablespoon peppercorns — whole
18	ounces apple jelly
18	ounces apricot preserves
3	tablespoons dry mustard
8	ounces horseradish
8	ounces cream cheese — softened
	crackers

Combine all ingredients except cream cheese in blender. **Blend** to smooth.

Refrigerate until ready to use. (Keeps several weeks in refrigerator.)

On serving plate, **place** block of cream cheese . **Pour** sauce over cream cheese.

Serve with crackers.

Per Serving: 175 Calories; 4g Fat (20.7% calories from fat); 1g Protein; 35g Carbohydrate; 1g Dietary Fiber; 12mg Cholesterol; 74mg Sodium.

Exchanges: 0 Grain(Starch); 0 Lean Meat; 1 Fat; 2 1/2 Other Carbohydrates.

> "This recipe is a great hostess gift.
> Friends love having a delicious appetizer on hand. "

pepperoni pizza spread

Susan Ferry, IL

serves 12 • yields 6 cups

2	cups shredded mozzarella cheese
2	cups shredded cheddar cheese
1	cup mayonnaise — (not salad dressing)
1	cup pepperoni slices — chopped
4	ounces mushroom stems and pieces — drained and chopped
1/2	cup onion — chopped
1/2	cup green pepper — chopped
6	ounces ripe olives — drained and chopped
1	cup stuffed green olives — chopped
	crackers — crostini or french bread

Preheat oven to 350 degrees.

In large mixing bowl, **combine** first 9 ingredients.

Transfer to 11x7x2 inch baking dish.

Bake, uncovered, 350 degrees, 25-30 minutes or until edges are bubbly and lightly browned.

Serve with crackers, crostini or french bread.

Per Serving: 401 Calories; 38g Fat (82.7% calories from fat); 14g Protein; 4g Carbohydrate; 1g Dietary Fiber; 59mg Cholesterol; 924mg Sodium.

Exchanges: 2 Lean Meat; 1/2 Vegetable; 0 Fruit; 4 1/2 Fat.

Serving buffet style was used centuries ago. However, it became evident it was more economical to control portions by having guests served at the table.

tidbits

"don't rush when you brush
or your teeth will turn into mush"

Christine, Age 8

pineapple dip

Mary Beth Thornton, IL

serves 12

1	pineapple — halved lengthwise
8	ounces cream cheese — softened
1/4	cup chutney
1/4	teaspoon dry mustard
	toasted almonds

Per Serving: 98 Calories; 7g Fat (59.9% calories from fat); 2g Protein; 9g Carbohydrate; 1g Dietary Fiber; 21mg Cholesterol; 58mg Sodium.

Exchanges: 0 Grain(Starch); 0 Lean Meat; 1/2 Fruit; 1 Fat.

From pineapple half, **scoop** out pineapple and chop.

In mixing bowl, **combine** chopped pineapple with cream cheese, chutney and dry mustard. **Mix** well.

Place cream cheese mix in pineapple shell.

Top with toasted almonds.

Serve with crackers.

dislodge food with dental floss—
never with a sharp instrument.

dentalfill-ins
smokeless tobacco

Use of any tobacco product can increase your risk of developing oral cancer and gum disease. Like cigars and cigarettes, smokeless tobacco products contain a variety of toxins associated with cancer. Sores in the mouth lasting more than two weeks need a dentist's attention.

- Smokeless tobacco can irritate your gum tissue, causing it to recede or pull away from your teeth.
- Once gum tissue recedes, the roots of your teeth are exposed, increasing your risk for tooth decay and sensitivity to hot and cold foods and drinks.
- Sugars, often added to enhance the flavor of smokeless tobacco, can increase your risk for tooth decay.
- Smokeless tobacco also typically contains sand and grit, which can wear down your teeth.

"floss, floss, floss everyday to run those cavities far, far away"

Logan, Grade 4

36

ingredients:

eating soup

Soup is often served as a separate course at a more formal meal. It can be in a flat, brimmed soup "plate" or in a smaller bowl or cup.

- The soup spoon is held the way a pencil is held, steadied between your index and middle fingers, except that the thumb is turned up rather than down (as when writing).

- Soup is spooned away from you toward the center of the plate. Sip the soup from the side of the spoon.

- The soup plate may be tipped away from you in order to fill the spoon with the last sips. Place the spoon on the soup plate when you have finished.

- A rounded bouillon spoon may be used for soup served in a two-handled cream soup bowl or bouillon cup. Place the spoon on the saucer between sips and when you have finished—never in the bowl or cup.

- Do not blow on soup or stir to cool. Skim a little off the top close to the edge.

- Do not put crackers or bread in soup while dining out.

- Hearty soups or stews with a lot of liquid should be eaten with a larger spoon.

- When eating hearty soups and stews, bring the spoon to your mouth with the front toward your mouth instead of sipping off the side.

"take care of your pearly whites, keep your smile nice and bright"

Michael, Grade 5

barley vegetable soup
Barbara Mattern, IN

serves 10 • yields 10 cups

1	pound ground beef
16	ounces canned tomatoes
2	medium onions — chopped
1/4	cup ketchup
2	teaspoons basil, sweet — dried
1	tablespoon beef bouillon granules
5	cups water
2	medium carrots — diced
2	stalks celery — sliced
1/3	cup pearl barley
1	bay leaf

In skillet, **brown** ground beef. **Drain**.

In stockpot, **combine** all ingredients, including cooked ground beef.

Bring to boil, **reduce** heat, **simmer** about 1 hour.

Remove bay leaf. **Serve** hot.

Per Serving: 196 Calories; 12g Fat (55.9% calories from fat); 9g Protein; 13g Carbohydrate; 3g Dietary Fiber; 39mg Cholesterol; 288mg Sodium.

Exchanges: 1/2 Grain(Starch); 1 Lean Meat; 1 Vegetable; 2 Fat; 0 Other Carbohydrates.

" This is an old family recipe that is always a hit when I serve it. "

cookquotes

broccoli soup

Suzanne Bowden, TX

serves 8

2	tablespoons butter
1	tablespoon flour
1	teaspoon salt
1	teaspoon pepper
5	cups milk
1 1/2	cups fresh broccoli — chopped
3	tablespoons green onion — chopped
2	cups shredded cheddar cheese — fresh

Per Serving: 242 Calories; 17g Fat (63.9% calories from fat); 13g Protein; 9g Carbohydrate; 1g Dietary Fiber; 58mg Cholesterol; 551mg Sodium.

Exchanges: 0 Grain(Starch); 1 Lean Meat; 0 Vegetable; 1/2 Non-Fat Milk; 2 1/2 Fat.

In small saucepan, **melt** butter. **Stir** in flour, salt and pepper to form paste.

In large saucepan, **heat** milk. **Add** broccoli, onions and butter mix.

Cook until vegetables are tender and soup is thickened.

Add cheese, **heat** just until melted.

Serve hot.

" Delicious homemade hot soup. When served with crusty bread creates a great meal for the family. "

brunswick stew

Jean Weathers, GA

serves 20

3	pounds whole chicken
3	pounds lean beef roast
3	pounds lean pork roast
3	medium onions — chopped
64	ounces diced tomatoes — (4 cans)
5	tablespoons worcestershire sauce
21	ounces ketchup — (1 1/2 bottles)
1	tablespoon pepper sauce
2	bay leaves
6	ounces chili sauce — (1/2 bottle)
1/2	teaspoon dry mustard
1/2	stick butter
6	tablespoons vinegar
32	ounces creamed corn — (2 cans)
15	ounces english peas — (1can)

In large heavy pot, **place** meat seasoned with salt and pepper.

Add onions, **cover** with water. **Cook** until meat falls off bone (several hours).

Remove from heat. **Allow** to cool. **Tear** meat into shreds and **return** to stock.

Add next 8 ingredients. **Cook** 1 hour, **stirring** occasionally to prevent sticking.

Add last 3 ingredients. **Cook** until thick.

Ladle into bowls. **Serve** hot.

Per Serving: 475 Calories; 27g Fat (50.5% calories from fat); 33g Protein; 26g Carbohydrate; 3g Dietary Fiber; 122mg Cholesterol; 652mg Sodium.

Exchanges: 1 Grain(Starch); 4 Lean Meat; 1 Vegetable; 2 1/2 Fat; 1/2 Other Carbohydrates.

" Created in Brunswick, Georgia. Enjoyed all over the world. Traditionally served with barbecue or local seafood, my family's favorite! "

cheddar chowder

Christy Blake, IN

serves 4

2	cups potatos — chopped
1/4	cup carrot — sliced
1/4	cup onion — chopped
1/2	cup celery — chopped
1/4	teaspoon pepper
2	cups boiling water
1/4	cup margarine
1/4	cup flour
2	cups milk
1	cup cooked ham — chopped
2	cups shredded cheddar cheese

In stockpot, **combine** all vegetables, pepper and boiling water.

Cover, **simmer** 10 minutes. DO NOT DRAIN.

In small saucepan, **make** white sauce: **melt** margarine, **stir** in flour until all absorbed, gradually **pour** in milk, **stirring** constantly until smooth.

Add white sauce to vegetable-water mixture. **Stir.**

Over low heat, **add** ham and cheese, **stirring** until cheese is melted.

Serve.

Per Serving: 563 Calories; 38g Fat (60.3% calories from fat); 27g Protein; 29g Carbohydrate; 2g Dietary Fiber; 95mg Cholesterol; 1013mg Sodium.

Exchanges: 1/2 Grain(Starch); 3 Lean Meat; 1/2 Vegetable; 1/2 Non-Fat Milk; 5 1/2 Fat.

" A hearty soup everyone will enjoy. Add more or less vegetables or ham depending on your taste or diet. "

quotes

The word soup is derived from the Latin term *suppare*, which means "to soak." The liquid was poured over bread for sustenance and was called sop.

tidbits

chicken chipotle stew

Beth Gavzer, IL

serves 12

3	pounds boneless, skinless chicken — cubed
3	cups onions — chopped
1	tablespoon olive oil
6	cloves garlic — minced
2	cups red potato — peeled and chopped
1 1/2	cups carrots — chopped
1/4	cup tomato paste
1 1/2	cups ground cumin
4	cans chicken broth — fat free
43	ounces diced tomato — (3 cans) do not drain
1	package fresh mushrooms — sliced or halved
1	small can diced green chiles — or 3 chopped chipotles - spicy!
2	tablespoons fresh cilantro — chopped

In dutch oven coated with cooking spray, **brown** chicken. **Remove** and keep warm.

Add olive oil to dutch oven, **heat**. **Add** onions, **saute** 5 minutes.

Add garlic. **Saute** 1 minute.

Add remaining ingredients except cilantro and chicken. **Bring** to boil, reduce heat. **Simmer** 30 minutes.

Add cilantro and chicken. **Simmer** 15 minutes.

Serve hot.

Per Serving: 239 Calories; 6g Fat (21.3% calories from fat); 27g Protein; 22g Carbohydrate; 4g Dietary Fiber; 53 mg Cholesterol; 397mg Sodium.

Exchanges: 1/2 Grain(Starch); 3 Lean Meat; 2 Vegetable; 1/2 Fat.

"toss me some floss, give me some paste, and none of my teeth will go to waste"

Courtney & Riley, Grade 5

Eat a balanced diet and limit between meal snacks.

christmas soup

Joyce Ludlow, IN

serves 6

1/4	cup butter — or margarine, melted
1/2	cup red pepper — chopped
1/2	cup flour
6	cups chicken broth
10	ounces frozen chopped spinach — thawed and drained
2	cups cooked chicken — chopped
1/4	teaspoon nutmeg
1	cup half and half

In soup pot, **melt** butter. **Stir** in red pepper, **cook** 2 - 3 minutes.

Stir in flour. Mixture will be doughy.

Add chicken broth. **Cook** to slightly thick and bubbly.

Add spinach, chicken, nutmeg and half and half. **Stir.**

Heat mixture through. **Serve** hot.

Per Serving: 293 Calories; 16g Fat (49.8% calories from fat); 23g Protein; 13g Carbohydrate; 2g Dietary Fiber; 75mg Cholesterol; 929mg Sodium.

Exchanges: 1/2 Grain(Starch); 2 1/2 Lean Meat; 1/2 Vegetable; 0 Non-Fat Milk; 2 1/2 Fat.

" This soup gets its name from the red and green vegetables it uses. It is good any time of year. "

cream of artichoke soup

Kathy Kne, OH

serves 8

2	tablespoons butter
1/2	cup carrot — chopped
1/2	cup onion — chopped
1/2	cup celery — chopped
1/2	cup mushrooms — chopped
1/2	cup butter
1/4	cup flour
1	quart chicken broth
1	package frozen artichoke hearts — cooked and drained
1	bay leaf
3/4	teaspoon salt
1/2	teaspoon cayenne
1/4	teaspoon thyme
1/4	teaspoon sage
1	cup whipping cream — or fat free half and half
1	dozen raw oysters — undrained (optional)

Per Serving: 282 Calories; 26g Fat (83.3% calories from fat); 5g Protein; 7g Carbohydrate; 1g Dietary Fiber; 86mg Cholesterol; 776mg Sodium.

Exchanges: 0 Grain(Starch); 1/2 Lean Meat; 1/2 Vegetable; 0 Non-Fat Milk; 5 Fat; 0 Other Carbohydrates.

In skillet, **melt** 2 tablespoons butter then **saute** chopped vegetables 15 minutes.

In soup pot, **melt** 1/2 cup butter. **Add** flour. **Cook** 5 minutes.

Add sauteed vegetables, broth, artichoke hearts and seasonings. **Simmer** 30 minutes.

Whisk in cream. **Add** oysters, if desired. **Heat** thoroughly.

Ladle into bowls. **Pass** the pepper sauce.

" An unusual soup that is also very easy to make with ingredients you always have at home! Give it an extra kick with a dash of pepper sauce "

"floss your teeth every day to get plaque out of the way"

Sarah, Grade 4

creamy parsnip soup
Kathy Kne, OH

serves 8

1/2	pound salt pork — slivered, or 4 tablespoons butter or margarine
1	onion — chopped
3	medium parsnips — chopped
1 1/2	quarts vegetable broth — or chicken broth
1/2	teaspoon salt
1/8	teaspoon white pepper
2	tablespoons butter
2	tablespoons flour
1	cup cream — or fat free half and half
	parsley flakes — to garnish

Per Serving: 509 Calories; 36g Fat (63.6% calories from fat); 8g Protein; 39g Carbohydrate; 7g Dietary Fiber; 60mg Cholesterol; 1806mg Sodium.

Exchanges: 2 1/2 Grain (Starch); 0 Lean Meat; 0 Vegetable; 7 1/2 Fat.

In skillet, **melt** salt pork (or 4 tablespoons butter). **Fry** onions and parsnips until lightly browned.

Pour browned vegetables into soup kettle, **add** vegetable or chicken stock. **Cook** until parsnips are tender.

Pour into food processor, **puree**.

In small saucepan, **melt** 2 tablespoons butter. **Blend** in flour. **Cook** 3 - 5 minutes. DO NOT ALLOW TO BROWN.

Stir butter-flour mix into soup to thicken.

Just before serving, **add** cream.

Ladle into bowls, **garnish** with parsley.

Pass the pepper sauce for added kick.

"An imaginative soup made with a vegetable that is less commonly encountered - excellent!"

quotes

gazpacho soup

Molly Baker, IL

serves 4

15	ounces consomme — or vegetable broth
1 1/4	cups tomato juice
1 1/4	cups onion — chopped
2 1/2	cups cucumbers — chopped
2 1/2	cups tomato — chopped
1	tablespoon vegetable oil
2	tablespoons wine vinegar
2 1/2	teaspoons salt
2 1/2	cups peppers — chopped

In large bowl, **combine** all ingredients.

Season to taste with pepper sauce and worcestershire sauce.

Chill and **serve**.

Per Serving: 133 Calories; 4g Fat (25.4% calories from fat); 6g Protein; 22g Carbohydrate; 5g Dietary Fiber; 0mg Cholesterol; 1903mg Sodium.

Exchanges: 1/2 Lean Meat; 3 1/2 Vegetable; 1/2 Fat; 0 Other Carbohydrates.

harvest pumpkin soup

Jenny Dalen, WA

serves 6

10 3/4	ounces condensed cream of potato soup
1	soup can water
1	soup can milk
15	ounces pumpkin puree
2	tablespoons butter
1	teaspoon salt
1/4	teaspoon black pepper
1/2	teaspoon garlic powder
1/2	teaspoon ginger
	pinch paprika — for garnish

In a saucepan, over medium heat, **combine** all ingredients, except paprika.

Bring to boil, **reduce** heat to low. **Simmer** 15 minutes.

Ladle into bowls, **sprinkle** with paprika to garnish.

If desired, may also **garnish** with toasted pumpkin seeds or croutons.

Per Serving: 114 Calories; 6g Fat (47.9% calories from fat); 3g Protein; 13g Carbohydrate; 2g Dietary Fiber; 18mg Cholesterol; 824mg Sodium.

Exchanges: 1/2 Grain(Starch); 1 Vegetable; 0 Non-Fat Milk; 1 Fat.

" A fun Fall soup. Pair with a green salad and crusty bread, follow with warm caramel apple cider. mmm ! "

lentil soup kuppin

Gretchen Frydyrchowicz, IL

serves 8 • yields 16 cups

2	cups lentils — picked clean and rinsed
3	cups beef broth — or 3 cups water mixed with 4 beef bouillon cubes
4	ribs celery — chopped
4	carrots — chopped
1 1/2	cups canned tomatoes — drained and chopped
1/4	cup olive oil
1	onion — chopped
1/2	cup fresh parsley — minced
1/2	pound pancetta — (Italian cured pork belly) or ham
2	cloves garlic — minced
1 1/2	teaspoons salt
1/2	teaspoon freshly ground pepper
7	cups water
2	tablespoons fresh lemon juice
1/2	cup parmesan cheese — grated

In soup kettle, **combine** all ingredients except lemon juice and parmesan cheese.

Bring to boil, **reduce** heat. Simmer, covered, 1 1/2 hours. **Skim** froth as needed.

Just before serving, **discard** meat, if desired.

Stir in lemon juice.

Ladle into bowls. **Sprinkle** with parmesan.

Serve.

Per Serving: 358 Calories; 11g Fat (27.7% calories from fat); 29g Protein; 37g Carbohydrate; 17g Dietary Fiber; 24mg Cholesterol; 1848mg Sodium.

Exchanges: 2 Grain (Starch); 3 Lean Meat; 1 1/2 Vegetable; 0 Fruit; 1 1/2 Fat.

mushroom bisque

Susan Ferry, IL

serves 12 • yields 3 quarts

5	cups chicken broth
1	pound fresh mushrooms — washed, trimmed, sliced
1	medium onion — finely chopped
1	teaspoon salt
1/2	teaspoon white pepper
1/4	teaspoon pepper sauce
1/2	cup butter
1/2	cup flour — may need 3/4 cup
1	quart whole milk
1	cup whipping cream

Per Serving: 234 Calories; 18g Fat (70.0% calories from fat); 7g Protein; 11g Carbohydrate; 1g Dietary Fiber; 59mg Cholesterol; 623mg Sodium.

Exchanges: 1/2 Grain(Starch); 0 Lean Meat; 1/2 Vegetable; 1/2 Non-Fat Milk; 3 1/2 Fat.

In soup kettle, **bring** chicken broth to boil. **Add** mushrooms and onion, **return** to boil.

Reduce heat, **add** salt, pepper and pepper sauce. **Simmer** 30-40 minutes.

In saucepan, **melt** butter. **Whisk** in flour, small amounts at a time, until thoroughly mixed.

Cook about 2 minutes. (This is called a roux.)

Meanwhile, in another saucepan, **bring** milk to boil and immediately **pour** into roux. **Whisk** to smooth.

Sauce will first look curdled, then lumpy. **Whisk** 2 - 4 minutes to produce a creamy white sauce.

Combine white sauce with mushroom broth. **Add** cream.

Serve.

"candy will give you tooth decay; see your dentist to feel okay"

Zach, Grade 4

park city oven stew

Janice Gerritsen, UT

serves 8

2	pounds beef cubes
10	medium potatoes — cubed
10	carrots — cut into chunks
1	package dried onion soup
2	bay leaves
1	can cream of mushroom soup
1	can cream of celery soup
1	can tomato soup, condensed
1	soup can water — or milk

Per Serving: 507 Calories; 25g Fat (43.6% calories from fat); 26g Protein; 46g Carbohydrate; 5g Dietary Fiber; 78mg Cholesterol; 963mg Sodium.

Exchanges: 2 1/2 Grain(Starch); 3 Lean Meat; 2 Vegetable; 3 Fat.

Preheat oven to 250 degrees.

In a large casserole or pan with a tight lid, **make** a layer of half the beef then half the vegetables.

Top with remaining beef, then remaining vegetables.

Sprinkle dried soup mix over the top. **Add** bay leaves.

In bowl, **combine** canned soups and water or milk. **Pour** over stew mixture.

Cover tightly. **Bake** 250 - 275 degrees, 6 - 8 hours.

Serve hot.

Passed down from a neighbor,
Marcia Cowley Keen.

" This easy stew is named after a famous ski resort in Utah.

It has a great and unique flavor. Everyone I 've ever served it to loves it.

To make it healthier, I use low fat canned soups. "

"my teeth are so white and bright,
you don't have to walk a mile
to see my smile"

Charles, Age 7

slow cooked corn chowder

Shirley Walsh, LA

serves 16 • yields 2 quarts

2 1/2	cups milk
1	can (15 ounces) creamed corn
1	can (15 ounces) corn
1	can (10 3/4 ounces) cream of mushroom soup — undiluted
1	cup hash browns, frozen — or refrigerated
1	large onion — chopped
2	tablespoons butter — or margarine
2	teaspoons dried parsley — flaked
2	teaspoons cajun seasoning

In slow cooker, **combine** all ingredients.

Cover. **Cook**, on low, 6 hours.

Serve hot.

Variations: Add 1 cup cubed, fully cooked ham or cooked shrimp.

Add chicken bouillion cube or 2, to personal taste. May increase milk to desired consistency.

Per Serving: 69 Calories; 3g Fat (43.4% calories from fat); 2g Protein; 8g Carbohydrate; 1g Dietary Fiber; 9mg Cholesterol; 152mg Sodium.

Exchanges: 1/2 Grain(Starch); 0 Lean Meat; 0 Vegetable; 0 Non-Fat Milk; 1/2 Fat; 0 Other Carbohydrates.

stuffed pepper soup

Pat McLaughlin, IL

serves 10

2	pounds ground beef — browned, drained
28	ounces tomato sauce
28	ounces diced tomatoes — undrained
1 1/2	cups white rice
2	cups green pepper — diced
1	tablespoon beef stock — or 2 beef boullion cubes and **2** cups water
1	tablespoon granulated garlic
1/4	cup packed brown sugar
	salt and pepper — to taste

In large soup pot, **combine** all ingredients. **Bring** to boil.

Reduce heat. **Cover**. **Simmer** 1/2 hour.

Ladle into soup bowls, **garnish** with shredded cheese. **Serve** hot.

May increase or decrease rice to desired consistency.

Per Serving: 455 Calories; 25g Fat (48.7% calories from fat); 19g Protein; 39g Carbohydrate; 3g Dietary Fiber; 77mg Cholesterol; 567mg Sodium.

Exchanges: 1 1/2 Grain(Starch); 2 Lean Meat; 2 Vegetable; 3 1/2 Fat; 1/2 Other Carbohydrates.

"don't eat candy, it's not right
unless you brush
day and night"

Caroline, Grade 3

vegetable rice soup

Jan Hagedorn, IN

serves 8

1	medium onion — chopped
1	cup celery — chopped
1	cup carrots — sliced
2	cloves garlic — minced
28	ounces chicken broth — (2 cans)
16	ounces tomatoes — diced
1/2	cup mild picante sauce
1/2	cup rice — uncooked
2	teaspoons basil

In large pot, **combine** all ingredients. **Bring** to boil.

Reduce heat, **simmer** 20 minutes.

Add water to desired consistency, **simmer** 10 more minutes.

Ladle into bowls. **Serve** hot.

May add 2 cooked, chopped
chicken breasts, if desired.

Per Serving: 91 Calories; 1g Fat (9.1% calories from fat);
4g Protein; 17g Carbohydrate; 2g Dietary Fiber; 0mg Cholesterol;
466mg Sodium.

Exchanges: 1/2 Grain(Starch); 0 Lean Meat; 1 1/2 Vegetable; 0 Fat.

" Easy, Tasty, Healthy "

vichyssoise

Linda Manning, IL

serves 12

7	green onions — sliced diagonally, reserve 2 green onions for garnish
1	small sweet onion — finely chopped
4	ounces butter
6	medium potatoes — peeled and chopped
1	quart chicken broth
1	teaspoon salt
4	cups half and half
1/2	teaspoon white pepper
	dash celery salt
1	cup heavy cream

Per Serving: 309 Calories; 25g Fat (71.0% calories from fat); 6g Protein; 17g Carbohydrate; 1g Dietary Fiber; 78mg Cholesterol; 556mg Sodium.

Exchanges: 1/2 Grain(Starch); 0 Lean Meat; 1/2 Vegetable; 1/2 Non-Fat Milk; 5 Fat.

In large soup kettle, **melt** butter. **Saute** 5 green onions and sweet onion.

Add potatoes, chicken broth and salt. **Cook** until potatoes are soft.

In blender, **liquefy** potato broth. **Return** to kettle.

Add half and half and remaining seasonings. **Chill.**

In electric mixer, **whip** cream. **Fold** into chilled potato broth about 30 minutes before serving.

Chill until ready to serve.

Ladle into bowls. **Garnish** with reserved raw, chopped green onions.

"i brush twice a day and my dentist says, hooray"

Reiser, Age 12

diet for oral surgery patients

Following an extraction or placement of an implant, dental patients should temporarily adjust their diets. The following are general guidelines for diet and mouth care. Your dentist will give you complete information about your surgery.

general/iv anesthesia

- If you are having surgery in the morning, do not eat or drink after midnight.
- If you are having surgery in the afternoon, eat a light breakfast at least six hours before surgery. A light breakfast consists of liquids, one egg, cereal or a piece of toast.

  Do not eat fatty foods, such as sausage or bacon.

the first 24 hours after surgery:

- Do not chew until the numbness is gone.
- Eat foods cold or at room temperature—never hot.
- Desirable foods include milkshakes, ice cream, applesauce, gelatin or pudding, yogurt, cottage cheese, soups (at room temperature), soft drinks and powdered food supplements.
- Do not rinse; this will allow blood clots to form and reduce chances of dry socket.

after the first 24 hours:

- Liquid and soft foods are desirable—but eat your regular diet (if you feel you can). Begin rinsing.

mouth care

- The cleaner you keep your mouth after surgery, the faster and better you will heal.
- Rinse gently and carefully four or five times daily, especially after meals, using a warm, salt-water rinse (1/4 t. in a glass of water) or a warm mouthwash.
- Brush your teeth to maintain cleanliness.

"if I brush my teeth white and bright each day, my dentist will say, your teeth are the best, they pass the test"

Cassie, Age 8

salads

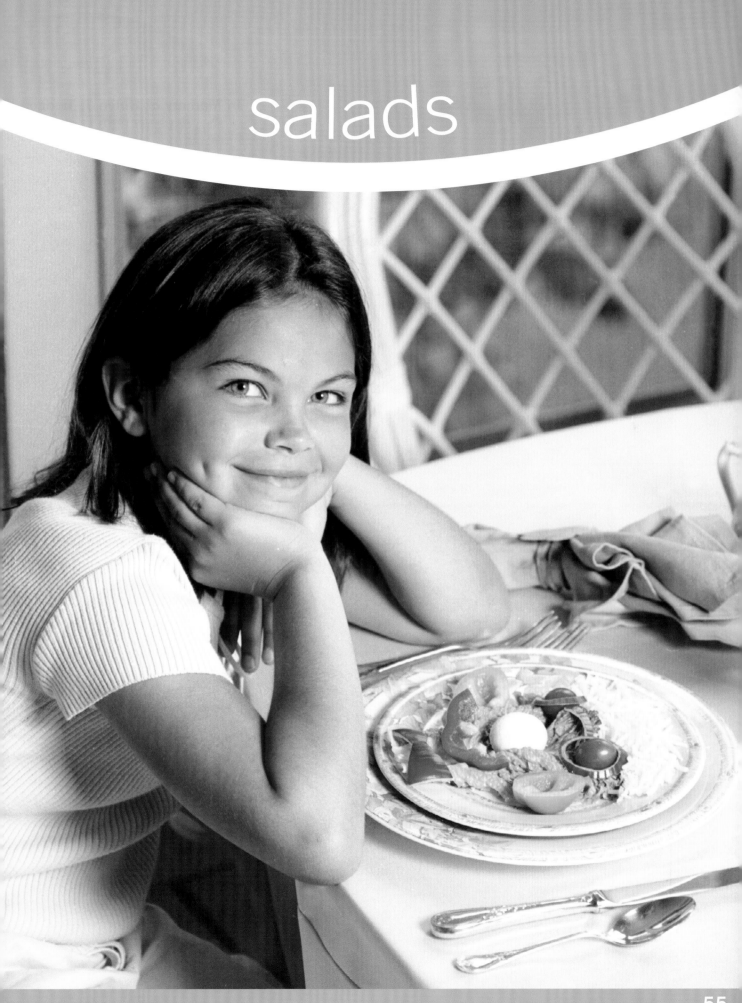

ingredients:

eating salad

A salad can be served as a separate course, a main course or as a side to the meal. Knowing when the salad will be served has to do with placement of the fork.

- If the salad fork is on the outside of the place setting, salad will be served before the main course.

- If the salad fork is next to the dinner plate and the dinner fork is on the outside, the salad will be served in the Continental fashion, after the main course.

- Use a knife and salad fork when cutting is required

- Cut one bite at a time.

- Use only the salad fork if the knife is not needed.

- If salad is your main course, use the dinner fork for eating.

- The salad will be at the left side of the dinner plate if it accompanies the meal.

"10" salad dressing

Tenley Ysseldyke, IL

serves 2

3	tablespoons safflower oil
1	tablespoon dijon mustard
1	tablespoon red wine vinegar
	salt and pepper — to taste

In bowl, **mix** all ingredients together.

Pour over your favorite salad greens.

Garnish with slivered almonds and freshly sliced parmesan cheese curls.

Per Serving: 187 Calories; 21g Fat (97.3% calories from fat); trace Protein; 1g Carbohydrate; trace Dietary Fiber; 0mg Cholesterol; 94mg Sodium.

Exchanges: 0 Lean Meat; 4 Fat; 0 Other Carbohydrates.

12 hour germany slaw

Margo Martin, IN

serves 10

1	large head of cabbage — shredded
1	large bermuda onion — thinly sliced
1	green pepper — chopped
1	cup sugar
1	cup cider vinegar
3/4	cup salad oil — prefer peanut oil
1	tablespoon celery seed
1	tablespoon sugar
1	teaspoon dry mustard

In an 8 quart (2 gallon) stainless steel or glass bowl , **pack** cabbage, onion and pepper in layers.

Pour sugar over top. DO NOT STIR.

In saucepan, **mix** remaining ingredients, **bring** to hard boil.

Immediately **remove** from heat, **pour** over cabbage and sugar layers. DO NOT STIR.

Seal tightly. (Plastic wrap works well.)

Let **stand** in refrigerator 12 hours, then **toss** and **serve**.

Per Serving: 263 Calories; 17g Fat (54.8% calories from fat); 2g Protein; 30g Carbohydrate; 3g Dietary Fiber; 0mg Cholesterol; 18mg Sodium.

Exchanges: 0 Grain(Starch); 0 Lean Meat; 1 Vegetable; 3 1/2 Fat; 1 1/2 Other Carbohydrates.

"Easy, prepare the day before. Keeps in refrigerator for two weeks."

"brush your teeth everyday to scare away tooth decay."

Anthony, Grade 3

blackeyed pea salad
Kathy Gotcher, TN

serves 8

2	cans (14 ounce) corn — drained (use one white, one yellow)
2	cans (14 ounce) blackeyed peas — drained and rinsed
1/2	cup green onion — diced
1/2	cup celery — diced
1/4	cup sugar — or substitute
3	tablespoons corn oil — or canola
2	tablespoons red wine vinegar — optional
1/2	cup Italian salad dressing, (may use low-fat)

In large serving bowl, **combine** all ingredients. **Mix** well.

Refrigerate overnight.

Serve. **Store** leftovers in refrigerator.

Per Serving: 301 Calories; 13g Fat (37.5% calories from fat); 11g Protein; 38g Carbohydrate; 5g Dietary Fiber; 0mg Cholesterol; 133mg Sodium.

Exchanges: 2 Grain(Starch); 1/2 Lean Meat; 0 Vegetable; 2 1/2 Fat; 1/2 Other Carbohydrates.

" This is a delicious salad, serve cold on a hot day. High in protein, low in fat.

I also like this with pita bread chips as a salsa. "

blueberry
congealed salad

Jean Weathers, GA

serves 8

1	large box gelatin powder, unsweetened — blackberry
2 1/2	cups boiling water
1	small can crushed pineapple
1	can blueberries — not blueberry pie filling
8	ounces softened cream cheese
8	ounces sour cream
1/2	cup sugar or substitute

In serving bowl, **dissolve** gelatin in boiling water.

Add pineapple and blueberries, including juices. **Congeal**.

In mixing bowl, **combine** cream cheese, sour cream and sugar (or substitute) until smooth.

Spread cream cheese mix on top of congealed mix.

If desired, **garnish** with chopped nuts.

Refrigerate until ready to serve.

Per Serving: 240 Calories; 16g Fat (58.0% calories from fat); 4g Protein; 22g Carbohydrate; 1g Dietary Fiber; 44mg Cholesterol; 104mg Sodium.

Exchanges: 1/2 Lean Meat; 1/2 Fruit; 0 Non-Fat Milk; 3 Fat; 1 Other Carbohydrates.

" Passed down from my friend, Cathy Baughman. Everyone I have served this to has asked for the recipe. I serve it almost every holiday. "

Robert May was a noted English cookbook author from the 1600's. In a book entitled Aceteria, he describes serving salad with "oyl" (of good quality) and vinegar. The book was dedicated to salads. Even before the 1600's, it has been documented that raw or boiled vegetables were served like a salad with an oil and vinegar dressing. They were referred to as *salients*.

tidbits

broccoli slaw

Shannon Brasseale, IN

serves 6

2	teaspoons sesame seeds
1/2	cup slivered almonds
1	teaspoon butter — melted
1	cup sugar
1/2	cup cider vinegar
1/4	cup vegetable oil
1	teaspoon salt
1/2	teaspoon pepper
1	package ramen noodles — chicken flavored
4	green onions — chopped
16	ounces broccoli slaw

In skillet, **toast** sesame seeds and almonds in butter. **Set** aside.

In saucepan, **cook** sugar, vinegar, oil, salt, pepper and flavor packet from noodles, until sugar is dissolved.

DO NOT COOK NOODLES. **Allow** mixture to cool.

In large serving bowl, **break** noodles. **Add** broccoli slaw and dressing. **Toss** to coat.

Serve.

Per Serving: 322 Calories; 17g Fat (45.2% calories from fat); 4g Protein; 42g Carbohydrate; 1g Dietary Fiber; 8mg Cholesterol; 367mg Sodium.

Exchanges: 1/2 Grain(Starch); 1/2 Lean Meat; 0 Vegetable; 3 Fat; 2 1/2 Other Carbohydrates.

" Passed down from Jackie Brasseale. " quotes

cauliflower salad

Marie Robison, MO

serves 12

1	medium head cauliflower — broken up and sliced
16	ounces French cut frozen green beans — thawed
1/2	pound fresh mushrooms — sliced
1	large red onion — sliced, separated into rings
1	teaspoon dried basil
1	teaspoon dried oregano
8	ounces reduced calorie Italian salad dressing

In large bowl, **combine** first 6 ingredients.

Add dressing, **toss** to coat.

Cover, refrigerate at least 2 hours before serving.

Per Serving: 55 Calories; 2g Fat (31.2% calories from fat); 2g Protein; 8g Carbohydrate; 3g Dietary Fiber; 1mg Cholesterol; 165mg Sodium.

Exchanges: 0 Grain(Starch); 1 1/2 Vegetable; 1/2 Fat; 0 Other Carbohydrates.

chick pea
mushroom salad

Carol Cooke, MO

serves 4

1	can garbanzo beans — (chick peas), drained
1/4	cup parsley, fresh — chopped
1/4	cup onion — chopped
1/2	teaspoon garlic — chopped
3	tablespoons fresh lemon juice
2	tablespoons olive oil
1/2	teaspoon salt
1	pinch pepper
1	cup fresh mushrooms — sliced
1/2	cup black olives — or green olives, sliced

In small salad bowl, **combine** all ingredients. **Toss** to coat.

Chill and **serve**.

Per Serving: 273 Calories; 12g Fat (37.0% calories from fat); 10g Protein; 34g Carbohydrate; 10g Dietary Fiber; 0mg Cholesterol; 427mg Sodium.

Exchanges: 2 Grain(Starch); 1/2 Lean Meat; 1/2 Vegetable; 0 Fruit; 2 Fat.

" This is a fun side dish to take when there is a crowd. A small helping livens your plate. "

"brush your teeth every night so they will be healthy and bright"

O'Cean, Grade 2

"if you don't brush your teeth day and night, all the germs will be in sight"

Francie, Grade 3

chicken salad for the holidays

Connie Slyby, IN

serves 12

1	cup mayonnaise
1	teaspoon paprika
1	teaspoon seasoned salt
1 1/2	cups dried cranberries
1	cup celery — chopped
1/2	cup green pepper — minced
2	green onions — chopped
1	cup pecans — chopped
4	cups cooked chicken — cubed
	ground black pepper — to taste

In large bowl, **mix** first 3 ingredients.

Add next 5 ingredients.

Add chicken. **Mix** well.

Season with pepper, as desired.

Chill and **serve**.

Per Serving: 278 Calories; 24g Fat (74.4% calories from fat); 16g Protein; 3g Carbohydrate; 1g Dietary Fiber; 46mg Cholesterol; 263mg Sodium.

Exchanges: 0 Grain(Starch); 2 Lean Meat; 0 Vegetable; 0 Fruit; 2 1/2 Fat; 0 Other Carbohydrates.

"Can be used for a salad or in a sandwich."

christmas eve salad

Kathy Kne, OH

serves 8

8	small cooked beets — sliced, may use canned beets
4	oranges — peeled and chopped (remove white membrane)
4	red apples — unpeeled, cored and diced
1	fresh pineapple — cored, peeled and chopped, may use canned pineapple chunks (1 pound, 14 ounce)
3	limes — peeled and chopped (remove white membrane)
4	bananas — peeled and sliced
1	head iceberg lettuce — or equivalent amount bibb or boston
1/4	cup sugar — as needed
2	pomegranates — seeds only
1	cup peanuts — halved or chopped
1	cup salad dressing — tart french or orange juice

Save some thin slices of oranges, apples, pineapple, limes and banana for garnish.

In the bottom of a large salad bowl, **place** torn lettuce.

Arrange fruits over lettuce, sprinkling with sugar if desired.

Arrange top layer attractively, using all reserved fruit slices and beets.

Sprinkle pomegranate seeds and chopped peanuts over all.

Just before serving, **pour** on French dressing or orange juice (or pass dressing for diners to add their own).

Mix gently.

Per Serving: 346 Calories; 10g Fat (24.1% calories from fat); 8g Protein; 64g Carbohydrate; 9g Dietary Fiber; 0mg Cholesterol; 51mg Sodium.

Exchanges: 0 Grain(Starch); 1/2 Lean Meat; 1 1/2 Vegetable; 3 Fruit; 1 1/2 Fat; 1/2 Other Carbohydrates.

" This is a beautiful, delicious salad with interesting tastes and textures.

Makes a colorful, bold statement on a buffet table. "

"healthy teeth and healthy gums make your life fun, fun, fun"

Ryan, Grade 2

curried fruit and rice salad

serves 8

Dorothy Unger, IL

3	cups cooked rice — warm
1	large apple — cut 1/2" thick cubes, sprinkled with 2 teaspoons lemon juice
1	cup seedless grapes — red or green
2/3	cup golden raisins
2	cups celery — sliced thin
1/2	cup scallions — with tops, sliced thin
1/3	cup safflower oil
1 1/2	teaspoons white vinegar
1 1/2	teaspoons dijon mustard
1 1/2	teaspoons curry powder
	salt and pepper — to taste
1/4	cup mayonnaise
1	teaspoon dijon mustard
1	teaspoon honey
	salt — to taste

In large bowl, **combine** first 6 ingredients. **Set** aside.

In a large jar, **combine** next 6 ingredients to make marinade. **Shake** well.

Pour marinade over rice mixture. **Chill.**

In small bowl, **combine** last 4 ingredients. **Mix** well.

Add mayonnaise mix to chilled mixture. **Toss** well. **Serve**.

Per Serving: 295 Calories; 15g Fat (45.4% calories from fat); 3g Protein; 39g Carbohydrate; 2g Dietary Fiber; 2mg Cholesterol; 91mg Sodium.

Exchanges: 1 1/2 Grain(Starch); 0 Lean Meat; 1/2 Vegetable; 1 Fruit; 2 1/2 Fat; 0 Other Carbohydrates.

frozen yogurt salad
Carol Heimann, AZ

serves 12

2	cartons yogurt — strawberry
15	ounces crushed pineapple — drained
20	ounces frozen strawberries — thawed

Per Serving: 83 Calories; 1g Fat (14.3% calories from fat);
2g Protein; 17g Carbohydrate; 1g Dietary Fiber; 5mg Cholesterol;
20mg Sodium.

Exchanges: 1 Fruit; 0 Non-Fat Milk; 0 Fat; 0 Other Carbohydrates.

In large mixing bowl, **combine** all ingredients. **Blend** well.

Freeze in large plastic mold. **Thaw** about 30 minutes before serving.

May **spoon** into 12 paper-lined muffin pans, **freeze**.

After freezing, **remove** from pans, **store** in plastic bags or plastic container. **Thaw** 15 minutes before serving.

"From a long ago neighbor, this recipe can be made with any yogurt and fruit; use your imagination! Children like it and it's especially good during summer in Arizona."

grape salad
Connie Larsen, GA

serves 8

8	ounces sour cream
8	ounces cream cheese — softened
1/2	cup sugar — or substitute
1/2	teaspoon vanilla
1	pound grapes — red
1	pound grapes — white
1	cup brown sugar
1	cup pecans — chopped

Per Serving: 436 Calories; 25g Fat (49.3% calories from fat);
5g Protein; 53g Carbohydrate; 2g Dietary Fiber; 44mg Cholesterol;
108mg Sodium.

Exchanges: 0 Grain(Starch); 1/2 Lean Meat; 1 Fruit; 0 Non-Fat Milk;
5 Fat; 2 Other Carbohydrates.

In mixing bowl, **combine** first 4 ingredients. **Mix** well.

Add to grapes. **Mix** well.

In small bowl, **combine** brown sugar and pecans. **Mix** well. **Pour** over grape mix.

Refrigerate overnight. **Serve** chilled.

"brush and floss until your teeth are clean and watch how bright your smile will gleam"

Tyler, Grade 2

healthy fruit salad

Jean Barclay, UT

serves 36

6	ounces dried orange cranberries
16	ounces frozen blueberries
16	ounces frozen mixed tropical fruit
16	ounces frozen raspberries
2	cups seedless grapes — red or green
2	cups cantaloupe — chopped
16	ounces frozen boysenberries — or blackberries
2	cups miniature marshmallows — fruit flavored
2	bananas — sliced
2	kiwis — sliced
2	cans pineapple chunks in juice — drained
4	containers light blueberry yogurt
32	ounces fat free whipped topping

In very large bowl, **combine** all ingredients, **stir**.

Let **rest** half an hour, then **serve**.

May **add** mandarin oranges, maraschino cherries or any fruit that sounds good.

When available, **use** fresh fruits.

Per Serving: 129 Calories; 1g Fat (8.1% calories from fat); 2g Protein; 27g Carbohydrate; 2g Dietary Fiber; 3mg Cholesterol; 30mg Sodium.

Exchanges: 1 Fruit; 0 Non-Fat Milk; 0 Fat; 1/2 Other Carbohydrates.

" This is my original recipe. From adults to children, everyone raves about this one...and it is so easy ! "

lime fluff pear mold

Leah Gabrek, IN

serves 10

16	ounces pear halves in juice — drained, reserve juice
3	ounces lime gelatin powder
3	ounces cream cheese — cubed
2	cups whipped topping
	strawberries — for garnish

Per Serving: 133 Calories; 7g Fat (44.7% calories from fat); 2g Protein; 17g Carbohydrate; 1g Dietary Fiber; 9mg Cholesterol; 52mg Sodium.

Exchanges: 0 Lean Meat; 1/2 Fruit; 1 1/2 Fat; 1/2 Other Carbohydrates.

Drain pears, **save** juice. **Add** enough water to make 1 cup.

In saucepan, **heat** juice mix to boiling, **add** gelatin powder, **stir** until dissolved. **Cool** 5 minutes.

In blender, **mix** gelatin and cream cheese to smooth.

Add pears and **mix** until chopped.

Pour into bowl, **fold** in whipped topping. **Pour** into ring mold. **Chill**.

When ready to serve, **unmold** onto plate. **Place** strawberries in center of mold.

" This recipe is a favorite of the family. One time I didn't make it and everyone complained, so now it is enjoyed by all at every family dinner. "

"brush me, brush me, your teeth will say, if you don't, we might go away; but if you brush they will say, OK, OK, we think we'll stay"

Anna, Age 10

brush your teeth everyday, so you will wash those germs away

Cole, Grade 2

mandarin tossed salad

Barbara Mattern, IN

serves 8

salad

1	small head iceberg lettuce — broken , or bag of greens
3	green onions — sliced
11	ounces mandarin oranges in juice — drained

dressing

1/3	cup olive oil
3	tablespoons sugar
2	tablespoons vinegar
3/4	teaspoon salt
	dash pepper

topping

1/2	cup sliced almonds
2	tablespoons sugar
2	tablespoons water

Per Serving: 188 Calories; 14g Fat (63.3% calories from fat); 3g Protein; 15g Carbohydrate; 2g Dietary Fiber; 0mg Cholesterol; 210mg Sodium.

Exchanges: 0 Grain(Starch); 0 Lean Meat; 1/2 Vegetable; 0 Fruit; 2 1/2 Fat; 1/2 Other Carbohydrates.

In large salad bowl, **mix** all salad ingredients.

Add dressing. **Mix** well.

Top with prepared almonds. **Serve**.

dressing

In shaker, **mix** all dressing ingredients. **Shake** well.

topping

In microwaveable bowl, **mix** all topping ingredients.

Microwave on high, 2 1/2 minutes or until lightly toasted. **Stir** occasionally during cooking and when removing from oven.

" I use this recipe with sliced strawberries, pineapple or any fresh fruit. "

marty's salad

Marthiel Russell, TX

serves 18

10	ounces vermicelli — cooked
3	tablespoons lemon juice
2	tablespoons flavor enhancer
6	ounces black olives — chopped
1	cup celery — chopped
	green onion — to taste, chopped
1	green pepper — chopped
4	ounces chopped pimientos
1	pint salad dressing — not mayonnaise

Cook vermicelli as directed on package. **Marinate** overnight in lemon juice and flavor enhancer.

In salad bowl, **combine** next 5 ingredients. **Add** marinated pasta and salad dressing. **Mix** well.

Refrigerate at least 1 hour before serving. More time is better.

Will keep several days in refrigerator.

Per Serving: 70 Calories; 1g Fat (13.6% calories from fat); 2g Protein; 14g Carbohydrate; 1g Dietary Fiber; 0mg Cholesterol; 88mg Sodium.

Exchanges: 1 Grain(Starch); 0 Vegetable; 0 Fruit; 0 Fat.

minnie lee's frozen cranberry salad

Marietta Bishop, TN

serves 6

16	ounces cranberry sauce — whole berry
8	ounces crushed pineapple in juice
8	ounces sour cream

In a mixing bowl, **combine** all ingredients. **Mix** well.

Spoon equal amounts into cupcake papers. **Freeze.**

Keep frozen until ready to serve.

Per Serving: 218 Calories; 8g Fat (32.1% calories from fat); 2g Protein; 37g Carbohydrate; 1g Dietary Fiber; 17mg Cholesterol; 42mg Sodium.

Exchanges: 1/2 Fruit; 0 Non-Fat Milk; 1 1/2 Fat; 2 Other Carbohydrates.

" The color is a pale purple. Nice served in the Spring. "

out of this world ranch dressing

Connie Karlowicz, OH

serves 32 • yields 4 cups

1	cup oil
1/2	cup vinegar
1	cup sugar
1	tablespoon dry mustard
1	teaspoon paprika
1	teaspoon salt
1	teaspoon celery seed
10 3/4	ounces tomato soup, condensed
1	tablespoon worcestershire sauce

In electric mixer, **combine** all ingredients until sugar is dissolved.

Cover. **Refrigerate** 2 hours to allow flavors to blend.

Refrigerate any unused dressing.

Per Serving: 93 Calories; 7g Fat (66.0% calories from fat); trace Protein; 8g Carbohydrate; trace Dietary Fiber; 0mg Cholesterol; 124mg Sodium.

Exchanges: 0 Grain(Starch); 0 Lean Meat; 1 1/2 Fat; 1/2 Other Carbohydrates.

quick and easy fruit salad

serves 6

20	ounces pineapple chunks in juice — drained
11	ounces mandarin oranges in juice — drained
2	bananas — sliced
1	cup seedless grapes
10 1/2	ounces pie filling — apricot or cherry

In bowl, **combine** all fruits. **Mix** well.

Elizabeth Ferry, IL

Add pie filling, **mix**, **cover**.

Chill until ready to serve.

Fruits may be varied.

Per Serving: 128 Calories; trace Fat (2.0% calories from fat); 1g Protein; 33g Carbohydrate; 2g Dietary Fiber; 0mg Cholesterol; 6mg Sodium.

Exchanges: 2 Fruit.

ranch dressing

Melody Nord, ND

serves 32

2	cups mayonnaise — not salad dressing
1 1/2	cups buttermilk
2	teaspoons parsley flakes
2	teaspoons onion powder
1/2	teaspoon flavor enhancer
1/4	teaspoon garlic powder
1/4	teaspoon pepper
1	teaspoon salt

In 2 quart bowl, **mix** all ingredients together with wire whisk.

Refrigerate any unused portion.

Great as salad dressing,
veggie dip or on sandwiches.

Per Serving: 104 Calories; 12g Fat (95.5% calories from fat); 1g Protein; 1g Carbohydrate; trace Dietary Fiber; 5mg Cholesterol; 157mg Sodium.

Exchanges: 0 Grain(Starch); 0 Non-Fat Milk; 1 Fat.

" I teach high school Foods classes. Students love this hot on tostados, with chips or with any Mexican food. "

romaine-broccoli salad with red wine vinegar dressing

Sherry James, IN

serves 12

salad

3	ounces ramen noodles — broken
1	cup pecans — chopped
1/4	cup unsalted butter
1	bunch broccoli — broken
2	heads romaine lettuce — broken
4	green onions — chopped

dressing

1	cup sugar — or substitute
3/4	cup oil
1/2	cup red wine vinegar
1	tablespoon soy sauce
	salt and pepper — to taste

salad

In skillet, **brown** noodles and pecans in melted butter. **Set** aside.

In large salad bowl, **combine** all salad ingredients. **Mix.**

Pour approximately 1 cup dressing over salad just before serving.

Top salad with noodle-pecan mix. **Toss** and **serve**.

dressing

In bowl, **combine** all dressing ingredients.

Whisk until thoroughly mixed.

Unused dressing keeps several days.

If sugar substitute and olive oil are used this is great for diabetics or those watching carbohydrate intake.

Per Serving: 342 Calories; 24g Fat (60.4% calories from fat); 6g Protein; 30g Carbohydrate; 5g Dietary Fiber; 17mg Cholesterol; 113mg Sodium.

Exchanges: 1/2 Grain(Starch); 0 Lean Meat; 1 1/2 Vegetable; 4 1/2 Fat; 1 Other Carbohydrates.

"if you don't brush your teeth, you might meet your worst fear... having to wear head gear"

Martin, Age 10

spinach strawberry salad

Susan Beckett, IN

serves 10

salad

1	package spinach leaves, whole
2	pounds strawberries — sliced
1	small package almonds — toasted and sliced

dressing

1	cup sugar
1	teaspoon paprika
1/2	teaspoon prepared mustard
1	teaspoon worcestershire sauce
1	cup oil
1	teaspoon onion — minced
1/2	cup vinegar, cider
1/4	teaspoon poppy seeds
1/4	teaspoon sesame seeds

Per Serving: 383 Calories; 30g Fat (66.7% calories from fat); 3g Protein; 30g Carbohydrate; 4g Dietary Fiber; 0mg Cholesterol; 12mg Sodium.

Exchanges: 0 Grain(Starch); 1/2 Lean Meat; 0 Vegetable; 1/2 Fruit; 5 1/2 Fat; 1 1/2 Other Carbohydrates.

salad

In salad bowl, **layer** spinach, strawberries, then almonds. **Refrigerate** until ready to serve.

Pour dressing over salad just before serving. **Toss.**

dressing

In small bowl, **whisk** all dressing ingredients to blend thoroughly.

" This is a beautiful salad for summer picnics or carry-ins. It is always a big hit ! "

vegetable salad

Christy Blake, IN

serves 12

salad

1	large bunch broccoli — cut up
1	head cauliflower — cut up
1	can artichoke hearts — in water, sliced
1	can waterchestnuts — sliced
8	ounces fresh mushrooms — sliced
1	cup bacon — cooked and chopped

dressing

1	cup mayonnaise
2/3	cup vegetable oil
1/3	cup vinegar
1/2	cup sugar

Per Serving: 411 Calories; 38g Fat (79.2% calories from fat);
8g Protein; 14g Carbohydrate; 2g Dietary Fiber; 23mg Cholesterol;
443mg Sodium.

Exchanges: 0 Grain(Starch); 1 Lean Meat; 1 Vegetable; 5 Fat;
1/2 Other Carbohydrates.

salad

In large salad bowl, **combine** all salad ingredients.

Pour dressing over salad a few hours before serving. **Toss**.

dressing

In bowl, **mix** all dressing ingredients thoroughly. **Chill** until ready for use.

" This is very easy to put together. It tastes even better the next few days. "

**"brush your teeth twice a day;
so you'll keep the germs away"**

Liza, Grade 3

vermicelli asparagus toss

Mary Miller, OH

serves 10

1	pound asparagus — washed, cleaned
7	ounces vermicelli
1	cup grape tomatoes — halved
4	green onions — sliced
1/2	cup feta cheese
2	teaspoons basil
1 1/2	teaspoons thyme
1/4	teaspoon salt
2	tablespoons lemon juice
1/2	cup Italian salad dressing

Per Serving: 155 Calories; 7g Fat (42.4% calories from fat); 4g Protein; 19g Carbohydrate; 1g Dietary Fiber; 7mg Cholesterol; 231mg Sodium.

Exchanges: 1 Grain(Starch); 0 Lean Meat; 1/2 Vegetable; 0 Fruit; 1 1/2 Fat.

In large saucepan, **blanch** asparagus 1 minute. **Drain**. **Cut** into 2 inch pieces. **Set** aside.

Cook pasta as directed on package. **Drain**. **Rinse**. **Drain** again.

In large serving bowl, **place** pasta, asparagus, tomatoes, onions and feta.

In small bowl, **combine** remaining ingredients. **Pour** over salad. **Toss**.

Serve hot or cold.

"This awesome salad stands alone-and stands out at any luncheon! It was passed along from a friend and owner of an Irish boutique in Toledo."

"brush your teeth twice a day,
if you don't want tooth decay"

Thomas, Age 10

walnut pomegranate salad

Hannah Sammons, AZ

serves 8

salad

1	cup sugar
1	bag walnuts — halved
2	bags lettuce — spring mix or european
1	package gorgonzola cheese — cubed
1	pomegranate — seeded and peeled (optional)

dressing

1/2	cup vegetable oil
1/4	cup red wine vinegar
1/4	cup vinegar, cider
3/4	teaspoon salt
3/4	teaspoon pepper
2	tablespoons sugar
1/8	teaspoon tarragon

Per Serving: 355 Calories; 24g Fat (57.2% calories from fat); 5g Protein; 35g Carbohydrate; 1g Dietary Fiber; 3mg Cholesterol; 251mg Sodium.

Exchanges: 0 Grain(Starch); 1/2 Lean Meat; 0 Vegetable; 0 Fruit; 4 1/2 Fat; 2 Other Carbohydrates.

salad

In skillet, **melt** sugar to brown. DO NOT BURN.

Add walnuts and coat. **Turn** out on waxed paper, **break** into pieces. **Set** aside.

In salad bowl, **combine** lettuce, cheese, pomegranate and walnut pieces.

Just before serving **prepare** dressing, **pour** over salad. **Toss** and **serve**.

dressing

In bowl, **whisk** all dressing ingredients until well blended.

" Great holiday salad. "

75

bottled water and
tooth decay prevention

If bottled water is the main source of drinking water for your family, they may be missing the decay-preventive benefits of fluoride. The majority of bottled waters do not contain the optimal levels (0.7-1.2 ppm) of fluoride.

How can you make sure you — and especially your children — are getting the right amount of fluoride protection?

• Check the bottled water label for fluoride content or contact the company and ask what level of fluoride the water contains. (Amounts of fluoride are the same whether they are reported in parts per million or milligrams per liter.)

• Don't overlook home water treatment systems, such as reverse osmosis and distillation units, which may remove the fluoride from water supplies. Read the manual or contact the manufacturer to determine their effect on fluoride levels.

Since 1950, the American Dental Association and the United States Public Health Service have continuously and unreservedly endorsed the optimal fluoridation of community water supplies as a safe and effective public health measure for the prevention of dental decay. Studies show that water fluoridation can reduce the amount of cavities children get in their baby teeth by as much as 60% and can reduce tooth decay in permanent adult teeth by nearly 35%.

"brushing teeth improves your smile and helps it last for quite a while"

Paige, Grade 6

vegetables

ingredients:

eating vegetables

Vegetables are almost always served with the main course, and some can be difficult to eat.

- Whole artichokes are eaten with the fingers. Remove each leaf separately, dip the soft end in sauce, pull it through your teeth to remove the edible portion and discard the remainder. Cut away the thistle before exposing the heart. Then, cut into pieces and eat with a fork.

- Asparagus is cut into bite-size pieces and eaten with a fork. In Europe, it is eaten with the fingers or asparagus tongs.

- Corn on the cob is served only at casual meals. Butter and season several rows at a time—not the whole ear at once. Hold the ear firmly with the fingers of both hands.

- Baked potatoes are eaten from the skin with a fork. You may eat the skin with a knife and fork. Do not mash potatoes on your plate.

- Chips and shoestring potatoes are eaten with your fingers.

- French fries are eaten with a fork or fingers. If served with food that requires a fork, like fish, they are eaten with a fork. If served with food eaten with fingers, like a hamburger on a bun, they are eaten with the fingers.

- Celery, olives, pickles and radishes can be taken from the serving tray with your fingers and placed on the side of your dinner plate or bread and butter plate. Celery and radishes may be dipped in salt and eaten with the fingers. Large olives with a pit are eaten in several bites, discarding the pit on the side of the plate. Small stuffed olives are eaten whole.

allie's creamed celery

Joanne Parrot, MO

serves 8

5	cups celery — diced
1	teaspoon salt — (omit if on low sodium diet)
1/4	teaspoon pepper
1/4	cup butter
1	tablespoon onion — finely chopped
1/2	cup chicken broth — or bouillon
1 1/2	tablespoons flour
1	cup half and half
1/2	cup slivered almonds — optional

Per Serving: 164 Calories; 14g Fat (74.6% calories from fat); 4g Protein; 7g Carbohydrate; 2g Dietary Fiber; 27mg Cholesterol; 451mg Sodium.

Exchanges: 0 Grain(Starch); 0 Lean Meat; 1/2 Vegetable; 0 Non-Fat Milk; 2 1/2 Fat.

In medium saucepan, **place** first 6 ingredients. **Cover. Bring** to boil.

Lower heat, **cook** slowly 15 minutes.

Stir in flour. **Add** cream. **Cook** 1 minute.

Stir in almonds, if desired. **Pour** into serving dish.

Serve immediately.

Easy to prepare. Celery can be diced the day before.

"Especially good as a side dish with poultry.

Passed down from my Great Aunt Allie, this is a treasured

tradition of our family Thanksgiving dinner. "

quotes

"you're the boss, when you floss"

Joshua, Age 11

infants' teeth can be harmed by letting babies fall asleep with a bottle of anything other than water.

brussels sprouts in brown butter

Susan Barsness, IL

serves 6

10	ounces frozen brussels sprouts
6	ounces sliced almonds
1/2	stick butter
	salt to taste

Per Serving: 253 Calories; 23g Fat (75.5% calories from fat); 8g Protein; 9g Carbohydrate; 4g Dietary Fiber; 21mg Cholesterol; 86mg Sodium.

Exchanges: 1/2 Grain(Starch); 1/2 Lean Meat; 1 Vegetable; 4 Fat.

In steamer, **steam** brussels sprouts to tender.

In saucepan, **melt** butter, **cook** to brown.

Add almonds and brussels sprouts.

Add salt to taste.

Serve immediately.

cooked cabbage and tomato sauce

Margaret Slyby, IN

serves 6

1	medium onion — chopped
1	tablespoon olive oil
1	head cabbage — coarsely chopped
1	small can tomato sauce
	salt and pepper to taste

Per Serving: 43 Calories; 2g Fat (46.1% calories from fat); 1g Protein; 5g Carbohydrate; 1g Dietary Fiber; 0mg Cholesterol; 250mg Sodium.

Exchanges: 1 Vegetable; 1/2 Fat.

In skillet, **brown** onion in olive oil.

Add cabbage. **Cook** and **stir** until tender.

Add tomato sauce. **Season** with salt and pepper.

Cook 10 minutes more, uncovered.

Serve immediately.

corn casserole

Shirley Walsh, LA

serves 20

1	stick margarine
1	small onion — chopped, or chopped green onion
1/4	green pepper — chopped
15	ounces corn — whole kernel, undrained
15	ounces creamed corn
8 1/2	ounces corn muffin mix
8	ounces sour cream
1	egg
	cajun seasoning to taste

Per Serving: 143 Calories; 9g Fat (53.8% calories from fat); 2g Protein; 15g Carbohydrate; 1g Dietary Fiber; 14mg Cholesterol; 258mg Sodium.

Exchanges: 1/2 Grain(Starch); 0 Lean Meat; 0 Vegetable; 0 Non-Fat Milk; 1 1/2 Fat; 1/2 Other Carbohydrates.

Preheat oven to 350 degrees. **Grease** 9x13 baking dish.

In skillet, **melt** margarine, **saute** onion and green pepper.

In bowl, **combine** whole kernel corn, creamed corn, corn muffin mix, sour cream and egg.

Season to taste with cajun seasoning.

Add sauteed onions and green peppers. **Mix** well.

Pour into prepared casserole dish. **Bake** 350 degrees, 45 minutes - 1 hour.

Should be golden brown and solid, but not dry.

Serve.

creamed spinach

Dr. David Slyby, IN

serves 6

10	ounces frozen chopped spinach
2	slices bacon — finely chopped
1/2	onion — chopped
2	tablespoons flour
1	teaspoon salt
	pepper — to taste
1	clove garlic — minced
1	cup whole milk

Per Serving: 62 Calories; 3g Fat (35.6% calories from fat); 4g Protein; 7g Carbohydrate; 2g Dietary Fiber; 7mg Cholesterol; 444mg Sodium.

Exchanges: 0 Grain(Starch); 0 Lean Meat; 1/2 Vegetable; 0 Non-Fat Milk; 1/2 Fat.

Cook spinach according to directions on package. **Drain**.

In skillet, **fry** bacon. **Add** onions and cook until tender, about 10 minutes.

Add flour, salt, pepper and garlic.

Slowly **add** milk, **stir** until thick.

Add spinach. **Mix** thoroughly.

Serve immediately.

" This is a family favorite. " quotes

fresh carrot puree

Catherine Capps, GA

serves 8

4	pounds carrots — peeled
1/2	cup unsalted butter — melted
1 1/2	cups chicken broth — warmed
1/2	cup fresh orange juice
3/4	teaspoon orange zest — grated
1/2	teaspoon ground cardamom
1	teaspoon salt
	pinch cayenne pepper

Per Serving: 203 Calories; 12g Fat (51.6% calories from fat); 3g Protein; 22g Carbohydrate; 6g Dietary Fiber; 31mg Cholesterol; 482mg Sodium.

Exchanges: 0 Grain(Starch); 0 Lean Meat; 4 Vegetable; 0 Fruit; 2 1/2 Fat.

Preheat oven to 350 degrees.

In saucepan, **cover** carrots with water, **cook** until tender. **Drain.**

In food processor, **combine** all ingredients. **Process** until smooth.

Increase seasonings, if desired.

Pour into 9x13 baking dish. **Cover.**

Bake 350 degrees, 25 minutes or until heated through.

Garnish with sour cream. **Serve.**

" Use this colorful dish as a side dish or substitute for heavy sauces.

This is healthy alternative to sweetened side dishes. "

Vegetables were originally eaten raw. Because of their water content, they were thought to cool the body. Lettuce and some vegetables were eaten after the meal as a palette cleanser before dessert. Today, salad is still often served after the main course in Europe.

"brush your teeth twice a day, we love to see you smile the whole day"

Amir, Grade 3

georgia caviar

Shari Carter, GA

serves 8

2	cans blackeyed peas — drained
1/2	cup onion — diced
1/2	cup green pepper — diced
1/2	clove garlic — whole
1/4	cup vinegar
1/4	cup sugar
1/4	cup oil
1/2	teaspoon salt
1/2	teaspoon pepper
	hot sauce — optional

In large bowl, **combine** all ingredients. **Mix** thoroughly.

Refrigerate 12 hours.

Remove and **discard** garlic clove. **Drain**.

Add hot sauce to taste.

Pour into serving dish. **Serve**.

Per Serving: 233 Calories; 7g Fat (27.7% calories from fat); 10g Protein; 33g Carbohydrate; 5g Dietary Fiber; 0mg Cholesterol; 141mg Sodium.

Exchanges: 1 1/2 Grain(Starch); 1/2 Lean Meat; 1/2 Vegetable; 1 1/2 Fat; 1/2 Other Carbohydrates.

Nice side dish.

"your white bright teeth need a brush and some paste; take care of your smile so it won't go to waste"

Harrison, Age 7

green beans with peppers, olives and capers

Dorothy Unger, IL

serves 8

1	pound fresh or frozen green beans
1/4	cup extra virgin olive oil
7 1/4	ounces (jar) red peppers — peeled, drained, cut in 1/2 inch slices
2	large cloves garlic — minced
6	ounces oil-cured black ripe olives
1/4	cup capers — rinsed and drained
1	teaspoon dried oregano
3	tablespoons fresh parsley — chopped
1/2	teaspoon salt
1/4	teaspoon pepper
	pinch hot pepper flakes

Cook green beans according to directions on package. **Drain**. **Set** aside.

Meanwhile, in large skillet, **heat** olive oil over medium-low heat.

Add remaining ingredients. **Cook**, stirring, 2 minutes.

Add beans to sauce. **Toss** to coat. **Turn** into serving dish.

Serve hot or cold.

Per Serving: 163 Calories; 13g Fat (67.8% calories from fat); 2g Protein; 12g Carbohydrate; 4g Dietary Fiber; 0mg Cholesterol; 931mg Sodium.

Exchanges: 0 Grain(Starch); 2 Vegetable; 2 1/2 Fat; 0 Other Carbohydrates.

" My daughter Marilyn served this with cold poached chicken, curried rice and fruit salad. Tasty summer supper. "

grilled asparagus with orange dipping sauce

Lillie Sowell, TN

serves 8

2	tablespoons olive oil
1/4	teaspoon salt
2	tablespoons tarragon — divided, fresh is best
1	pound asparagus — trimmed
1/3	cup light mayonnaise
1	tablespoon orange juice
1/2	teaspoon orange peel — grated
1/2	teaspoon cayenne pepper
1/2	teaspoon anise seed — crushed, optional

Per Serving: 65 Calories; 5g Fat (71.3% calories from fat); 1g Protein; 4g Carbohydrate; 1g Dietary Fiber; 4mg Cholesterol; 118mg Sodium.

Exchanges: 0 Grain(Starch); 0 Lean Meat; 1/2 Vegetable; 0 Fruit; 1 Fat; 0 Other Carbohydrates.

In bowl, **whisk** together oil, salt and 1 tablespoon tarragon. **Pour** over trimmed asparagus. **Set** aside.

Light grill, or oven if broiling.

In another small bowl, **combine** next 4 ingredients, remaining tarragon, and anise, if using. **Set** aside.

Arrange asparagus in single layer on grill, or baking sheet if using oven.

Grill over medium heat, 7 minutes, or until tender, **turning** after 3 minutes.

If broiling, **cook** 5 minutes, **turning** once.

Place in serving dish. **Pour** orange sauce over. **Serve.**

" We prefer grilling because of the "smoky" flavor. "

"don't eat too much sweet or your teeth will fall out. and every year, go to a dentist to get a check-up in your mouth"

Michelle, Grade 4

jaw or facial pain? possible causes include toothache, sinus or TMD. a dentist can identify which one.

pea casserole

Dinah Catey, IN

serves 8

2	tablespoons butter
8	ounces sliced mushrooms
1/2	cup celery — sliced
1	can cream of mushroom soup, condensed — or cream of celery
20	ounces frozen peas — thawed
1	can bean sprouts — drained
1	can waterchestnuts — sliced, drained

Per Serving: 133 Calories; 6g Fat (40.2% calories from fat); 5g Protein; 15g Carbohydrate; 4g Dietary Fiber; 8mg Cholesterol; 426mg Sodium.

Exchanges: 1 Grain(Starch); 1/2 Vegetable; 1 Fat.

Preheat oven to 350 degrees. **Butter** 9x9 or 7x11 casserole dish.

In skillet, **melt** butter. **Saute** mushrooms and celery.

Add remaining ingredients. **Mix** thoroughly.

Pour into prepared casserole dish. **Bake** 350 degrees, 45 minutes.

Serve hot.

" Passed down from a former co-worker, Esther Shafer. "

"keep your teeth super clean, you might grow to marry a queen"

Matthew, Age 10

"tooth decay you will lack,
if what you eat is a healthy snack"

John, Grade 2

potato casserole

Debbie Preece, UT

serves 10

4	medium potatoes — boiled, peeled, coarsely grated
1/8	cup butter
1/2	can cream of chicken soup, condensed — undiluted
1/2	pint sour cream
1/3	cup onions — chopped
3/4	cup shredded cheddar cheese — mild

topping

1/2	cup potato chips — crushed
2	tablespoons butter — melted

Per Serving: 240 Calories; 17g Fat (63.0% calories from fat); 5g Protein; 17g Carbohydrate; 1g Dietary Fiber; 33mg Cholesterol; 284mg Sodium.

Exchanges: 1 Grain(Starch); 1/2 Lean Meat; 0 Vegetable; 0 Non-Fat Milk; 3 Fat.

Preheat oven to 350 degrees.

In large saucepan or microwave bowl, **warm** all ingredients except potatoes.

In large casserole dish, **combine** potatoes and warmed mix.

Sprinkle topping over potato mixture.

Bake 350 degrees, 45 minutes, in small casserole dish.

For 9x13 baking pan, double all ingredients except topping.

 A great casserole that can be frozen to use later. "

"brush your teeth morning and night to keep your teeth all of your life"

Natalie, *Age 5*

ruth's colorado beans

Linda Iczkovitz, IN

serves 20

1	pound bacon
1	large onion — diced
1	pound can lima beans — drained
1	pound can butter beans — drained
1	pound can Mexican-style chili beans — drained
1	pound can kidney or navy beans — drained,
1	pound can pork and beans — undrained
1	cup ketchup
1/2	cup brown sugar
2	teaspoons dry mustard

Preheat oven to 350 degrees.

In skillet, **fry** bacon to crisp, **drain**.

Add onion, **brown** in bacon drippings.

In large bowl, **combine** all ingredients. **Mix** well.

Pour into large casserole dish. **Bake** 350 degrees, 1 hour.

Serve.

Per Serving: 269 Calories; 12g Fat (38.4% calories from fat); 14g Protein; 28g Carbohydrate; 8g Dietary Fiber; 20mg Cholesterol; 598mg Sodium.

Exchanges: 1 1/2 Grain(Starch); 1 1/2 Lean Meat; 0 Vegetable; 1 1/2 Fat; 1/2 Other Carbohydrates.

" Delicious side dish for those summer barbeques.

Serve with a juicy burger off the grill. Very rich in flavor! "

spinach
mushroom casserole

Jan Hagedorn, IN

serves 8

1	tablespoon butter
1	pound fresh mushrooms — washed, use stems and caps
3	packages frozen spinach — thawed
1	teaspoon salt
4	green onions — chopped
1/4	cup butter — melted
1	cup grated cheddar cheese — divided garlic salt to taste

Per Serving: 151 Calories; 12g Fat (69.4% calories from fat); 7g Protein; 6g Carbohydrate; 3g Dietary Fiber; 34mg Cholesterol; 474mg Sodium.

Exchanges: 1/2 Lean Meat; 1 Vegetable; 2 Fat

Preheat oven to 350 degrees.

In skillet, **melt** 1 tablespoon butter, **saute** mushroom stems and caps to brown.

In 10 inch casserole dish, **put** spinach, salt, green onions, and 1/4 cup butter.

Sprinkle with 1/2 cup cheese.

Arrange mushrooms over spinach.

Season with garlic salt.

Cover with remaining cheese.

Bake 350 degrees, 20 minutes.

Serve.

"A great make ahead dinner party casserole. Refrigerate until ready to use.

We've been using this recipe for more than 30 years"

"eat good foods, brush twice a day, then you won't get tooth decay and you'll have more time to play yaa"

Morgan, Grade 3

> **"floss and paste keep them clean, nice and bright they will seem"**
>
> Sweta, Grade 4

steve's favorite green bean casserole

Doris Cunningham, NC

serves 8

2	tablespoons butter
2	tablespoons flour
1	teaspoon salt
1/4	teaspoon pepper
1	tablespoon sugar
1	small onion — grated
1	pint sour cream
1/2	pound swiss cheese — grated
1	can fried onion rings
2	cans French-style green beans — drained

Preheat oven to 400 degrees. **Grease** casserole dish.

In saucepan, **combine** all ingredients, except last 3. **Cook** and **stir** until thick.

Add beans. **Pour** into prepared casserole.

Bake 400 degrees, 20 minutes. **Remove** from oven. **Sprinkle** top with cheese and onion rings.

Bake additional 5 minutes or until cheese is melted.

Serve hot.

Per Serving: 285 Calories; 23g Fat (71.6% calories from fat); 11g Protein; 10g Carbohydrate; trace Dietary Fiber; 60mg Cholesterol; 407mg Sodium.

Exchanges: 0 Grain(Starch); 1 Lean Meat; 1/2 Vegetable; 0 Non-Fat Milk; 4 Fat; 0 Other Carbohydrates.

" Son Steve's favorite. From a friend. " quotes

sweet potatoes with cranberry orange glaze

Robin Larson, UT

serves 12

6	sweet potatoes — peeled and cut lengthwise
1/2	cup cranberries
1/4	cup orange juice
1	cup brown sugar
	zest from one orange

Per Serving: 118 Calories; trace Fat (1.6% calories from fat); 1g Protein; 29g Carbohydrate; 2g Dietary Fiber; 0mg Cholesterol; 13mg Sodium.

Exchanges: 1 Grain(Starch); 0 Fruit; 1 Other Carbohydrates.

Preheat oven to 350 degrees.

Bake sweet potatoes, 350 degrees, 45 minutes or until golden brown and fork tender.

Meanwhile, in saucepan, **combine** rest of ingredients. **Boil** 5 minutes. **Strain**.

Place sweet potatoes in serving dish. **Pour** over glaze.

Serve hot.

" This is lots better then traditional yams with brown sugar.
Less fat, better taste. My kids never eat yams, but they love these! "

**"hold on wait a while;
you're going to get a brighter smile"**

Garrett, Grade 4

"brush, brush every day,
brush all the germs away"

I'Zarious, Grade 2

tomato pie

Jane Lange, KY

serves 16

1	pie shell, deep dish — baked and cooled
2	large tomatoes — peeled and thickly sliced, divided
1	bunch green onions — chopped, divided
	salt and pepper to taste
1	teaspoon dried basil — or 1 tablespoon fresh basil
1	tablespoon flour
12	slices bacon — fried and crumbled
1	cup mayonnaise
1/2	cup parmesan cheese — grated
1/2	cup mozzarella cheese — or any white cheese

Preheat oven to 350 degrees.

Cover bottom of pie shell with layer of half the tomatoes.

Sprinkle with salt and pepper, basil and flour.

Layer remaining tomatoes over first layer, **sprinkle** with remaining green onions.

In small bowl, **mix** mayonnaise and cheeses. **Spread** over tomatoes sealing top of pie.

Bake 350 degrees, 30-40 minutes.

Let **sit** a few minutes before cutting. **Serve** hot.

Per Serving: 204 Calories; 19g Fat (79.7% calories from fat); 4g Protein; 6g Carbohydrate; 1g Dietary Fiber; 14mg Cholesterol; 290mg Sodium.

Exchanges: 1/2 Grain(Starch); 1/2 Lean Meat; 0 Vegetable; 2 Fat.

"Use no-fat mayo and no-fat cheese for a healthier recipe."

vegetarian meatloaf

Jerilyn Bird, FL

serves 8

24	ounces cottage cheese — no fat, small curd
2 1/2	cups bran cereal
2	large eggs
3/4	cup margarine — melted
3/4	cup pecan flour — (finely chopped pecans)
1	medium onion — finely chopped
1	cup seasoned bread crumbs
2	tablespoons parsley
2	tablespoons soy sauce
1	tablespoon garlic powder
14 1/2	ounce can stewed Italian tomatoes

Per Serving: 422 Calories; 21g Fat (43.5% calories from fat); 22g Protein; 40g Carbohydrate; 5g Dietary Fiber; 54mg Cholesterol; 1333mg Sodium.

Exchanges: 2 Grain(Starch); 2 Lean Meat; 1 1/2 Vegetable; 3 1/2 Fat.

Preheat oven to 350 degrees. **Grease** 9x13 baking dish.

In large mixing bowl, **combine** all ingredients except stewed tomatoes. **Mix** thoroughly using a spoon.

Place mix in prepared pan. **Flatten** and **cover** with foil.

Bake 350 degrees, 45 minutes.

Meanwhile, in food processor, **blend** tomatoes and dash of garlic powder, for a few seconds. **Set** aside.

After 45 minutes, **remove** loaf from oven, uncover, **top** with tomato sauce. **Return** to oven.

Bake 30 more minutes, uncovered.

Cut into squares. **Serve**.

— From a friend, Natalie Weaver.

" This is very healthy. For variety, form the mix into patties (like burgers), bake and serve on buns. "

yellow squash casserole

Patsy Mitchener, IN

serves 8

4	yellow squash — sliced thin
1	medium onion — diced
1	egg — beaten
2	tablespoons butter — or margarine
1/2	pound processed American cheese
	salt and pepper — to taste
1/2	cup crackers — crushed

Per Serving: 222 Calories; 14g Fat (57.1% calories from fat); 9g Protein; 15g Carbohydrate; 2g Dietary Fiber; 58mg Cholesterol; 636mg Sodium.

Exchanges: 1/2 Grain(Starch); 1 Lean Meat; 1/2 Vegetable; 2 Fat.

Preheat oven to 350 degrees. **Butter** 9 inch casserole dish.

In steamer, **steam** squash and onion until tender.

Add egg and butter. **Mix**.

Stir in cheese until melted.

Add salt and pepper to taste.

Cover with crackers.

Bake 350 degrees, 20 - 30 minutes or until bubbly.

Serve hot.

usda food pyramid guidelines

A healthy diet contributes not only to dental health—but also to overall health!

Based on years of research, the United States Department of Agriculture suggests seven dietary guidelines. The USDA food pyramid is meant to help you choose what and how much to eat from each food group—thus providing the nutrients you need, while limiting calories, fat, cholesterol, sugar and sodium.

- Eat a variety of foods to get the energy, protein, vitamins, minerals and fiber you need for good health.

- Balance the food you eat with physical activity and maintain or improve your weight to reduce your chances of having high blood pressure, heart disease, a stroke, certain cancers and the most common kind of diabetes.

- Choose a diet with plenty of grain products, vegetables and fruits, which provide needed vitamins, minerals, fiber and complex carbohydrates and which can help you lower your intake of fat.

- Choose a diet low in fat, saturated fat and cholesterol to reduce your risk of heart attack and certain types of cancer and to help you maintain a healthy weight.

- Choose a diet moderate in sugars. A diet with lots of sugars has too many calories and too few nutrients for most people and can contribute to tooth decay.

- Choose a diet moderate in salt and sodium to help reduce your risk of high blood pressure.

- If you drink alcoholic beverages, do so in moderation. Alcoholic beverages supply calories but little or no nutrients. Drinking alcohol is also the cause of many health problems and accidents and can lead to addiction.

knocked out tooth? put it in milk
and take it to the dentist quickly!

ingredients:

eating pasta

Pasta is an Italian word for "dough" and is a type of noodle made a variety of ways: round, short sections, like penne; thin long strings, such as spaghetti; flat long forms, notably egg noodles; and wide shapes, such as lasagna. The width and length of the noodle determine whether the pasta is cut or wound around the tines of a fork.

- When pasta, such as spaghetti, is served on a plate or in a shallow bowl, it is eaten with a fork. Wind two or three strands around the tines of the fork balanced against the side of the plate or a spoon.

- Using the spoon in one hand as a base to steady the fork while winding the noodles is frowned upon in some parts of Italy.

- Wide noodles, such as lasagna, are cut with a fork.

- When ravioli is served in a deep bowl, it is eaten with a spoon.

- One-dish meals or casseroles are usually eaten with a fork. Use a knife to cut large pieces of meat or vegetables. If the dish is very juicy, a spoon may be used.

- If you are dining in a formal restaurant or attempting to make a good impression, avoid ordering food that is difficult to eat, such as spaghetti.

apple-pecan stuffing

Sue Ryser, UT

serves 8

1	cup chicken broth
1/2	cup celery — chopped
1/4	cup onion — chopped
4	tablespoons butter — or margarine
1/2	teaspoon salt
4	cups whole wheat bread crumbs — dry (about 8 slices)
1	large peeled apple — cored and diced
1/2	cup pecans — chopped
1	teaspoon ground sage
1/3	teaspoon cinnamon
1/8	teaspoon pepper

Per Serving: 320 Calories; 14g Fat (37.5% calories from fat) 9g Protein; 43g Carbohydrate; 7g Dietary Fiber; 16mg Cholesterol; 603mg Sodium.

Exchanges: 2 1/2 Grain(Starch); 0 Lean Meat; 0 Vegetable; 0 Fruit; 2 1/2 Fat.

Preheat oven to 350 degrees. **Prepare** bird or **grease** 2 quart casserole dish.

In medium saucepan, **combine** first 5 ingredients. **Simmer** 5 minutes or until vegetables are tender.

In large mixing bowl, **combine** remaining ingredients. **Pour** broth mix over, **toss** gently.

Stuff loosely into bird or pour into prepared casserole dish.

Cover. **Bake** 350 degrees, 25-30 minutes.

" Whole wheat bread and bits of apple make this a holiday winner. "

"brush and floss three times a day to chase the sugar bugs away"

Taryn, Kindergarten

asparagus cheese sauce for pasta

Dorothy Unger, IL

serves 4

10	ounces frozen asparagus
8	ounces cream cheese
1/2	cup milk
1/8	teaspoon white pepper
2	tablespoons parmesan cheese
2	teaspoons fresh thyme — tarragon or basil

Per Serving: 246 Calories; 22g Fat (76.9% calories from fat) 9g Protein; 6g Carbohydrate; 1g Dietary Fiber; 68mg Cholesterol; 235mg Sodium.

Exchanges: 0 Grain(Starch); 1 Lean Meat; 1/2 Vegetable; 0 Non-Fat Milk; 4 Fat.

Cook asparagus as directed on package.

Meanwhile in a saucepan, **heat** cream cheese, milk and white pepper until cheese is softened.

Stir in parmesan cheese and spice.

Add more milk if needed.

Toss asparagus and sauce with hot pasta.

Garnish with additional herbs and pink peppercorns or almonds.

Serve hot.

"fluoridated water makes my teeth harder; drink it everyday. it reduces tooth decay"

Kathryn, Age 8

baked bananas

Janie Quinn, PA

serves 4

1 1/2	teaspoons butter
2	bananas
2	teaspoons cranberry juice
4	teaspoons maple syrup
1/4	teaspoon cinnamon

Per Serving: 86 Calories; 2g Fat (16.8% calories from fat)
1g Protein; 19g Carbohydrate; 1g Dietary Fiber; 4mg Cholesterol;
16mg Sodium.

Exchanges: 0 Grain(Starch); 1 Fruit; 1/2 Fat; 1/2 Other
Carbohydrates.

Preheat oven to 400 degrees.

In a baking dish, **melt** butter in heated oven, about 5 minutes.

Slice banana in half lengthwise then crosswise,
forming quarters.

Turn quarters in butter to coat. **Sprinkle** with remaining
ingredients.

Bake 400 degrees, 10 minutes.

Serve warm.

" Deliciously sweet, melts in your mouth

without feeling guilty or deprived. "

Pasta is a food attributed to France, Japan and China.

It was introduced to Europe by Marco Polo.

tidbits

cheesy apples

Shari Carter, GA

serves 6

16	ounces canned apple slices — (not pie filling)
1	cup granulated sugar
1	stick butter — or margarine
1/2	pound processed American cheese — cubed
3/4	cup flour

Per Serving: 514 Calories; 28g Fat (47.5% calories from fat); 10g Protein; 58g Carbohydrate; 2g Dietary Fiber; 77mg Cholesterol; 700mg Sodium.

Exchanges: 1 Grain(Starch); 1 Lean Meat; 1 Fruit; 4 1/2 Fat 2 Other Carbohydrates.

Preheat oven to 350 degrees. **Butter** casserole dish.

In prepared casserole dish, **place** apples to form one layer. **Set** aside.

In mixing bowl, **cream** sugar and butter. **Add** cheese and flour. **Mix** well.

Spread cheese mix over layer of apples.

Bake 350 degrees, 30-35 minutes.

Serve warm.

" Wonderful as a side dish with ham, pork or baked chicken. "

"brush and brush every day,
it will take your smile a long way"

Janay, Grade 3

lip or tongue bitten? clean gently
and apply a cold compress;
if bleeding won't stop, go to the ER.

chicken artichoke rice
Susan Martindale, MS

serves 10

2	jars (6 ounces each) marinated artichoke hearts
1	package rice — chicken flavored
3	small onions — finely chopped
1/2	bell pepper — chopped
12	olives — stuffed
1	tablespoon mayonnaise
3/4	teaspoon curry powder

Drain artichoke hearts. **Reserve** oil. **Chop**.

Cook rice as directed on package.

In large serving bowl, **mix** artichokes, rice, onions, bell pepper and olives. **Add** reserved oil to taste.

Add mayonnaise and curry.

Serve at room temperature.

This dish is better if prepared
a day ahead of serving.

Per Serving: 103 Calories; 2g Fat (19.3% calories from fat)
2g Protein; 19g Carbohydrate; 1g Dietary Fiber; trace Cholesterol;
73mg Sodium.

Exchanges: 1 Grain(Starch); 1/2 Vegetable; 0 Fruit; 1/2 Fat.

confetti rice
Jill Martin, CA

serves 8

1	cup onion — chopped
1/2	cup green pepper — chopped
1	clove garlic — minced
3	tablespoons butter
1 1/2	cups rice — uncooked
2	cups beef broth — boiling hot
1 1/2	teaspoons salt
1/4	teaspoon pepper
1/2	teaspoon basil
3	medium tomatoes — cut into small wedges

Preheat oven to 350 degrees.

In large skillet, **saute** onion, green pepper and garlic in butter until tender.

Add rice. **Cook** 2 minutes more.

Turn into shallow 2 quart dish. **Stir** in boiling broth and seasonings.

Place tomato wedges on top of rice. **Cover** tightly.

Bake 350 degrees, 35 - 40 minutes or until rice is tender and broth is absorbed.

Per Serving: 200 Calories; 5g Fat (21.4% calories from fat)
6g Protein; 33g Carbohydrate; 2g Dietary Fiber; 12mg Cholesterol;
770mg Sodium.

Exchanges: 2 Grain(Starch); 1/2 Lean Meat; 1 Vegetable; 1 Fat.

couscous with dried cranberries

Connie Slyby, IN

serves 4

1 1/4	cups chicken broth
1 1/2	cups dried cranberries
1	tablespoon butter
	salt and pepper — to taste
1	cup couscous — uncooked

In 2 quart saucepan, **combine** broth, cranberries, butter and seasonings. **Boil.**

Add couscous. **Cover**, remove from heat. Let **stand** 5 minutes.

Fluff with fork. **Serve.**

Per Serving: 202 Calories; 4g Fat (16.3% calories from fat); 7g Protein; 34g Carbohydrate; 2g Dietary Fiber; 8mg Cholesterol; 272mg Sodium.

Exchanges: 2 Grain(Starch); 0 Lean Meat; 0 Fruit; 1/2 Fat.

cranberry-pear chutney

Beth Gavzer, IL

serves 8

4	cups fresh cranberries — or frozen
1 1/2	cups brown sugar, packed
2	cups water
2	Bosc pears — or Asian, peeled and diced
1	alapeno pepper — seeded, minced
1	cup golden raisins
2	tablespoons lime juice

In large saucepan, over medium-high heat, bring first 3 ingredients to **boil.**

Reduce heat. **Simmer**, stirring occasionally, until cranberries start to pop and release juices, (about 10 minutes).

Add remaining ingredients. **Simmer** 5 minutes. **Remove** from heat. **Cool.**

Cover. Refrigerate up to 2 days.

Per Serving: 267 Calories; trace Fat (1.2% calories from fat); 1g Protein; 69g Carbohydrate; 4g Dietary Fiber; 0mg Cholesterol; 21mg Sodium.

Exchanges: 0 Vegetable; 2 Fruit; 0 Fat; 2 1/2 Other Carbohydrates.

" Serve as a relish for pork or poultry. "

escalloped pineapple

Jan Miller, IN

serves 6

1/4	cup butter
1/2	cup granulated sugar
2	eggs
22	ounces crushed pineapple — drained
6	slices white bread — cubed

Per Serving: 283 Calories; 10g Fat (31.3% calories from fat); 4g Protein; 46g Carbohydrate; 1g Dietary Fiber; 83mg Cholesterol; 232mg Sodium.

Exchanges: 1 Grain(Starch); 1/2 Lean Meat; 1 Fruit; 2 Fat; 1 Other Carbohydrates.

Preheat oven to 350 degrees. **Grease** casserole dish.

In large mixing bowl, **cream** butter and sugar.

Beat in eggs, one at a time.

Stir in pineapple.

Fold in bread cubes.

Turn into prepared casserole dish. **Bake** 350 degrees, 1 hour.

Serve warm.

"Pineapple usually glazes ham, but this pineapple is used to accompany ham. Easy, healthy, tasty!"

favorite fettuccini

Patti White, GA

serves 8

8	ounces fettuccini — fresh
1/2	cup butter — or margarine
3/4	cup half and half
3/4	cup grated parmesan cheese
1/2	teaspoon salt
1/2	teaspoon freshly ground pepper
2	teaspoons chopped fresh basil

Per Serving: 271 Calories; 17g Fat (55.7% calories from fat); 8g Protein; 23g Carbohydrate; 1g Dietary Fiber; 45mg Cholesterol; 401mg Sodium.

Exchanges: 1 1/2 Grain(Starch); 1/2 Lean Meat; 0 Vegetable; 0 Non-Fat Milk; 3 Fat.

Cook pasta as directed on package. **Drain**. **Set** aside.

In same pot used to cooked pasta, **heat** butter and half and half until butter is melted.

Stir in cheese, salt and pepper.

Return pasta to pot; **toss** to coat with sauce. **Sprinkle** with basil.

Pour into serving dish. **Serve** immediately.

fresh pasta with goat cheese and scallops

Dr. Ronnie Weathers, GA

serves 8

2	cups whipping cream
4	ounces goat cheese — california, cut into chunks
1	pound bay scallops — patted dry
	salt and pepper
1/4	stick butter
16	ounces fresh pasta — (or make your own with a pasta machine)
40	asparagus — baby, blanched and trimmed to 4 inches
1	bunch fresh basil — (about **1** cup) stemmed, julienned,divided
2	tablespoons fresh chives — snipped

Per Serving: 527 Calories; 32g Fat (53.9% calories from fat); 23g Protein; 38g Carbohydrate; 2g Dietary Fiber; 164mg Cholesterol; 208mg Sodium.

Exchanges: 2 Grain(Starch); 2 Lean Meat; 1/2 Vegetable; 0 Non-Fat Milk; 6 Fat.

In saucepan, **boil** cream and cheese until reduced to 1 1/2 cups. **Set** aside.

Season scallops with salt and pepper.

In large heavy skillet over high heat, **melt** butter. **Add** scallops. **Saute** on both sides until firm, about 1 minute.

Cook pasta as directed on package, until just tender but firm to bite. **Drain**.

Reheat cream mix.

Set aside 8 scallops, 20 asparagus and 2 tablespoons basil.

Stir remaining scallops, asparagus and basil into sauce. **Add** to pasta. **Toss** well.

Season generously with salt and pepper.

Mound pasta on plates. **Decorate** with reserved scallops, asparagus and basil. **Sprinkle** with chives.

Serve.

green chiles rice

Dr. Dan Martindale, MS

serves 12

1/4	cup butter — or margarine
1	cup onion — chopped
4	cups white rice — freshly cooked
2	cups sour cream
1	cup cottage cheese — cream style
1	large bay leaf — crumbled
1/2	teaspoon salt
1/8	teaspoon pepper
3	cans (4 ounces each) green chiles — drained, halved lengthwise, leaving seeds

Per Serving: 368 Calories; 13g Fat (31.4% calories from fat); 9g Protein; 54g Carbohydrate; 1g Dietary Fiber; 29mg Cholesterol; 229mg Sodium.

Exchanges: 3 1/2 Grain(Starch); 1/2 Lean Meat; 1/2 Vegetable; 0 Non-Fat Milk; 2 1/2 Fat.

Preheat oven to 375 degrees. Lightly **grease** 2 quart casserole dish.

In large skillet, **melt** butter, **add** onions. **Saute** until golden, about 5 minutes.

Remove from heat. **Stir in** hot rice, sour cream, cottage cheese, bay leaf, salt and pepper. **Toss** lightly to mix well.

Add green chiles. **Mix**.

Bake, uncovered, 375 degrees, 25 minutes or until bubbly and hot.

Serve hot.

green rice bake

Hazel Adams, GA

serves 6

2	eggs — slightly beaten
2	cups milk
3/4	cup instant rice — uncooked
1/3	cup onion — finely chopped
10	ounces frozen chopped spinach — cooked and drained
4	ounces shredded cheddar cheese
1/2	teaspoon garlic salt

Per Serving: 208 Calories; 11g Fat (45.7% calories from fat); 12g Protein; 17g Carbohydrate; 2g Dietary Fiber; 93mg Cholesterol; 382mg Sodium.

Exchanges: 1/2 Grain(Starch); 1 Lean Meat; 1/2 Vegetable; 1/2 Non-Fat Milk; 1 1/2 Fat; 0 Other Carbohydrates.

Preheat oven to 325 degrees.

In large mixing bowl, **combine** eggs and milk.

Add remaining ingredients.

Pour into shallow baking dish.

Bake 325 degrees, 35 - 40 minutes or until firm.

macaroni casserole

Shirley Walsh, LA

serves 10

1	pound lean ground beef — or ground turkey
4	cups spaghetti sauce
2	packages (10 ounce) frozen chopped spinach — cooked and drained
7	ounces macaroni — cooked and drained
1	cup shredded mozzarella cheese
1/2	cup soft bread crumbs
2	eggs — beaten
1/4	cup olive oil

Per Serving: 427 Calories; 24g Fat (49.6% calories from fat); 19g Protein; 36g Carbohydrate; 7g Dietary Fiber; 82mg Cholesterol; 664mg Sodium.

Exchanges: 1 Grain(Starch); 1 1/2 Lean Meat; 4 Vegetable; 3 1/2 Fat.

Preheat oven to 350 degrees. **Cook** spinach and macaroni according to directions on packages, **drain**.

In large skillet, **brown** ground meat. **Add** spaghetti sauce, **simmer** 5 -10 minutes.

Combine spinach, macaroni and remaining ingredients.

Spread mixture in 9x13 baking dish. **Top** with meat mixture.

Bake 350 degrees, 30 minutes or until very hot.

Let **stand** 5 - 10 minutes before serving.

orzo with parmesan

Connie Slyby, IN

serves 4

2	tablespoons butter
1	cup orzo — uncooked
14	ounces chicken broth
1/4	cup fresh basil — chopped
1/2	cup parmesan cheese
	salt and pepper — to taste
	parsley

In large skillet, **melt** butter. **Add** orzo pasta and **saute** until lightly browned.

Stir in broth, **boil**. **Reduce** heat, **cover**. **Simmer** 15-20 minutes or until pasta is cooked.

Add basil and cheese.

Season with salt and pepper. **Garnish** with parsley.

Serve warm.

Per Serving: 269 Calories; 10g Fat (33.9% calories from fat); 12g Protein; 32g Carbohydrate; 1g Dietary Fiber; 23mg Cholesterol; 563mg Sodium.

Exchanges: 2 Grain(Starch); 1 Lean Meat; 0 Vegetable; 1 1/2 Fat.

parmesan-basil rice pilaf

Jill Martin, CA

serves 7

1	teaspoon olive oil
1	teaspoon minced garlic
2	cups long-grain rice — uncooked
1/2	cup water
2	cans (14.25 ounce each) chicken broth — fat-free
1	cup frozen peas — thawed
1/2	cup shredded parmesan cheese — fresh
1/4	cup green onions — chopped
1/2	teaspoon dried basil
1/4	teaspoon pepper

In saucepan, over medium-high heat, **warm** oil. **Add** garlic. **Saute** until lightly browned.

Add rice. **Cook** 2 minutes. **Stir** constantly.

Stir in water and broth. **Bring** to boil. **Cover**. Reduce heat. **Cook** over medium-low heat 20 minutes or until liquid is absorbed.

Remove from heat. **Fluff** with fork. **Add** remaining ingredients. **Toss** well.

Serve immediately.

Per Serving: 251 Calories; 3g Fat (11.1% calories from fat); 8g Protein; 46g Carbohydrate; 2g Dietary Fiber; 4mg Cholesterol; 342mg Sodium.

Exchanges: 3 Grain(Starch); 1/2 Lean Meat; 0 Vegetable; 1/2 Fat.

pasta for company

Susan Ferry, IL

serves 10

1	cup frozen chopped broccoli
1	cup snow peas — frozen
1	cup frozen peas — baby
1	tablespoon olive oil
12	fresh mushrooms — sliced
2	tomatoes — chopped
1/2	cup fresh parsley — chopped
4	teaspoons minced garlic
1	pound linguine — or fettuccini, cooked
1	cup whipping cream
1/2	cup parmesan cheese — freshly grated
1/2	cup butter
1/3	cup fresh basil — chopped
	strips red pepper — or carrot

Per Serving: 393 Calories; 22g Fat (48.8% calories from fat); 10g Protein; 41g Carbohydrate; 3g Dietary Fiber; 61mg Cholesterol; 205mg Sodium.

Exchanges: 2 1/2 Grain(Starch); 0 Lean Meat; 1 Vegetable; 0 Non-Fat Milk; 4 Fat.

In large saucepan, **blanch** broccoli, snow peas and baby peas in boiling water, 3-4 minutes. **Rinse** in cold water. **Drain**. **Set** aside.

In medium skillet, **heat** olive oil. **Add** mushrooms. **Saute** 2 -3 minutes.

Add tomatoes, parsley, garlic. **Saute** 2-3 minutes. **Set** aside.

Drain cooked pasta. In large bowl, **add** whipping cream, parmesan cheese, butter and basil. **Toss** well.

Add blanched vegetable and mushroom mixture. **Toss** gently.

Garnish with red pepper strips or carrot strips, for color.

Serve immediately.

"brushing before hitting the sack can keep away plaque"

Zach, Grade 3

pasta with fresh tomatoes

Jill Martin, CA

serves 8

3	quarts water
12	ounces vermicelli — uncooked
4	cups diced tomatoes — seeded
3	tablespoons fresh oregano — chopped
3	tablespoons green onion — minced
3	tablespoons lemon juice — fresh
1	tablespoon olive oil
1	teaspoon coriander seeds — crushed
1/4	teaspoon salt
1/8	teaspoon crushed red pepper
2	cloves garlic — minced

In large pot, bring water to boil. **Add** pasta. **Cook** 5 minutes. **Drain**.

In large pasta bowl, **combine** tomatoes and remaining ingredients.

Add pasta to tomato mix. **Toss** well.

Serve immediately.

Per Serving: 189 Calories; 2g Fat (10.3% calories from fat); 5g Protein; 39g Carbohydrate; 1g Dietary Fiber; 0mg Cholesterol; 86mg Sodium.

Exchanges: 2 Grain(Starch); 1 Vegetable; 0 Fruit; 1/2 Fat.

rice noodle casserole

Kathy Kne, OH

serves 15

1/2	pound rice noodles — very thin
1	stick butter — or margarine
2	cups instant rice
2	cans (10 3/4 ounce) onion soup
2	cans(10 3/4 ounce) chicken broth
1	can water
1	water chestnuts, canned — chopped
1	teaspoon soy sauce

Preheat oven to 350 degrees.

In large pan, **brown** noodles in butter or margarine.

Add remaining ingredients. **Mix** well.

Place in 3 quart casserole dish.(shallow or deep)

Bake 350 degrees, 45 minutes or until heated through.

Can be made day ahead, refrigerate and heat before serving.

Per Serving: 169 Calories; 7g Fat (35.3% calories from fat); 2g Protein; 25g Carbohydrate; trace Dietary Fiber; 17mg Cholesterol; 330mg Sodium.

Exchanges: 1 1/2 Grain(Starch); 0 Lean Meat; 1/2 Vegetable; 1 Fat.

" Nothing could be easier or tastier than this ! A great dish for a potluck. "

rice pilaf

Lori Daby, CA

serves 4

2	tablespoons butter
2	angel hair nests — (capellini)
1	can (10 3/4 ounce) chicken broth
2	cans water
1/2	teaspoon salt
1	cup converted rice

Per Serving: 282 Calories; 6g Fat (20.3% calories from fat);
7g Protein; 49g Carbohydrate; trace Dietary Fiber;
16mg Cholesterol; 520mg Sodium.

Exchanges: 3 Grain(Starch); 0 Lean Meat; 1 Fat.

In 3 quart saucepan, over medium-high heat, **melt** butter.

Meanwhile, **crush** pasta into small pieces. **Brown** pasta in butter, careful not to burn.

Add remaining ingredients in order listed.

Reduce heat, **simmer** 20 -30 minutes or until liquid is absorbed.

Serve warm.

This is very easy. It makes a wonderful side dish for any grilled meat or fish.

diet for orthodontic patients

Orthodontic patients need to adjust their diets to protect their braces—and their teeth. The following are general diet guidelines to follow when you have braces. Your orthodontist will give you detailed information about what not to eat and how to care for your teeth.

foods that damage braces

- All hard, gummy, sticky, sugar-intense foods and drinks should be avoided. These types of foods damage and bend wires and break brackets and bands. Examples of hard foods not to eat include nuts, popcorn, hard candy, hard chips, hard pretzels, hard breads, hard cereal and pizza crust. Examples of gummy foods not to eat include all candy with the word "gummy" and other chewy candy, like caramels and toffee.

- Replace high-sugar soft drinks with sugar-free drinks.

- Eat soft fruits instead of sugary desserts.

- Cut raw vegetables (like carrots) and hard fruits (like apples) into very small pieces and nibble carefully.

- Never chew ice cubes!

- Never chew gum!

cleaning your mouth

Braces trap food. Failing to brush after eating causes permanent stains on your teeth and results in increased risk of decay and cavities.

- Brush after every meal and snack—with a soft toothbrush or a brush made especially for orthodontic patients.

- Floss with the aid of floss threaders or a special orthodontic toothbrush.

- Use a fluoride rinse to help clean and strengthen your teeth.

visiting your family dentist

Continue your regular 6-month cleanings and check ups. This is an important part of keeping everything in your mouth clean and healthy.

"to keep your smile beautiful and bright, brush and floss both day and night"

Leah, Grade 3

tex-mex

tex-mex

ingredients:

eating pick-up and messy food

Most cultural groups have pick-up food. Sandwiches and wraps of all kinds fall into this category.

- If it is essential to make a good impression over a meal, avoid foods that are hard and messy to eat.

- If you are comfortable with your dining partners, eat whatever you want.

- If in doubt about how to eat a certain food, watch someone who knows—or ask.

- Soft or hard-shell wraps, like tacos, may be eaten with your hands.

- Most sandwiches may be picked up and eaten. However, if they are too large to get in your mouth easily, or are open faced, use a knife and fork.

- Chips with salsa or dip may be eaten with your fingers.

- Double dipping is not polite if you share the dip with anyone else.

tex-manners

never put aspirin on an aching tooth. it can burn your gums.

aileen's mexican dip

Aileen Ottenweller, IN

serves 8

2	cans refried beans
3	avocados — ripe
3	tablespoons lemon juice
1/4	teaspoon salt
1/4	teaspoon pepper
1	cup sour cream
3/4	cup mayonnaise
1	package taco seasoning mix
1/2	head shredded lettuce
2	tomatoes — chopped
1	bunch green onions — chopped
2	cups shredded cheddar cheese
1	large bag tortilla chips

In flat dish with 2 inch sides, **spread** refried beans.

In medium bowl, **mash** avocados. **Stir** in lemon juice, salt and pepper. **Spread** over beans.

In small bowl, **mix** sour cream, mayonnaise and taco seasoning mix. **Spread** over avocados.

Sprinkle remaining ingredients, except chips, in order listed.

Serve with chips.

Variation: Add black olives and/or jalapeno peppers.

Per Serving: 534 Calories; 45g Fat (72.9% calories from fat); 14g Protein; 24g Carbohydrate; 6g Dietary Fiber; 50mg Cholesterol; 945mg Sodium.

Exchanges: 1 Grain(Starch); 1 Lean Meat; 1/2 Vegetable; 1/2 Fruit; 0 Non-Fat Milk; 6 Fat; 0 Other Carbohydrates.

" Aileen has been making this recipe for about 4 years. It is a favorite at the lake. She always brings two, one for the family and one for Grandma Jan. "

"keep your teeth shiny and bright, brush them in the day and night"

Candace, Grade 4

awesome south of the border dip

Martha Lester, KY

serves 12

8	ounces sour cream
8	ounces cream cheese — softened
1	can bean dip — jalapeno, or milder
1/4	cup picante sauce — optional
2	teaspoons dried parsley
8	ounces shredded cheddar cheese — divided
8	ounces shredded monterey jack cheese — divided

Per Serving: 258 Calories; 23g Fat (78.4% calories from fat); 12g Protein; 2g Carbohydrate; trace Dietary Fiber; 66mg Cholesterol; 339mg Sodium.

Exchanges: 0 Grain(Starch); 1 1/2 Lean Meat; 0 Vegetable; 0 Non-Fat Milk; 3 1/2 Fat.

Preheat oven to 325 degrees.

With electric mixer on medium speed, **beat** sour cream and cream cheese until smooth.

Add bean dip, picante sauce, parsley, 1 1/4 cup shredded cheddar cheese and 1 1/4 cup monterey jack cheese.

Pour mix into quiche dish. **Sprinkle** with remaining cheeses.

Bake 325 degrees, 35 - 45 minutes.

Let **stand** at room temperature 10 minutes before serving.

Serve with tortilla chips.

" Make this impressive dip when company is coming and you are short on time. It always wins lots of compliments and is frequently requested. "

oral health habits are vital during puberty, menstruation, pregnancy and menopause.

black bean corn salsa
Carol Cooke, MO

serves 30 • yields 2 quarts

30	ounces black beans — rinsed and drained
16	ounces white corn — shoe peg, drained
6	tablespoons lime juice
6	tablespoons olive oil — or less
1/2	teaspoon cumin
1/2	cup red onion — chopped
1/4	cup fresh cilantro — chopped
1/2	teaspoon salt
1	cup tomatoes — seeded and chopped

In large bowl, **combine** all ingredients.

Cover and **refrigerate** until ready to serve.

Serve with scoop type tortilla chips.

Best if made a day ahead.

Per Serving: 137 Calories; 3g Fat (21.0% calories from fat); 7g Protein; 21g Carbohydrate; 5g Dietary Fiber; 0mg Cholesterol; 40mg Sodium.

Exchanges: 1 1/2 Grain(Starch); 1/2 Lean Meat; 0 Vegetable; 0 Fruit; 1/2 Fat.

"brush your teeth three times a day and you won't have to pay"

Dalton, Age 9

blackeyed pea salsa

Debra Ann Grimes, TN

serves 40

1	can blackeyed peas — drained
1	can tomatoes — drained and chopped
1	can diced green chiles
1	bunch green onions — chopped
1/8	cup pepper rings — zesty, chopped
3	tablespoons olive oil
1	tablespoon white wine vinegar
1/2	teaspoon kosher salt
1/2	teaspoon fresh ground pepper
6	cloves garlic — minced

In 2 1/2 quart bowl, gently **mix** all ingredients.

Cover. **Chill** at least 8 hours for flavors to meld.

Serve with restaurant style white corn chips.

Per Serving: 25 Calories; 1g Fat (38.0% calories from fat);
1g Protein; 3g Carbohydrate; 1g Dietary Fiber; 0mg Cholesterol;
25mg Sodium.

Exchanges: 0 Grain(Starch); 0 Lean Meat; 0 Vegetable; 0 Fat;
0 Other Carbohydrates.

Before silverware was used, people ate with their hands. It was considered a sign of refinement to eat with the thumb and first two fingers, instead of the whole hand. Queen Elizabeth I of England was said to have worn gloves while eating and to change them between courses.

tidbits

easy cheesy salsa

Jocelyn Lance, VA

serves 6

2	cups shredded monterey jack cheese
1	avocado — diced
1	medium tomato — diced
4	ounces green chiles — diced
3	green onion — diced
1/2	cup sliced olives
1/4	cup fresh cilantro — chopped
1	cup Italian salad dressing — or less
	salt and pepper — to taste

In serving bowl, **combine** all ingredients except salad dressing.

Add salad dressing, **stir** to coat.

Refrigerate until ready to serve. **Serve** with tortilla chips.

Per Serving: 403 Calories; 37g Fat (79.7% calories from fat); 11g Protein; 10g Carbohydrate; 2g Dietary Fiber; 34mg Cholesterol; 616mg Sodium.

Exchanges: 1 1/2 Lean Meat; 1/2 Vegetable; 1/2 Fruit; 6 1/2 Fat.

fresh tomato salsa

Paula Oldag, IN

serves 24

6	cups tomatoes — chopped
1	small onion — minced
1	jalapeno chile pepper — seeded and minced
1/4	cup fresh cilantro — chopped
2	tablespoons vegetable oil
1	tablespoon white vinegar
1/2	teaspoon salt

In large serving bowl, **combine** all ingredients. **Mix**.

Cover. Refrigerate until ready to serve.

Per Serving: 22 Calories; 1g Fat (49.2% calories from fat); trace Protein; 3g Carbohydrate; 1g Dietary Fiber; 0mg Cholesterol; 49mg Sodium.

Exchanges: 1/2 Vegetable; 0 Fat; 0 Other Carbohydrates.

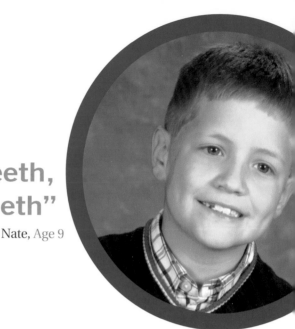

"if you floss your teeth, you won't have to toss you teeth"

Nate, Age 9

green chile chicken taco

Mary Beth Thornton, IL

serves 8

1	pound tomatillos — 10-12 medium, husked and rinsed
5	serrano peppers or 3 jalapenos, stemmed and chopped
4	cloves garlic — peeled and chopped
1 1/2	tablespoons vegetable oil
2	cups chicken broth
	salt to taste
4	cups cooked chicken — shredded
2/3	cup cilantro — chopped

Per Serving: 182 Calories; 7g Fat (33.9% calories from fat); 24g Protein; 6g Carbohydrate; 1g Dietary Fiber; 60mg Cholesterol; 251mg Sodium.

Exchanges: 0 Grain(Starch); 3 Lean Meat; 1 Vegetable; 1/2 Fat.

Preheat oven to 350 degrees.

On cookie sheet with sides, **place** tomatillos. **Roast** until soft, about 5 minutes per side. (They should have black spots.)

Remove from oven, **cool**.

In food processor, **mix** cooled tomatillos, juice from cookie sheet, chiles and garlic. **Process** to smooth puree.

In medium saucepan, over high heat, **heat** oil. When very hot, **add** puree all at once. **Stir** until thick and dark, about 5 minutes.

Reduce heat. **Add** broth. **Simmer** over medium heat, 8 - 10 minutes.

Season with salt to taste, (about 2 teaspoons).

Stir in chicken and cilantro. **Cool** completely.

Serve in soft or hard taco shells.

Top with sour cream, shredded cheddar cheese, diced tomatoes, and/or lettuce, if desired.

jack's casa dias

Jan Hagedorn, IN

serves 15

2	pounds lean ground beef or chicken
1	packet taco seaoning mix
30	6-inch flour tortillas
2	pounds shredded 2% cheddar cheese
1	can refried beans

Per Serving: 890 Calories; 43g Fat (43.9% calories from fat); 39g Protein; 84g Carbohydrate; 5g Dietary Fiber; 109mg Cholesterol; 1177mg Sodium.

Exchanges: 5 1/2 Grain(Starch); 3 1/2 Lean Meat; 6 Fat.

In skillet, **brown** ground beef, **add** taco seasoning mix, (may need to add a little water).

Assemble casa dias: (repeat 15 times)

Spread one tortilla with refried beans.

Add approximately 1/4 cup hamburger mix.

Sprinkle with cheese.

Place another tortilla on top.

Microwave on high, 2 minutes or **bake** 400 degrees in oven, 5 minutes or **Cook** on griddle, 350 degrees, 2 minutes each side.

" The grandkids and I developed this one weekend at the lake cottage. It is now a favorite at the Hagedorn House, especially with Jack. We use our pancake griddle to cook and slice with a pizza cutter. "

"good night brush right, don't let the tooth bugs bite"

Alley, Age 12

"don't do what your toothless granddaddy done, brush and floss so you can keep your teeth till you're 101"

Holly, Grade 5

light black bean soup

Karole Kaldahl, NE

serves 4

1	red pepper — sweet, chopped
1	onion — chopped
1	cup carrots — chopped
2	cloves garlic — minced
14 1/2	ounces chicken broth — light
1 1/2	cups water
45	ounces black beans, canned — rinsed and drained
3	tablespoons Italian seasoning
1/8	teaspoon red pepper — crushed, optional
1/8	teaspoon black pepper
1/4	cup vinegar
1/2	cup sour cream, light

Spray dutch oven with cooking spray.

Over medium-low heat, **cook** first 4 ingredients, covered, about 5 minutes or until vegetables are tender.

Remove from heat. **Stir** in remaining ingredients except vinegar and sour cream.

In food processor or blender, **place** half soup mix. **Blend** until smooth. **Repeat** with other half.

Return to dutch oven. **Bring** to boil, **reduce** heat.

Simmer, covered, 10 minutes.

Add vinegar. **Stir** well.

Serve with dollop sour cream on top.
May be doubled.

Per Serving: 340 Calories; 4g Fat (10.7% calories from fat); 21g Protein; 54g Carbohydrate; 20g Dietary Fiber; 2mg Cholesterol; 1332mg Sodium.

Exchanges: 3 Grain(Starch); 1 1/2 Lean Meat; 1 1/2 Vegetable; 0 Fat; 0 Other Carbohydrates.

" A healthy soup recipe which is a family favorite. May be made in advance. "

low-fat cornbread

Sarah Looper, GA

serves 9

1	cup all-purpose flour
1	cup self-rising cornmeal
1/4	cup sugar
1	tablespoon baking powder
4	egg whites
1	cup skim milk
1/4	cup applesauce

Per Serving: 140 Calories; 1g Fat (4.2% calories from fat);
5g Protein; 29g Carbohydrate; 1g Dietary Fiber; trace Cholesterol;
370mg Sodium.

Exchanges: 1 1/2 Grain(Starch); 0 Lean Meat; 0 Fruit; 0 Non-Fat
Milk; 0 Fat; 1/2 Other Carbohydrates.

In medium bowl, **combine** first 4 ingredients, **stir** with whisk.

In small bowl, **mix** last 3 ingredients.

Add milk mixture to cornmeal mixture, **stir** until moistened.

Bake 400 degrees, 20-25 minutes, in an 8x8 square pan.

Serve warm.

mexican cornbread

Imo Slaten, OR

serves 18

18	ounces corn muffin mix
1	cup creamed cottage cheese
3	eggs
1/4	cup milk
1/4	cup red and green bell peppers

Per Serving: 144 Calories; 5g Fat (30.4% calories from fat);
4g Protein; 20g Carbohydrate; 2g Dietary Fiber; 33mg Cholesterol;
373mg Sodium.

Exchanges: 1/2 Lean Meat; 0 Vegetable; 0 Non-Fat Milk; 1 Fat;
1 1/2 Other Carbohydrates.

Preheat oven to 400 degrees. **Place** paper liners in 18 muffin cups.

In mixing bowl, **combin**e all ingredients. **Mix** until thoroughly moistened and slightly lumpy.

Pour into prepared muffin cups, **filling** each approximately half full.

Bake 400 degrees, 15 minutes.

Remove from oven. **Serve** warm.

" My aunt lived most of her life in southern California.
She had a Mexican flair to most of her recipes. "

mexican fudge

Mary Higgins, IL

serves 20 • yields 81 cubes

2	cups shredded cheddar cheese
2	cups shredded monterey jack cheese
1/2	cup green taco sauce
3	eggs

Per Serving: 98 Calories; 8g Fat (72.4% calories from fat); 6g Protein; trace Carbohydrate; 0g Dietary Fiber; 50mg Cholesterol; 139mg Sodium.

Exchanges: 1 Lean Meat; 1 Fat.

Preheat oven to 350 degrees.

In bowl, **combine** 2 cheeses.

In another bowl, **add** taco sauce and eggs. **Blend**.

Spoon half the cheese mixture into 9x9 baking pan. **Drizzle** with taco sauce mixture.

Add remaining cheese mix.

Bake 350 degrees, 30 minutes.

To serve, **cut** baked cheese mix into one-inch squares. **Place** on torti

" Ole! " quotes

southwest grits

DebraAnn Grimes, TN

serves 4

14 1/2	ounces chicken broth
1/2	cup water
1/2	cup quick-cooking grits — not instant
1	cup shredded sharp cheddar cheese
4	ounces diced green chiles

Per Serving: 212 Calories; 10g Fat (44.2% calories from fat); 11g Protein; 18g Carbohydrate; trace Dietary Fiber; 30mg Cholesterol; 542mg Sodium.

Exchanges: 1 Grain(Starch); 1 Lean Meat; 1/2 Vegetable; 1 1/2 Fat.

In 2 quart saucepan, **bring** chicken broth and water to boil.

Stir in grits, **return** to boil.

Reduce heat to low, **cover**, **simmer** 10 minutes, until thick and tender. **Stir** frequently to prevent sticking.

Stir in cheese and chiles.

Serve immediately.

" This is a quick, easy, tasty side dish. It is also easy to consume when wearing braces! " quotes

spanish rice

Jenny Zehner, PA

serves 8

3	tablespoons salad oil or olive oil
1	cup rice — uncooked
1/2	cup onions — finely chopped
2	cloves garlic — minced
1/2	cup green pepper — chopped
#2	can stewed tomatoes — chopped
	salt to taste
	dash cayenne
1	teaspoon chili powder

In skillet, **heat** oil. **Add** rice, **cook** over medium heat, until lightly browned.

Add onions, garlic, green pepper. **Cook** until onions are clear.

Add tomatoes and seasonings. **Cover.**

Simmer 25 minutes or until rice is tender.

Serve warm.

Per Serving: 138 Calories; 5g Fat (35.1% calories from fat); 2g Protein; 20g Carbohydrate; 1g Dietary Fiber; 0mg Cholesterol; 5mg Sodium.

Exchanges: 1 Grain(Starch); 1/2 Vegetable; 1 Fat.

taco soup

Dinah Catey, IN

serves 10 • yields 3 1/2 quarts

1	pound lean ground beef
1	small onion — chopped
14 1/2	ounce can tomatoes, diced
4 1/2	ounce can green chiles
15 1/2	ounce can Mexican-style chili beans — undrained
15 1/4	ounce can whole kernel corn — undrained
15	ounce can tomato sauce
1	envelope taco seasoning mix
1	envelope ranch salad dressing mix
1 1/2	cups water

In dutch oven, **cook** ground beef and onion until tender. **Drain.**

Add all other ingredients. **Bring** to boil.

Reduce heat. **Simmer**, uncovered, 15 minutes. **Stir** occasionally.

Ladle into bowls. **Serve** hot.

Suggested toppings: sour cream, shredded lettuce, shredded cheddar cheese, corn or tortilla chips.

Per Serving: 565 Calories; 13g Fat (17.5% calories from fat); 31g Protein; 102g Carbohydrate; 22g Dietary Fiber; 34mg Cholesterol; 3431mg Sodium.

Exchanges: 4 Grain(Starch); 2 Lean Meat; 7 1/2 Vegetable; 1 Fat; 0 Other Carbohydrates.

" A hearty, healthy soup. Even the kids like it! Serve with relishes and fresh fruit for a quick, satisfying lunch or supper. "

dentalfill-ins
sugarless gum and mints

ADA-member dentists recommend chewing sugarless gum—and using sugarless mints.

- Chewing a stick of sugarless gum stimulates saliva flow, which works as a natural mouthwash. Saliva dissolves the sulfur molecules that cause bad breath, neutralizes acids produced by plaque bacteria and helps clear the mouth of food.

- Sugarless gum and sugarless mints may also help eliminate after-dinner heartburn. A study published in the *New England Journal of Medicine* almost 20 years ago documented the power of saliva to ease heartburn, and new research demonstrates that chewing sugarless gum for 30 minutes after a meal dramatically eases acid reflux.

- Chewing sugarless gum may also stave off a "sweet-tooth" attack.

- For children who love to blow bubbles, there are many sugarless bubble gums.

poultry

poultry

ingredients:

eating poultry

Poultry is eaten in a variety of different ways, depending on whether the meal is formal, informal or family-style.

- At a formal dinner, chicken is eaten with a knife and fork.

- At an informal meal, the knife and fork are used to remove as much meat from the main body of the chicken as possible; to eat the rest of the meat, the bones are held with fingers and taken with the teeth.

- At a family meal, chicken with a bone attached is eaten with a fork and fingers.

- It is appropriate to eat fried chicken with your fingers at a picnic or casual family gathering.

- Turkey should be eaten with a knife and fork.

table manners

asian turkey salad

Dorothy Unger, IL

serves 2

salad

2	cups cooked turkey — diced
2/3	cup chow mein noodles — packaged
2/3	cup celery — diced
2/3	cup red bell pepper — diced
2/3	cup green onions — thinly sliced
2	cups iceberg lettuce — chopped

dressing

1	medium clove garlic — peeled
1	inch square fresh ginger — peeled
6	tablespoons rice wine vinegar
2	tablespoons honey
2	tablespoons sesame oil

Per Serving: 555 Calories; 26g Fat (40.7% calories from fat) 45g Protein; 39g Carbohydrate; 4g Dietary Fiber; 106mg Cholesterol; 213mg Sodium.

Exchanges: 1/2 Grain(Starch); 5 1/2 Lean Meat; 2 Vegetable 3 1/2 Fat; 1 1/2 Other Carbohydrates.

salad

In 2 quart bowl, **combine** all ingredients, except iceberg lettuce.

Add dressing. **Toss** until well mixed and evenly coated.

Add lettuce. **Serve**.

dressing

In running food processor or blender, **add** garlic and ginger. **Process** until finely minced.

Stop food processor, scrape sides. **Add** vinegar, honey and sesame oil. **Mix** well.

" Different from usual recipes for left-over turkey. Use as main course. "

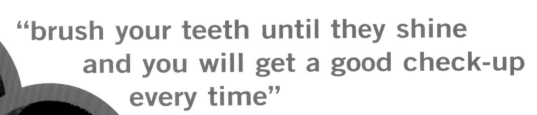

"brush your teeth until they shine and you will get a good check-up every time"

Alex and Ryan, Grade K & 2

blackened cajun chicken

Mary Beth Thornton, IL

serves 6

6	chicken breast halves
1	cup butter — melted
1 1/2	tablespoons paprika
1	teaspoon salt
1 1/2	teaspoons onion powder
1 1/2	teaspoons garlic powder
1 1/2	teaspoons cayenne pepper
1/2	teaspoon white pepper
1/2	teaspoon black pepper
1/2	teaspoon thyme
1/2	teaspoon oregano

Per Serving: 533 Calories; 44g Fat (74.8% calories from fat)
31g Protein; 3g Carbohydrate; 1g Dietary Fiber; 176mg Cholesterol;
760mg Sodium.

Exchanges: 0 Grain(Starch); 4 1/2 Lean Meat; 6 Fat.

Coat both sides chicken breasts with butter. **Set** aside.

In shallow pan, **combine** all spices. **Coat** both sides buttered chicken with mixed spices.

In hot skillet, **melt** enough butter to grease the bottom. **Saute** chicken over high heat, 3 - 5 minutes each side.

Serve hot.

"clean teeth are happy teeth"

Brittany Elise, Grade 4

chicken lasagna

Kendell Christensen and Debbie Brown, IL

serves 8

6	lasagna noodles
1	tablespoon butter
8	ounces fresh mushrooms — sliced
2	cups cooked chicken breast — diced
2	cups cooked ham — diced
1/3	cup butter
1/3	cup flour
3	cups milk
1 1/2	cups shredded parmesan cheese
3/4	teaspoon dried basil — or 2 teaspoon fresh basil
1/2	teaspoon salt
1/4	teaspoon pepper
1/2	cup whipping (heavy) cream

Per Serving: 656 Calories; 31g Fat (42.6% calories from fat) 34g Protein; 59g Carbohydrate; 2g Dietary Fiber; 118mg Cholesterol; 1011mg Sodium.

Exchanges: 3 1/2 Grain(Starch); 3 Lean Meat; 1/2 Vegetable; l 1/2 Non-Fat Milk; 4 Fat.

Preheat oven to 350 degrees. **Coat** 9x13 baking pan with cooking spray.

Cook noodles as directed on package. **Drain** and **set** aside.

In large skillet, **melt** 1 tablespoon butter over medium heat, **cook** mushrooms to tender. **Drain.**

In large bowl, **combine** chicken, ham and mushrooms. **Set** aside.

In skillet, **melt** 1/3 cup butter, **stir** in flour until bubbly.

Gradually **add** milk, **cook** and **stir** constantly until bubbly.

Add cheeses, spices and cream. **Cook** until melted and thick.

Combine cheese mixture with chicken mixture.

In prepared 9x13 baking dish, **alternate** meat, noodles, meat, noodles, ending with meat.

Bake 350 degrees, covered with foil, 30 minutes, (may take longer).

Remove from oven, let **stand** 10 minutes before serving

The custom of breaking the wishbone dates back to Roman times. The person getting the larger piece says, "Lucky break," and makes a silent wish. Wishbone "etiquette" dictates that placing your finger on the head of the bone for leverage is not polite. Letting the bone dry before snapping makes it easier to break.

tidbits

"candy means holes
and holes mean candy,
so don't even think
candy means dandy"

Hunter, Age 7

chicken pecan tart

Diane Obenauer, OH

serves 8

pastry dough

1	cup flour
1	cup shredded cheddar cheese
3/4	cup pecans — finely chopped
1/2	teaspoon salt
1/4	teaspoon paprika
1/3	cup vegetable oil

filling

3	eggs — beaten
1/2	cup chicken broth
1	cup sour cream
1/4	cup mayonnaise
3/4	teaspoon salt
1/4	teaspoon dried dill weed
3	drops hot pepper sauce
1/2	cup shredded sharp cheddar cheese
1/4	cup onion — minced
2	cups cooked chicken — chopped

Per Serving: 491 Calories; 38g Fat (69.4% calories from fat)
22g Protein; 16g Carbohydrate; 1g Dietary Fiber
137mg Cholesterol; 616mg Sodium.

Exchanges: 1 Grain(Starch); 2 1/2 Lean Meat; 0 Vegetable; 0 Non-Fat Milk; 6 Fat; 0 Other Carbohydrates.

pastry dough

Preheat oven to 350 degrees.

In mixing bowl, **combine** all ingredients except oil, **mix** well.

Stir in oil. **Reserve** 1/2 cup mixture.

Press remainder in 11 inch tart pan or 10 inch quiche or pie dish.

Bake 350 degrees, 15 minutes. Let **stand** to cool before filling.

filling

In large bowl, **combine** first 7 ingredients, **mix** well.

Add cheese and onion. **Mix** well.

Place chicken in cooled crust, **pour** filling over.

Sprinkle reserved pastry crumbs over top.

Bake 350 degrees, 45 minutes or until knife inserted in middle comes out clean.

" Low-fat is O.K. but do not use no-fat sour cream or mayonnaise. "

prevent plaque by brushing twice a day.

chicken rolls

Debbie Preece, UT

serves 16

3	ounces cream cheese — softened
1/2	teaspoon poultry seasoning
4	ounces mushrooms — drained, sliced
1	boiled chicken — deboned, cut in bite-size pieces
1	package seasoned bread stuffing — rolled into fine powder
2	cans rolls — refrigerator, crescent
1/2	cup margarine — melted.

Per Serving: 310 Calories; 23g Fat (66.4% calories from fat)
18g Protein; 8g Carbohydrate; 1g Dietary Fiber; 91mg Cholesterol;
365mg Sodium.

Exchanges: 1/2 Grain(Starch); 2 1/2 Lean Meat; 0 Vegetable; 3 Fat.

Preheat oven to 375 degrees.

In mixing bowl, **combine** first 4 ingredients. **Mix** well. **Set** aside.

In another bowl, **add** spices from box to finely rolled stuffing mix. **Pour** into a shallow dish.

Roll out and separate crescent rolls. **Place** approximately 1/4 cup chicken mixture on each roll. **Fold** into a ball.

Dip chicken roll in margarine. **Roll** in stuffing mix to coat. **Place** on cookie sheet with sides.

Bake 375 degrees, 15-20 minutes or until lightly browned. **Serve** hot.

May freeze.

" Passed down from my mother-in-law Norma Preece Nelson.

If frozen, easy to thaw and microwave for a quick meat. "

cold poached chicken with dill

Dorothy Unger, IL

serves 6

6	chicken breast halves without skin — boneless
1	cup vegetable oil
1/2	cup tarragon vinegar
1	teaspoon salt
1/2	teaspoon garlic salt
1/2	teaspoon seasoned salt
2	green onions, with tops — finely chopped
1/4	cup parsley — chopped
1/4	cup fresh dill chopped, plus fresh dill sprigs
	lemons or limes — sliced

Per Serving: 455 Calories; 38g Fat (74.7% calories from fat)
27g Protein; 1g Carbohydrate; trace Dietary Fiber;
68mg Cholesterol; 718mg Sodium.

Exchanges: 4 Lean Meat; 0 Vegetable; 7 1/2 Fat; 0 Other
Carbohydrates.

In large skillet, **poach** chicken for 5 - 7 minutes per side. (Total cooking time, 10 -15 minutes.)

In large plastic bag, **combine** remaining ingredients except dill sprigs and fruit. **Mix** well.

Add chicken to bag, seal. **Marinate** in refrigerator several hours or overnight, turning occasionally.

Remove chicken from bag. **Arrange** on serving platter, **garnish** with dill sprigs and fruit slices.

Serve.

"after eating an apple a day
you should always brush
to keep the plaque away"

Gary, Grade 4

"before your teeth turn black as the night, go to your dentist and make them white"

Max, Age 12

crockpot chicken cantonese

Lori Maurer, IN

serves 4

4	chicken breasts without skin, boneless — cut in strips
1	onion — sliced
1	green pepper — cut in strips
1	can (15 ounce) tomato sauce
6	tablespoons brown sugar — or substitute
3	tablespoons red wine vinegar
1	teaspoon salt
4	teaspoons worcestershire sauce

Place all ingredients in crockpot. **Mix**.

Cook on low 6 hours or on high 3 hours.

Serve over rice.

May add mushrooms, carrots or other favorite veggies.

Per Serving: 223 Calories; 2g Fat (6.7% calories from fat) 29g Protein; 23g Carbohydrate; 2g Dietary Fiber; 68mg Cholesterol; 1036mg Sodium.

Exchanges: 4 Lean Meat; 1 1/2 Vegetable; 1 Other Carbohydrates.

dixie's chicken and fettuccini casserole

Dixie Hummel, MO

serves 8

1/4	cup butter
1/4	cup flour
1	cup milk
1	cup chicken broth
1	large cooked chicken — boned and cut up
5	ounces fettuccini — cooked and drained
2	cups sour cream
10	ounces frozen spinach — cooked and drained
6	ounce jar mushrooms
8	ounces waterchestnuts, canned — sliced
4	ounces pimiento
1/2	cup onion — chopped
1/2	cup celery — chopped
1/3	cup lemon juice
2	teaspoons seasoned salt
1/2	teaspoon cayenne
1	teaspoon paprika
1	teaspoon salt
1	teaspoon pepper
1 1/2	cups shredded monterey jack cheese

Per Serving: 427 Calories; 27g Fat (55.7% calories from fat) 19g Protein; 29g Carbohydrate; 3g Dietary Fiber; 79mg Cholesterol; 794mg Sodium.

Exchanges: 1 Grain(Starch); 1 1/2 Lean Meat; 1 1/2 Vegetable 0 Fruit; 1/2 Non-Fat Milk; 4 1/2 Fat; 0 Other Carbohydrates.

Preheat oven to 300 degrees. **Butter** large casserole dish.

In large saucepan, **melt** butter. **Add** flour, stirring constantly.

Add milk and broth. **Stir** until thickened.

Add remaining ingredients except cheese. **Mix.**

Pour into prepared casserole dish. **Top** with cheese.

Bake 300 degrees, 25 - 30 minutes.

Serve.

One of my favorite recipes. It has a delicious sauce! I have served it as a luncheon dish and as an entree accompanied by a salad and French bread.

easy bake chicken

Jan Hagedorn, IN

serves 6

6	small chicken breasts
1	small bottle Russian salad dressing
1	small jar apricot preserves
1	package onion soup mix

Per Serving: 728 Calories; 48g Fat (60.1% calories from fat) 62g Protein; 10g Carbohydrate; 1g Dietary Fiber; 193mg Cholesterol; 1121mg Sodium.

Exchanges: 0 Grain(Starch); 8 1/2 Lean Meat; 4 Fat; 1/2 Other Carbohydrates.

Preheat oven to 300 degrees. Use cooking spray to **grease** 9x13 baking dish.

Place chicken in prepared 9x13 baking dish.

In mixing bowl, **combine** other ingredients, **mix** well. **Pour** over chicken.

Bake 300 degrees, 2 hours.

Serve hot, with rice.

"This is really easy but the taste is gourmet."

fruited chicken

Gretchen and Craig Frydyrchowich, IL

serves 6

1	large onion
6	chicken breasts without skin — boneless
1/3	cup orange juice
2	tablespoons soy sauce
2	tablespoons worcestershire sauce
2	tablespoons dijon mustard
1	tablespoon grated orange peel
2	cloves garlic — minced
1/2	cup dried apricots — chopped
1/2	cup dried cranberries

Per Serving: 312 Calories; 3g Fat (9.7% calories from fat) 56g Protein; 12g Carbohydrate; 2g Dietary Fiber; 137mg Cholesterol; 610mg Sodium.

Exchanges: 7 1/2 Lean Meat; 1/2 Vegetable; 1/2 Fruit; 0 Fat 0 Other Carbohydrates.

In 5 quart slow cooker, **place** onion and chicken.

In separate bowl, **combine** remaining ingredients, except fruits. **Pour** over chicken.

Sprinkle with apricots and cranberries.

Cover. Cook on low, 7 - 8 hours or until chicken juices run clear.

Serve over rice.

granny's meatloaf

Maureen Szish, PA

serves 4

2	eggs — slightly beaten
1/2	cup bread crumbs
1	pound ground poultry
1/2	celery stalk — finely chopped
1/2	carrot — grated
1/2	small onion — grated
1/8	green pepper — finely chopped
1	clove garlic — minced
1	tablespoon parsley — minced
1/2	teaspoon salt
1/4	teaspoon pepper
2	ounces tomato sauce

Preheat oven to 350 degrees. Use cooking spray to **grease** 1 1/2 quart loaf pan.

In large bowl, **mix** all ingredients except tomato sauce.

Shape into loaf, **place** in prepared loaf pan.

Spread tomato sauce over top.

Bake 350 degrees, 1 hour.

Per Serving: 103 Calories; 3g Fat (26.3% calories from fat); 5g Protein; 14g Carbohydrate; 1g Dietary Fiber; 94mg Cholesterol; 505mg Sodium.

Exchanges: 1/2 Grain(Starch); 1/2 Lean Meat; 1/2 Vegetable; 1/2 Fat.

" Meatloaf made with ground poultry is yummy. Slice any leftovers for sandwiches and freeze in individual packets for a busy day lunch. "

"make sure you brush up and down so you can smile without a frown"

Kyle, Grade 4

hot chicken salad

Barbara Wise, IN

serves 8

2	cups cooked chicken — cubed
1	cup celery — chopped
1	cup cooked rice
3/4	cup mayonnaise
1	teaspoon onion juice
1	teaspoon lemon juice
1	teaspoon salt
1	can waterchestnuts, canned — drained
3	hard-boiled eggs — chopped
1	can cream of chicken soup, condensed

topping

1/8	pound butter — melted
1/2	cup cornflake crumbs — or cracker crumbs

Per Serving: 371 Calories; 29g Fat (68.4% calories from fat); 15g Protein; 14g Carbohydrate; 1g Dietary Fiber; 135mg Cholesterol; 811mg Sodium.

Exchanges: 1 Grain(Starch); 2 Lean Meat; 0 Vegetable; 0 Fruit; 3 Fat.

Preheat oven to 350 degrees. **Grease** 2 quart casserole.

In large bowl, **combine** all ingredients, except topping. **Spread** in prepared casserole dish.

In small bowl, **combine** topping ingredients. **Mix** well. **Sprinkle** on top of chicken mix.

Bake 350 degrees, 1 hour or until bubbles.

Serve hot.

oven barbequed chicken

Karla Daubenspeck, FL

serves 6

6	chicken breast halves without skin — boneless
1/3	cup onion — chopped
3/4	cup ketchup
1/2	cup water
1/3	cup white vinegar
3	tablespoons brown sugar
1	tablespoon worcestershire sauce
1	teaspoon dry mustard
1/4	teaspoon salt
1/8	teaspoon pepper

Per Serving: 187 Calories; 2g Fat (8.0% calories from fat); 28g Protein; 15g Carbohydrate; 1g Dietary Fiber; 68mg Cholesterol; 549mg Sodium.

Exchanges: 0 Grain(Starch); 4 Lean Meat; 0 Vegetable; 0 Fat; 1 Other Carbohydrates.

Preheat oven to 350 degrees. **Coat** 9x13 baking dish with cooking spray.

Brown chicken over medium heat in large skillet, coated with cooking spray. **Transfer** to prepared baking dish.

Recoat skillet, **cook** onion over medium heat, until tender.

Stir in remaining ingredients, bring to boil. **Reduce** heat, simmer 15 minutes. **Pour** over chicken.

Bake, uncovered, 350 degrees, 45 - 55 minutes or until chicken juices run clear and meat thermometer reads 170 degrees.

Serve hot.

oven chicken parmesan

Debbie Raucci, IL

serves 8

28	ounces spaghetti sauce
1/2	cup grated parmesan cheese
1/4	cup dry bread crumbs
1	teaspoon dried oregano — crushed
1	teaspoon dried basil — crushed
1/2	teaspoon garlic salt
8	chicken breast halves without skin — boneless
3	tablespoons butter — melted
1	cup shredded mozzarella cheese

Per Serving: 359 Calories; 16g Fat (39.7% calories from fat)
35g Protein; 19g Carbohydrate; 4g Dietary Fiber; 97mg Cholesterol;
922mg Sodium.

Exchanges: 0 Grain(Starch); 4 1/2 Lean Meat; 3 Vegetable
2 1/2 Fat; 0 Other Carbohydrates.

Preheat oven to 400 degrees.

Pour spaghetti sauce into 15x10 jellyroll pan.

In small bowl, **combine** parmesan cheese, bread crumbs and seasonings.

Dip each chicken breast in butter, then **coat** thoroughly with bread crumb mix.

Place chicken over spaghetti sauce in pan.

Bake 400 degrees, 25 minutes. **Remove** from oven.

Top with mozzarella, **return** to oven. **Bake** additional 5 minutes or until cheese is melted and chicken is cooked through.

Serve hot. Can be served with pasta.

" See how easy? And it tastes good! " quotes

"brush and floss every day so you don't scare your teeth away"

Danielle, Age 8

smoked turkey cheese ball

Bobbie Keller, LA

serves 12

1	cup ground turkey — smoked
8	ounces cream cheese
3	tablespoons mayonnaise
1/2	cup pecans — chopped
3	tablespoons parsley
1	clove garlic — minced (optional)

In mixing bowl, **combine** first 3 ingredients. **Mix** well. **Roll** into a ball.

In shallow container, **mix** remaining ingredients. **Roll** turkey-cheese ball in pecan mix. **Coat** completely.

Refrigerate. Will keep several days in refrigerator, if wrapped in plastic wrap.

When ready to serve, **remove** from refrigerator. Let **stand** at room temperature 30 minutes. **Serve** with crackers.

Per Serving: 149 Calories; 14g Fat (82.8% calories from fat) 5g Protein; 1g Carbohydrate; trace Dietary Fiber; 37mg Cholesterol; 94mg Sodium.

Exchanges: 0 Grain(Starch); 1/2 Lean Meat; 0 Vegetable; 2 Fat.

turkey reuben sandwiches

Janice Gerritsen, UT

serves 1

2	slices rye bread
1	teaspoon dijon mustard
1	tablespoon mayonnaise
1/4	pound turkey — sliced thin
1	Swiss cheese slice
2	tablespoons sauerkraut
1	tablespoon butter

Combine mustard and mayonnaise, **spread** on one slice bread.

On other slice of bread, **place** turkey and cheese.

Spoon sauerkraut on cheese.

Close sandwich. **Butter** both sides of sandwich. In covered frying pan, over medium heat, **grill**. **Turn** to brown both sides.

Serve hot.

Per Serving: 625 Calories; 41g Fat (58.0% calories from fat) 33g Protein; 33g Carbohydrate; 5g Dietary Fiber; 123mg Cholesterol; 1007mg Sodium.

Exchanges: 2 Grain(Starch); 3 1/2 Lean Meat; 0 Vegetable 4 1/2 Fat; 0 Other Carbohydrates.

" This is a hot sandwich with a healthier meat and a delicious taste. "

mouthguard protection

Anyone who participates in sports with a significant risk of injury should wear a mouthguard. This includes a wide range of sports like football, hockey, basketball, baseball, gymnastics and volleyball.

- A properly fitted mouthguard can help cushion a blow to the face that otherwise might result in injury to the mouth.

- Since a mouthguard typically covers the upper teeth, it will help cushion a blow to the face and help prevent broken teeth and injuries to the lips, tongue, face and jaw.

- Your dentist can make a custom mouthguard that will fit comfortably and offer the best protection for your smile.

- A properly fitted mouth protector will stay in place while you are wearing it, making it easy to talk and breathe.

beef

beef

ingredients:

knife and fork etiquette

There are two styles of eating, American and Continental. In the United States, using either method — or a combination of both — is acceptable. Holding the knife and fork correctly is basic to either style.

- Open your hands, palms up. Place the knife and fork on the open hands, letting the knife handle and half of the fork rest in the palm of each hand. The remainder rests on the index fingers.

- Grasp the knife and fork and turn your hands over, resting your index fingers along the handles. You are ready to cut.

- Do not place the knife and fork on your plate like two oars in a rowboat.

- Once you pick up utensils, they should never touch the table again.

- Do not hold the knife and fork like a dagger.

continental style

tablemanr

beef and avocado salad
Kendell Christensen, IL

serves 6

4	avocados - peeled and sliced thin
2	pounds beef roast - rare, sliced thin
1	red onion - sliced thin
8	plum tomatoes - sliced thin
1/2	cup vegetable oil
1/4	cup olive oil
1/2	cup red wine vinegar
2	teaspoons dijon mustard
2	teaspoons salt
1/4	teaspoon pepper
2	tablespoons capers - drained
	parsley - chopped, to taste

Arrange layers of first 4 ingredients in casserole dish.

Combine remaining ingredients in a mixing bowl and **mix** well.

Pour over layers.

Marinate several hours.

Serve cold with hard rolls or french bread.

Per serving: 803 Calories; 72g Fat (78.2% calories from fat); 28g Protein; 17g Carbohydrate; 5g Dietary Fiber; 87mg Cholesterol; 855mg Sodium.

Exchanges: 0 Grain(Starch); 3 1/2 Lean Meat; 1 Vegetable; 1/2 Fruit; 12 Fat; 0 Other Carbohydrates.

beef beyond belief
Jan Miller, IN

serves 12

6	pounds flank steak
1/4	cup soy sauce
2	tablespoons red wine vinegar
1 1/2	teaspoons ground ginger
4	green onions - chopped
3	tablespoons honey
1 1/2	teaspoons garlic powder
3/4	cup oil

Place steak in large shallow pan. **Set** aside.

In small bowl, **combine** all other ingredients. **Pour** over steak.

Marinate meat at least 6 hours, or overnight, in refrigerator.

Remove from marinade, **broil or grill** to taste.

To serve, **carve** against the grain into thin slices.

Per serving: 544 Calories; 37g Fat (62.6% calories from fat); 44g Protein; 6g Carbohydrate; trace Dietary Fiber; 116mg Cholesterol; 502mg Sodium.

Exchanges: 0 Grain(Starch); 6 1/2 Lean Meat; 0 Vegetable; 4 Fat; 1/2 Other Carbohydrates.

" This melt-in-your mouth beef is grand for large family gatherings. "

classic cabbage rolls
Susan Barsness, IL

serves 4 • yields 8 rolls

1	medium cabbage - cored
1 1/2	cups onion, chopped, divided
1	tablespoon butter
2	14.5 oz cans Italian tomato - stewed
4	cloves garlic - minced
2	tablespoons brown sugar
1 1/2	teaspoons salt - divided
1	cup rice - cooked
1/4	cup ketchup
2	tablespoons worcestershire sauce
1/4	teaspoon pepper
1	pound lean ground beef
1/4	pound Italian sausage - bulk
1/2	cup 100% vegetable juice (optional)

Per serving: 703 Calories; 36g Fat (46.6% calories from fat); 31g Protein; 63g Carbohydrate; 5g Dietary Fiber; 114mg Cholesterol; 1393mg Sodium.

Exchanges: 2 1/2 Grain (Starch); 3 1/2 Lean Meat; 3 Vegetable; 5 Fat; 1/2 Other Carbohydrates.

In dutch oven, **cook** cabbage in boiling water, 10 minutes or until outer leaves are tender, drain. **Rinse** in cold water.

Remove eight large outer leaves, **set** aside (Refrigerate remaining cabbage for another use.)

Saute 1 cup onion in butter until tender. **Add** tomatoes, garlic, brown sugar and 1/2 teaspoon salt.

Simmer 15 minutes, **stirring** occasionally.

Meanwhile, **combine** rice, ketchup, worcestershire sauce, pepper, remaining onion and salt in a bowl.

Add beef and sausage. **Mix** well.

Remove thick vein from cabbage leaves for easier rolling. **Place** about 1/2 cup meat mixture on each leaf; **fold** in sides.

Roll up leaf to completely enclose filling, starting at an unfolded edge.

Place roll seam-side down in a skillet. **Top** with tomato-garlic sauce. **Cover** and **cook** over medium-low heat for 1 hour.

Add vegetable juice, if desired.

Reduce heat to low. **Cook** 20 minutes longer or until rolls are heated through and meat is no longer pink.

Serve hot.

"brushing is like flushing you just don't forget"

Madeleine, Grade 5

dr. denny's
holiday beef tenderloin

Dr. Dennis Manning, IL

serves 12

1/4	cup coarsely ground pepper (your choice, black, green, red or white)
2	tablespoons garlic salt
1	teaspoon basil — dried
4	tablespoons butter — melted
6	pounds beef tenderloin — whole

Per serving: 684 Calories; 56g Fat (74.8% calories from fat); 41g Protein; 2g Carbohydrate; 1g Dietary Fiber; 172mg Cholesterol; 1174mg Sodium.

Exchanges: 0 Grain(Starch); 5 1/2 Lean Meat; 8 Fat; 0 Other Carbohydrates.

Allow tenderloin, any size, to come to room temperature. (Allow 1/2 pound meat per serving.)

Pre-heat oven to 400 degrees.

In a bowl, **combine** spices. **Pat** on tenderloin.

Sear tenderloin in melted butter in large skillet. (Brown on all sides, this takes approximately 5 minutes.)

Place in roasting pan.

Roast 400 degrees, 30 - 35 minutes, for rare to medium rare. (Do not over-roast.)

Let **rest** 10 minutes after removing from oven.

Slice and **serve**.

eye of round
serves 6

Diane Obenauer, OH

3	pounds roasted beef bottom round - trimmed of fat
1	tablespoon seasoned salt
3	medium onions - sliced thin

Any leftovers may be wrapped in portion packages and frozen.

Per serving: 520 Calories; 26g Fat (46.2% calories from fat); 63g Protein; 5g Carbohydrate; 1g Dietary Fiber; 179mg Cholesterol; 830mg Sodium.

Exchanges: 8 1/2 Lean Meat; 1 Vegetable; 0 Fat; 0 Other Carbohydrates.

Preheat oven to 300 degrees. Liberally **sprinkle** salt over meat.

Place 1/2 the onions, top with meat on very large piece of heavy-duty foil, **cover** with remaining onions. **Wrap** tightly.

Place in a baking pan . **Bake** 300 degrees, one hour per pound of meat.

Refrigerate overnight.

Unwrap, discard onions, **strain** the juice (if desired, reserve for making gravy or soup stock). **Slice** the meat.

May rewrap and reheat or serve cold.

" This is easy and always rates compliments.
It must be made one day ahead to slice well. "

"brush your teeth, avoid the sweets, keep them clean and snappy, then, when you sit in the dentist's chair you will both be happy"

Erin, Grade 4

"brush your teeth every day, it will fight tooth decay"

Chase, Grade 2

golden meatball casserole
Vivian Mason, TX

serves 6 • yields 18 meatballs

1	pound ground beef
1/2	cup fresh bread crumbs
1	egg
1	teaspoon salt
2	tablespoons oil
2	cups water
1	cup uncooked rice
2	large carrots - cut in quarters
1/2	cup chopped green pepper
1/4	cup chopped onion
1/2	pound cubed processed American cheese

Combine meat, bread crumbs, egg and salt. **Mix** lightly in large bowl.

Shape into meatballs.

In large skillet, **brown** meatballs on all sides in oil. **Drain.**

Add remaining ingredients except cheese. **Cover.** **Simmer** 25 minutes.

Remove cover, **add** cheese. **Heat** until cheese melts.

Serve hot.

Per Serving: 566 Calories; 38g Fat (60.3% calories from fat); 25g Protein; 31g Carbohydrate; 2g Dietary Fiber; 131mg Cholesterol; 990mg Sodium.

Exchanges: 1 1/2 Grain(Starch); 3 Lean Meat; 1/2 Vegetable; 5 1/2 Fat.

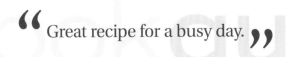

cookquotes " Great recipe for a busy day. "

grandmother lowe's smoked brisket

Linda Lowe, OK

serves 10

3	tablespoons liquid smoke flavoring
3	teaspoons garlic salt
2	teaspoons onion salt
2	teaspoons celery seed
5	pounds brisket, trimmed
3	tablespoons worcestershire sauce

In small bowl, **mix** first 4 ingredients. **Rub** mixture on brisket.

Wrap tightly in heavy duty aluminum foil. **Refrigerate** overnight.

Unwrap. **Add** worcestershire sauce. **Rewrap**. **Place** in baking pan.

Bake 225 degrees, approximately 9 hours.

Per Serving: 360 Calories; 17g Fat (43.8% calories from fat); 47g Protein; 1g Carbohydrate; trace Dietary Fiber; 141mg Cholesterol; 1174mg Sodium.

Exchanges: 0 Grain(Starch); 7 Lean Meat; 0 Fat; 0 Other Carbohydrates.

italian pot roast

Susan Martindale, MS

serves 4

2	pounds round steak — or London broil, trimmed, cut into cubes
2	teaspoons fresh garlic — crushed
1/4	teaspoon black pepper — ground
1 1/2	cups sliced fresh mushrooms
1	cup onion — chopped
1	1 pound can crushed tomatoes — unsalted
6	ounces tomato paste — unsalted
1/4	cup water
2	teaspoons dried italian seasoning
1 3/4	teaspoons beef bouillon granules

Preheat oven to 350 degrees. **Rinse** meat, **pat** dry with paper towel.

Spread garlic over meat. **Sprinkle** with pepper.

Coat large oven-suitable skillet with cooking spray.

Preheat over medium-high heat.

Brown meat in skillet, 2 minutes each side. **Remove** skillet from heat. **Spread** onions and mushrooms over meat.

In large mixing bowl, **combine** remaining ingredients. **Pour** over meat mix. **Cover** tightly.

Bake 350 degrees, 2 hours or until meat is tender.

Serve hot.

Accompany with spaghetti, linguini or another pasta, if desired.

Per Serving:: 500 Calories; 28g Fat (50.5% calories from fat); 47g Protein; 15g Carbohydrate; 3g Dietary Fiber; 135mg Cholesterol; 621mg Sodium.

Exchanges: 0 Grain(Starch); 6 Lean Meat; 3 Vegetable; 1 1/2 Fat.

korean bar-b-que

Carol Cooke, MO

serves 4

1 1/2	pounds thinly sliced flank steak
5	cloves garlic - pressed
1/2	cup soy sauce
3	tablespoons sesame oil
2	teaspoons ginger - minced or grated
3	tablespoons sugar
2	teaspoons white vinegar
2	teaspoons sesame seeds
1	teaspoon pepper
1/2	cup chopped scallions or onions

Per Serving: 469 Calories; 29g Fat (55.7% calories from fat); 36g Protein; 16g Carbohydrate; 1g Dietary Fiber; 87mg Cholesterol; 2179mg Sodium.

Exchanges: 0 Grain(Starch); 5 Lean Meat; 1 Vegetable; 3 Fat; 1/2 Other Carbohydrates.

Whisk all other ingredients together until well mixed.

Marinate steak in soy sauce mixture overnight, or several hours.

Lay foil over bar-b-que grill, **poke** full of holes with fork.

When grill is hot, **cook** meat on foil, 1 - 2 minutes per side. **Stir** or turn while grilling.

Serve hot.

Marinate the meat in a bag for easy coating or turning.

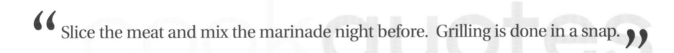

"Slice the meat and mix the marinade night before. Grilling is done in a snap."

"visit the dentist twice a year; if you don't, then plaque will appear"

Mackenzie, Grade 3

sour beef and dumplings

serves 4

Aunt Ruth Vanick, PA "Sister M. Helen Regina, OSF"

2	tablespoons pickling spice
1	pound beef round -- cut into 2 inch cubes, or your choice beef
1	medium onion -- cut in half
1	teaspoon sugar
1	pinch salt
1	cup vinegar
1 1/2	cups water -- divided
1	bo ginger snaps
1	tablespoon cornstarch

dumplings

8	medium potatoes
2	tablespoons flour
1	egg
	salt to taste

Per Serving: 507 Calories; 17g Fat (29.9% calories from fat); 31g Protein; 59g Carbohydrate; 5g Dietary Fiber; 118mg Cholesterol; 106mg Sodium.

Exchanges: 3 1/2 Grain(Starch); 3 1/2 Lean Meat; 1/2 Vegetable; 1 1/2 Fat; 1/2 Other Carbohydrates.

Place spices in a metal tea ball or cloth bag.

In a large Dutch oven, **place** beef, spice ball, onion, sugar, and salt.

Cover with vinegar and 1 cup water.

Bring to **boil**. Lower heat. **Simmer** until meat is tender (can be cut with a fork).

Remove spice ball. **Serve** with gravy.

gravy

In bowl, **soften** ginger snaps in small amount water.

Stir in cornstarch diluted in 1/2 cup water, until thickened.

Pour over beef in pot. **Heat**. **Serve** over potato dumplings.

potato dumplings
(One potato makes about 1 1/2 dumplings.)

In large pan, **boil** whole potatoes in skins. **Remove** skin while hot.

Rice, grate or coarse mash potatoes.

Add flour, egg and salt.

Shape into dumplings about the size of a small potato.

Fill large pan 3/4 full water. **Bring** water to boil.

Drop dumplings into boiling water. **Cook** about 5 minutes.

Dumplings will rise to top when done.

"A hit at the convent — and a dish we craved during Aunt Ruth's summer visits to the lake."

stroganoff
Jenny Lee Zehner, PA

serves 4

1 1/2	pounds venison — cut in 3-inch pieces
1	tablespoon fat
1	medium onion — sliced
1	clove garlic — minced
1	tablespoon ketchup
2	teaspoons worcestershire sauce
1	small can sliced mushrooms
1	can cream of mushroom soup
8	ounces sour cream

In large skillet, **brown** pieces of venison (or caribou) in fat.

Add onions and garlic, **cook** 5 minutes or until tender.

Add next 4 ingredients. **Simmer** 10 minutes.

Just before serving, **add** sour cream and reheat.

Serve over noodles or rice.

Per Serving: 409 Calories; 22g Fat (48.3% calories from fat); 42g Protein; 10g Carbohydrate; 1g Dietary Fiber; 174mg Cholesterol; 446mg Sodium.

Exchanges: 0 Grain(Starch); 5 1/2 Lean Meat; 1/2 Vegetable; 0 Non-Fat Milk; 3 1/2 Fat; 0 Other Carbohydrates.

" Adapted from my mother-in-law's beef stroganoff recipe. I use venison or caribou. "

Europeans used the American style of eating originally and brought it to the Colonies. After the settlement of America, Europeans switched to the Continental style of eating – leaving Americans as the only culture using the original method.

tidbits

- Food does not cause tooth decay — eating does.

- About 90 percent of all food contains sugars or starches that permit bacteria in dental plaque to produce acids. Bacterial acid attacking teeth for 20 minutes or more can lead to loss of tooth mineral and cavities.

- Processed starches can cause decay. Bread, crackers, pasta, pretzels and potato chips often take longer to clear the mouth than sugar — so the risk of tooth decay may last even longer.

- Science cannot tell us which foods have the highest or the least risk of decay.

- To cavity-causing bacteria, sugars are essentially the same, whether natural or processed. All types of sugars — and the foods that contain them — can play a role in tooth decay.

- Bacteria in the mouth can't tell the difference between the amount of sugar or starch in food. A lick of frosting can start the same acid attack as eating the whole cake.

"if you brush well, then your smile will be swell"

Samantha, Grade 3

pork

pork

ingredients:

continental and american style of eating

Food is cut the same way in both the American and the Continental style of eating..

- Hold the knife in your right hand with the index finger overlapping the blade about 1 inch and hold the fork, tines down, in your left hand.

- Cut one bite at a time.

- After cutting meat in the **American** style, rest the knife on the upper right edge of the plate. Switch the fork to your right hand and hold it as you would a pencil before raising it to your mouth. This is sometimes called the "zig zag" method.

- In the **Continental** style, bring the fork, tines down, to your mouth by twisting your wrist and raising your forearm slightly. The knife should stay in your right hand.

- It is acceptable to place a small amount of potatoes, rice or vegetables on the tines of the fork with the meat.

american style

birthday barbeque ribs

Kathy Moorman, OH

serves 8

5	pounds pork or beef backribs
1	can beef consomme
1	can condensed onion soup

sauce

1 1/2	cups ketchup
1/4	cup vinegar
1	tablespoon molasses
2	tablespoons brown sugar
1	onion — finely chopped

Per Serving: 140 Calories; 5g Fat (29.0% calories from fat) 6g Protein; 20g Carbohydrate; 1g Dietary Fiber; 14mg Cholesterol; 974mg Sodium.

Exchanges: 1/2 Lean Meat; 1/2 Vegetable; 1/2 Fat; 1 Other Carbohydrate.

Preheat oven to 350 degrees. Or use pressure cooker to manufacturer's directions.

Place ribs in large baking pan. **Cover** with soups and 1-2 cans water.

Bake 350 degrees, 2-3 hours.

Remove from oven. **Place** in clean roaster or large crock-pot.

In small mixing bowl, **combine** all sauce ingredients. **Pour** over ribs.

Bake additional 35-60 minutes.

Slow cooking provides the best result. As long as there is plenty of liquid, the longer ribs are in the oven, the more tender they will be.

" As a kid, ribs with my Dad's barbeque sauce — passed along from his Mom, my Gram — were my favorite "birthday meal". "

crock pot pork roast

Jackie Davis, IN

serves 8

4	pounds pork roast
1	package garlic and herb dry soup mix
1 1/2	cups water

Per Serving: 336 Calories; 21g Fat (58.7% calories from fat) 34g Protein; 0g Carbohydrate; 0g Dietary Fiber; 113mg Cholesterol; 102mg Sodium.

Exchanges: 5 Lean Meat; 1 1/2 Fat.

Place roast in crock pot.

Sprinkle about half the soup mix over the roast.

Pour water over the roast and soup mix.

Cook on low, 7 - 8 hours or until fork tender.

Serve.

crunchy ham casserole

Mary Higgins, IL

serves 6

2	cups elbow macaroni — cooked and drained
1 1/2	cups ham cubes — cooked, or luncheon meat
1	can cream of chicken soup, condensed
1/2	cup sour cream
1/2	cup milk
10	ounces frozen broccoli spears — cooked and drained
1	cup shredded cheddar cheese
2 3/4	ounces french fried onions — canned

Per Serving: 314 Calories; 17g Fat (49.6% calories from fat)
17g Protein; 23g Carbohydrate; 2g Dietary Fiber; 54mg Cholesterol;
920mg Sodium.

Exchanges: 1 Grain(Starch); 1 1/2 Lean Meat; 1/2 Vegetable
0 Non-Fat Milk; 2 1/2 Fat.

Preheat oven to 350 degrees.

In large bowl, **combine** cooked macaroni and ham. **Pour** into 9x13 baking dish.

In mixing bowl, **blend** soup, sour cream and milk. **Pour** 1/2 mix over macaroni and ham.

Arrange broccoli on top.

Pour remaining sauce over broccoli. **Sprinkle** with cheese.

Bake, uncovered, 350 degrees, 20 minutes.

Top with french fried onions, **bake** 5 minutes longer.

May substitute large can water packed chicken
and low-fat cream of chicken soup
or cheddar cheese soup.

ham and chicken casserole

Connie Slyby, IN

serves 6

1	package (6 ounces) long-grain wild rice
2	cups cooked chicken — cubed
1	cup ham cubes
1	can (10.75 ounces) cream of chicken soup, condensed
1	can (12 ounces) evaporated milk
1	cup shredded cheddar cheese
	pepper — to taste
1/4	cup parmesan cheese

Per Serving: 403 Calories; 18g Fat (39.5% calories from fat)
32g Protein; 28g Carbohydrate; 2g Dietary Fiber; 91mg Cholesterol;
886mg Sodium.

Exchanges: 1 1/2 Grain(Starch); 3 1/2 Lean Meat; 1/2 Non-Fat Milk
2 1/2 Fat.

Preheat oven to 350 degrees. **Grease** 2 quart baking dish.

Cook rice according to directions on package. **Pour** into prepared baking dish. **Top** with ham and chicken.

In a bowl, **combine** soup, milk, cheese and pepper. **Pour** over ham mix. **Top** with parmesan.

Bake, uncovered, 350 degrees, 30 minutes or until bubbly.

Serve warm.

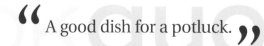

" A good dish for a potluck. "

ham loaf

Dinah Catey, IN

serves 8

loaf

3	cups ham — ground
1	egg
1	cup milk
3	cups crispy rice cereal
1/2	teaspoon dry mustard

sauce

1 1/2	cups brown sugar
2 1/2	tablespoons flour
1/2	cup water
1/2	cup vinegar, cider
1/2	teaspoon dry mustard

Per Serving: 275 Calories; 7g Fat (22.9% calories from fat) 12g Protein; 42g Carbohydrate; trace Dietary Fiber 56mg Cholesterol; 777mg Sodium.

Exchanges: 1 Grain(Starch); 1 1/2 Lean Meat; 0 Non-Fat Milk 1/2 Fat; 2 Other Carbohydrates.

loaf

Preheat oven to 350 degrees.

In large bowl, **combine** all ingredients, **place** in 9 inch loaf pan or 9 inch casserole dish, ungreased.

Bake 350 degrees, 1 hour.

Cover with sauce. **Bake** additional 30 minutes.

Serve hot.

sauce

In large bowl, **combine** all ingredients. **Mix** thoroughly.

Pour over ham loaf after it has baked 1 hour.

A good way to use scraps left from baked ham.
Use meat grinder to grind ham.

Hundreds of years ago, people of distinction were targets of poisoning. Covers were placed over food as it was carried the long distance from kitchen to table. A "cover" kept the heat in and protected the food from being poisoned until it reached the tasters, who then reassured the recipients the food was safe to eat. Today, the wrap on fast food mimics the idea of a cover for protection.

tidbits

italian meatballs
Christine Maggio, IL

serves 20 • yields 9 dozen

4	pounds ground pork
2	pounds ground sirloin
5	large eggs — lightly beaten
2	cups soft bread crumbs — homemade
1	cup Parmesan cheese — freshly grated
1/3	cup fresh parsley — chopped
6	cloves garlic — minced
1	teaspoon salt
1/2	teaspoon freshly ground black pepper

Per Serving: 394 Calories; 29g Fat (68.7% calories from fat) 27g Protein; 3g Carbohydrate; trace Dietary Fiber; 147mg Cholesterol; 301mg Sodium.

Exchanges: 0 Grain(Starch); 4 Lean Meat; 0 Vegetable; 3 1/2 Fat.

Preheat oven to 400 degrees. **Line** baking sheets with aluminum foil coated with cooking spray.

In large bowl, **combine** all ingredients, **mix** lightly.

Shape mixture into 1 1/2 inch balls.

Place meatballs on prepared baking sheets.

Bake 400 degrees, 18-20 minutes or until meatballs are done.

Serve immediately or freeze in airtight container up to 1 month.

To create a supper on the go, simply reheat in your favorite spaghetti sauce and serve over cooked pasta.

north coast pork roast
Suzann Glenn, OH

serves 8

5	pounds pork roast — boneless
1	teaspoon chili powder — divided
1/2	teaspoon garlic salt
1/2	teaspoon salt
1/2	cup apple jelly
1/2	cup ketchup
1	tablespoon vinegar
1	cup corn chips — crushed

Per Serving: 514 Calories; 28g Fat (50.3% calories from fat) 43g Protein; 20g Carbohydrate; 1g Dietary Fiber; 141mg Cholesterol; 615mg Sodium.

Exchanges: 0 Grain(Starch); 6 Lean Meat; 2 Fat; 1 Other Carbohydrates.

Preheat oven to 325 degrees.

Place roast fat side up on rack in shallow roasting pan.

In small bowl, **combine** 1/2 teaspoon chili powder, garlic salt and salt. **Rub** on roast. **Insert** meat thermometer.

Roast 325 degrees, 2-2 1/2 hours or to 165 degrees on meat thermometer.

In small saucepan, **combine** next 3 ingredients and remaining 1/2 teaspoon chili powder. **Simmer** 2 minutes.

Brush over roast. **Sprinkle** with corn chips.

Roast 10-15 minutes longer or to 170 degrees on meat thermometer. **Remove** to platter, let **stand** 10 minutes.

Add enough water to pan drippings, including corn chips, to measure 1 cup.

In saucepan, **bring** pan drippings mix to boil. **Serve** with roast.

pork chops made easy

Dr. Phil Catey, IN

serves 12

12	large pork chops — boneless, 1 inch thick, trimmed
	salt and pepper — to taste
1	large onion — cut into rings
12	tablespoons ketchup
12	tablespoons brown sugar
1/2	cup lemon juice — or more as needed

Per Serving: 287 Calories; 15g Fat (46.6% calories from fat) 23g Protein; 15g Carbohydrate; trace Dietary Fiber 74mg Cholesterol; 240mg Sodium.

Exchanges: 3 1/2 Lean Meat; 0 Vegetable; 0 Fruit; 1 Fat; 1 Other Carbohydrates.

Preheat oven to 400 degrees. **Prepare** large shallow baking pan with non-stick spray.

Place chops in single layer in prepared pan. DO NOT OVERLAP.

On top each chop **place** 1 or 2 rings of onion, 1 tablespoon ketchup and 1 tablespoon brown sugar.

Pour lemon juice approximately 1/4 inch deep around chops. **Cover** tightly with foil.

Bake 400 degrees, 1 hour.

Remove foil, **bake** additional 20-30 minutes until brown and tender.

Serve hot.

pork medallions with glazed apples

A. Paige Godat, TN

serves 2

1	teaspoon olive oil
1	pound pork tenderloin slices — cut 1/4" thick
2	large Granny Smith apples — peeled, cored, cut into 1/4 inch rings
1/3	cup apple juice, frozen concentrate — unsweetened, undiluted, thawed
2	teaspoons dijon mustard
1/4	teaspoon salt
1/4	teaspoon white pepper

Per Serving: 437 Calories; 11g Fat (21.9% calories from fat) 49g Protein; 36g Carbohydrate; 3g Dietary Fiber; 148mg Cholesterol; 457mg Sodium.

Exchanges: 0 Grain(Starch); 7 Lean Meat; 2 1/2 Fruit; 1/2 Fat 0 Other Carbohydrates.

Coat large skillet with cooking spray, **add** olive oil. **Place** over medium-high heat until oil is hot.

Add pork slices, **brown** on both sides. **Remove** from pan, pat dry. **Set** aside.

Coat skillet again with cooking spray, **place** over medium-high heat until hot.

Add apples, **saute** until tender. **Add** apple juice concentrate, bring to boil. **Stir** in mustard, salt and pepper.

Add pork. **Cook** until heated through.

Serve immediately.

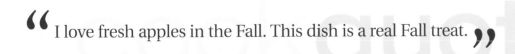

" I love fresh apples in the Fall. This dish is a real Fall treat. "

cookquotes

pork tenderloin

Dorothy Unger, IL

serves 4

1	large red pepper
1	clove garlic
1/2	cup heavy cream
6	tablespoons butter
2	tablespoons tomato paste
1/2	teaspoon dried sage — crumbled
1	teaspoon paprika — or more to taste
1/2	teaspoon salt
2	pounds pork tenderloin — cut into 2 tenderloins

Per Serving: 545 Calories; 36g Fat (60.1% calories from fat) 49g Protein; 5g Carbohydrate; 1g Dietary Fiber; 235mg Cholesterol; 632mg Sodium.

Exchanges: 0 Grain(Starch); 7 Lean Meat; 1/2 Vegetable; 0 Non-Fat Milk; 5 1/2 Fat.

In food processor, **chop** red pepper and garlic.

Add cream. **Process** to smooth.

In saucepan, **melt** butter. **Work** in tomato paste. **Add** to garlic puree.

Add spices. **Heat** through, (about 1 minute).

Brush tenderloins with 1/4 tomato sauce. Let **stand**, covered, at room temperature, 2 hours.

Preheat oven to 350 degrees. **Warm** sauce.

Baste tenderloins and **place** in a baking pan.

Bake 350 degrees, about 50 minutes or until meat thermometer inserted in center reads 160 degrees.

Baste every 10 minutes while roasting.

"if you don't believe in the tooth fairy, that's fine but you should believe in hygiene because it will make your teeth shine"

Ashley, Grade 5

the master's pork chops
Melodi Duwell, SC

serves 6

chops

6	pork chops — 1-inch thick
1/4	cup flour
1/2	teaspoon salt
1/2	teaspoon flavor enhancer
1/4	teaspoon pepper
1	egg — slightly beaten
2	tablespoons water
1 1/2	cups crackers — finely crushed
1	tablespoon butter
2	onions — finely chopped
1	clove garlic — minced

sauce

1/2	cup packed brown sugar
2	teaspoons dry mustard
1	cup water
2	tablespoons vinegar, cider
1	cup ketchup
3	ounces cream cheese
3	lemon slices
1	tablespoon butter — or margarine
1	tablespoon brown bouquet sauce — bottled

Per Serving: 731 Calories; 32g Fat (38.8% calories from fat);
32g Protein; 80g Carbohydrate; 3g Dietary Fiber; 131mg
Cholesterol; 1581mg Sodium.

Exchanges: 3 Grain(Starch); 3 1/2 Lean Meat; 1/2 Vegetable
0 Fruit; 4 Fat; 2 Other Carbohydrates.

chops

Coat chops in mixture of flour and seasonings. **Dip** both sides in blend of egg and water, then **coat** with cracker crumbs.

In large skillet, **brown** both sides of chops in hot butter. **Remove** from skillet, keep warm.

Add onion and garlic to remaining fat, **cook**, **stirring** occasionally, until onion is soft.

Return chops to skillet. **Pour** sauce over all. **Cover**, **cook** over low heat, about 50 minutes or until meat is tender.

Baste occasionally during cooking.

Serve chops with sauce on the side.

sauce

In saucepan, **mix** first 2 ingredients. **Stir in** water and vinegar.

In a mixing bowl, **blend** ketchup and cream cheese. **Add** to vinegar mix.

Add lemon slices and butter. **Heat** thoroughly, **stir** occasionally.

When ready for use, **remove** from heat, **mix in** bottled brown bouquet sauce.

eating disorders and dental health

Anorexia Nervosa and Bulimia Nervosa rob the body of adequate minerals, vitamins, proteins and other nutrients needed for good health—causing potential injury to teeth, muscles and major organs.

- Bulimia Nervosa is an eating disorder that harms your overall health and is particularly destructive to teeth. It involves secret, repeated binge eating followed by purging — self-induced vomiting, use of laxatives, fasting, diuretics or diet pills. The digestive system contains strong acids that break down food. When vomiting is used to purge food from the body, these acids attack tooth enamel. Repeated vomiting can severely erode tooth enamel, and over time, teeth will become worn and translucent. The mouth, throat and salivary glands may become swollen and tender, and bad breath may result.

- Anorexia Nervosa is an eating disorder characterized by an intense fear of weight gain, the desire to be thinner and an inability to maintain a minimally normal weight for height and age. It is self-induced starvation.

"it might be fun to jump on earth
if there were no gravity
i brush my teeth so
i don't get a cavity"

Morgan, Grade 4

fish & seafood

ingredients:

eating seafood

Seafood may be served as an appetizer, fish course or main course.

- When shrimp is served with the tails on, hold by the tail, dip in sauce, bite off and discard the tail.

- Shrimp cocktail is eaten with a seafood fork. Eat large shrimp in two bites or cut with a fork.

- When eating oysters, mussels and clams on the half-shell, hold with one hand and remove with an oyster fork. Dip in sauce and eat it in one mouthful. Mussels may be sucked from the shell.

- Seafood served on toothpicks may be eaten directly from the toothpick.

- When eating snails (also known as escargot), hold the shell with your fingers or tongs; remove it with an oyster fork, and eat whole. You may dip bread in garlic butter.

- To eat steamed clams, hold by the shell and lift out by the neck. Slip off the inedible neck sheathe; dip the clam in butter or broth, and eat in one bite.

- Fried clams are eaten with a fork.

- When eating lobster, crack the claws with a nutcracker and extract the meat with a seafood fork. Cut large pieces with a fork. Next, pull off and clean the small claws and suck as through a straw.

- Stuffed lobster and soft-shell crabs are eaten with a knife and fork.

- At a formal meal with several courses, the third course served is the fish course. A fish knife and fork are provided. If the fish is soft and boneless, it is correct to use only the fish fork. If you do not use the fish knife, leave it on the table until you are finished eating the fish. When you have finished, place the knife next to the fork on the plate in the 10:20 position.

catfish parmesan

Debbie Preece, UT

serves 6

2/3	cup parmesan cheese — grated
1/4	cup flour
1/2	teaspoon salt
1/4	teaspoon pepper
1	teaspoon paprika
1	egg — beaten
1/4	cup milk
6	catfish fillets
1/4	cup butter — melted
1/3	cup sliced almonds

Per Serving: 344 Calories; 20g Fat (53.3% calories from fat); 33g Protein; 7g Carbohydrate; 1g Dietary Fiber; 152mg Cholesterol; 505mg Sodium.

Exchanges: 1/2 Grain(Starch); 4 1/2 Lean Meat; 0 Non-Fat Milk 2 1/2 Fat.

Preheat oven to 350 degrees. Lightly **grease** a cookie sheet with sides.

In large shallow bowl, **combine** first 5 ingredients. **Mix** well.

In small bowl, **combine** egg and milk. **Mix** well.

Dip fillets in milk mixture then **dredge** in flour mix.

Arrange on prepared cookie sheet with sides. **Drizzle** with butter. **Sprinkle** with almonds.

Bake 350 degrees, 20 minutes or until fish flakes.

Serve hot.

"brush, brush to make them white, brush, brush to keep them strong and bright"

Alexia Rose, Kindergarten

sores in the mouth lasting longer than two weeks need a dentist's attention.

ceviche
Kathy Kne, OH

serves 8

1	pound cod — or any lean white fish, cut in 1/2inch cubes
1/3	cup fresh lemon juice
1/3	cup fresh lime juice
1/2	teaspoon salt
1/2	teaspoon dried oregano
1	tablespoon olive oil
1/3	cup fresh lemon juice
1/3	cup fresh lime juice
1/2	teaspoon salt
1/4	teaspoon white pepper
1/4	teaspoon ground cumin
1	medium tomato — finely chopped
1/2	medium onion — finely chopped
1	teaspoon vinegar
4	ounces tiny boiled shrimp
1	jalapeno pepper — seeded, finely minced
1	tablespoon fresh cilantro — finely chopped

Per Serving: 93 Calories; 2g Fat (21.9% calories from fat)
13g Protein; 5g Carbohydrate; 1g Dietary Fiber; 52mg Cholesterol;
331mg Sodium.

Exchanges: 0 Grain(Starch); 2 Lean Meat; 1/2 Vegetable; 0 Fruit;
1/2 Fat; 0 Other Carbohydrates.

In large bowl, **mix** first 5 ingredients. **Marinate** in refrigerator 2 hours. **Drain** completely.

In small bowl, **combine** next 6 ingredients. **Add** to drained fish.

In large bowl, **combine** next 6 ingredients. **Mix** well. **Add** to undrained fish mixture. Stir.

Refrigerate 8 hours or overnight.

Serve cold on lettuce leaf with tortilla chips.

The acid in the citrus juice actually "cooks" the fish so no heat is necessary.

" Something unique that is sure to win raves for the wonderful textures and flavors! "

cod for those who don't like fish

Dr. Ron Slyby, IN

serves 2

1	cod fillet — or haddock
	lemon juice — to taste
1	carrot — sliced, microwave to crunchy
1/2	onion — thinly sliced
1/4	green pepper — or red
1/2	tomato — cut into wedges
	seasoned salt — to taste

Per Serving: 131 Calories; 1g Fat (7.0% calories from fat) 22g Protein; 8g Carbohydrate; 2g Dietary Fiber; 50mg Cholesterol; 79mg Sodium.

Exchanges: 3 Lean Meat; 1 1/2 Vegetable.

Preheat oven to 350 degrees or preheat grill.

Place fish fillet on large enough piece of aluminum foil to wrap tightly.

Top fillet with lemon juice and vegetables. **Sprinkle** vegetables and fish with seasoned salt.

Wrap fish and vegetables tightly. **Bake** in 350 degree oven, or grill, 20 minutes or until fish is done.

company shrimp

Susan Barsness, IL

serves 20

1	pound butter
1	pound margarine
8	ounces worcestershire sauce
4	tablespoons ground black pepper
1	teaspoon ground rosemary
5	lemons — sliced
1	teaspoon hot pepper sauce
5	teaspoons salt
4	cloves garlic — crushed
10	pounds jumbo bay shrimp — unpeeled

Per Serving: 583 Calories; 41g Fat (63.0% calories from fat) 47g Protein; 7g Carbohydrate; trace Dietary Fiber; 395mg Cholesterol; 1389mg Sodium.

Exchanges: 0 Grain(Starch); 6 1/2 Lean Meat; 0 Vegetable; 0 Fruit; 7 1/2 Fat; 0 Other Carbohydrates.

Preheat oven to 400 degrees.

In large saucepan, **melt** butter and margarine.

Add remaining ingredients, except shrimp. **Mix** well.

Divide shrimp in two 9x13 pyrex dishes, **pour** sauce over. **Stir** well.

Bake 400 degrees, 15-20 minutes, turning once.

Serve immediately.

" Refrigerate to make a great shrimp salad the next day. "

"go the mile with a healthy smile"

David , Age 7

crustless crab quiche

Eleanora B. Perry, IL

serves 10

1/2	pound fresh mushrooms — sliced
2	tablespoons butter
4	eggs
1	cup light sour cream
1	cup cottage cheese
1	cup parmesan cheese
1	dash hot pepper sauce
2	cups shredded cheddar cheese — or your favorite
1	can crabmeat

Preheat oven to 350 degrees. **Grease** 10 inch pie plate.

In skillet, **saute** mushrooms in butter until tender.

In large mixing bowl, **blend** eggs, sour cream, cottage cheese, parmesan cheese and hot pepper sauce.

Add mushrooms, butter, your favorite shredded cheese and crab. **Mix**. **Pour** into prepared pie plate.

Bake 350 degrees, 45 minutes or until tests done.

Rest and **serve**.

Per Serving: 220 Calories; 15g Fat (61.6% calories from fat) 18g Protein; 4g Carbohydrate; trace Dietary Fiber; 125mg Cholesterol; 474mg Sodium.

Exchanges: 2 1/2 Lean Meat; 0 Vegetable; 2 Fat; 0 Other Carbohydrates.

" For variation add one cup chopped spinach or broccoli. "

easy creole shrimp

Melodi Duwell, SC

serves 4

1/2	cup onion — chopped
1/2	cup celery — chopped
1	clove garlic — chopped
3	tablespoons shortening
16	ounces tomatoes, canned
8	ounces tomato sauce
1/2	teaspoon salt
1	tablespoon sugar
1	tablespoon worcestershire sauce
1/2	teaspoon chili powder
1	dash hot pepper sauce
1/2	cup green pepper — chopped
4	ounces mushroom pieces — drained
2	tablespoons cornstarch
1	tablespoon water
1	pound shrimp — frozen and thawed, or canned, rinsed and drained

Per Serving: 298 Calories; 12g Fat (35.7% calories from fat) 26g Protein; 23g Carbohydrate; 3g Dietary Fiber; 173mg Cholesterol; 1005mg Sodium.

Exchanges: 1/2 Grain(Starch); 3 Lean Meat; 2 1/2 Vegetable; 2 Fat; 1/2 Other Carbohydrates.

In large skillet, **brown** onion, celery and garlic in shortening.

Add next 9 ingredients, **simmer** 45 minutes.

In small measuring cup, **mix** cornstarch into water. **Stir** into sauce to thicken.

Add shrimp. **Cover**. **Simmer** 3-5 minutes.

Serve over hot cooked rice.

"wearing a mouthguard when sports I play, keeps me smiling every day"

Jordan, Grade 3

"brush your teeth morning, noon and night, so your teeth are sparkling white"

Nick, Grade 3

grilled red salmon

Nicole Putt, PA

serves 8

4	pounds red salmon fillets
3	cloves garlic — crushed
1	tablespoon salt
3	limes — halved
2	tablespoons parsley — chopped
1	stick butter — sliced in 8 patties

Per Serving: 374 Calories; 19g Fat (47.2% calories from fat); 46g Protein; 3g Carbohydrate; trace Dietary Fiber; 149mg Cholesterol; 1070mg Sodium.

Exchanges: 6 1/2 Lean Meat; 0 Vegetable; 0 Fruit; 2 1/2 Fat.

Preheat grill.

Place salmon, skin side down, in long glass dish.

In small bowl, **combine** garlic and salt to form paste. **Rub** on salmon.

Squeeze juice from limes on fish. **Scrape** pulp and spread over fish.

Marinate 2 hours.

Spray grill rack with non-sticking cooking spray. **Place** fish, skin side down, on grill rack, over hot coals.

Cover grill keeping all dampers open.

Cook until flesh is firm and flakes, about 10-15 minutes. DO NOT TURN FISH OVER. DO NOT OVERCOOK.

Top each fillet with sprinkle of parsley and 1 pat butter.

Serve.

" This salmon is simple and stress-free to prepare because the ingredients can be found in most kitchens. Great for entertaining. "

halibut with
tomatoes and pine nuts

Stephen Williams, IN

serves 4

1/4	cup pine nuts
4 1/2	cups Roma tomatoes — peeled, seeded, coarsely chopped
3	tablespoons olive oil
3	cloves garlic — chopped
1	bay leaf
2	tablespoons fresh dill — chopped, or 1 tablespoon dried dill
1	cup water
1/2	teaspoon salt
	freshly ground pepper — to taste
28	ounces halibut — (4 fillets, about 7 ounces each)
	italian parsley — chopped
4	lemon wedges

Per Serving: 414 Calories; 20g Fat (41.3% calories from fat) 465g Protein; 18g Carbohydrate; 3g Dietary Fiber; 64mg Cholesterol; 396mg Sodium.

Exchanges: 0 Grain(Starch); 6 Lean Meat; 2 Vegetable; 2 1/2 Fat.

In heavy skillet, over medium heat, **toast** pine nuts, **stirring** to light color and fragrant, about 1-2 minutes. **Set** aside.

In large skillet, over medium heat, **warm** oil. **Saute** garlic in oil just to changing color.

Add bay leaf, dill and tomatoes. **Cook** gently, uncovered, 8-10 minutes.

Stir in water, salt and pepper. **Cook** another 10 minutes.

Carefully **lay** fish in a single layer on tomato mix. **Cover**. **Simmer**, until fish is opaque throughout, about 12-15 minutes.

DO NOT OVERCOOK.

Place on warmed plates. **Spoon** tomato mix over and around fillet.

Garnish with toasted pine nuts and parsley.

Serve immediately, with lemon wedge alongside fillet.

Variation: May substitute other flaky white fish such as bass, sea bass or snapper.

If tiny bones get in your mouth while eating fish, it is

proper to remove them with your thumb and index finger

and place them on the side of your plate.

Do not put them in your napkin.

tidbits

171

maple-mustard grilled salmon

Jean Weathers, GA

serves 4

1	cup maple syrup — sugarfree and preferably carbohydrate free
2	tablespoons prepared mustard
1/4	cup soy sauce
4	salmon fillets

Per Serving: 419 Calories; 6g Fat (13.7% calories from fat) 35g Protein; 55g Carbohydrate; trace Dietary Fiber; 88mg Cholesterol; 1244mg Sodium.

Exchanges: 5 Lean Meat; 1/2 Vegetable; 0 Fat; 3 1/2 Other Carbohydrates.

In large dish, **combine** syrup, mustard and soy sauce.

Marinate salmon fillets in mix at least 30 minutes.

Remove salmon from marinade, **grill**, 4-5 minutes per side.

Remove from grill, **pour** remaining marinade over salmon. **Serve** immediately.

" My own creation. I use this marinade on everything: fish, chicken, beef and pork. "

orange roughy

Anne Devitt, IN

serves 4

1	tablespoon butter
4	orange roughy fillets
	lemon pepper — to taste
	salt and pepper — to taste
4	ounces lemon juice, bottled

Per Serving: 111 Calories; 4g Fat (31.1% calories from fat) 17g Protein; 2g Carbohydrate; trace Dietary Fiber 30mg Cholesterol; 107mg Sodium.

Exchanges: 2 1/2 Lean Meat; 0 Fruit; 1/2 Fat.

Preheat oven to 350 degrees.

In baking pan with 1/2 inch sides, **melt** butter.

Place fillets in pan. **Sprinkle** with spices.

Pour lemon juice around fillets (so fillets are sitting in juice, not submerged).

Bake 350 degrees, uncovered, 20 minutes or until fish is cooked through and flaky.

Place in serving dish. May **pour** drippings over fillets, if desired, before serving.

Serve hot.

Variation: Preheat grill covered with foil (turn up sides to form tray). Melt butter on foil, add seasoned fillets, douse with lemon juice and worcestershire sauce. Grill until cooked through and flaky. About 10-14 minutes.

poached salmon with horseradish sauce

Kathy Kne, OH

serves 4

salmon

4	cups water
1	lemon — sliced crosswise
1	carrot — sliced crosswise
	stalk celery — sliced crosswise
1	teaspoon peppercorns
16	ounces salmon steaks — (4 - 4ounces each)

sauce

1/4	cup mayonnaise — reduced calorie
1/4	cup nonfat yogurt — plain
2	teaspoons prepared horseradish
1 1/2	teaspoons lemon juice
1 1/2	teaspoons chopped chives

Per Serving: 254 Calories; 16g Fat (54.2% calories from fat) 24g Protein; 6g Carbohydrate; 1g Dietary Fiber; 64mg Cholesterol; 187mg Sodium.

Exchanges: 0 Grain(Starch); 3 Lean Meat; 1/2 Vegetable; 0 Fruit 0 Non-Fat Milk; 1 Fat; 0 Other Carbohydrates.

salmon

In large skillet, **combine** first 5 ingredients.

Bring to boil over medium-high heat. **Cover, reduce** heat, **simmer** 10 minutes.

Add salmon steaks. **Cover, simmer** 10 minutes.

Remove skillet from heat. Let **stand** 8 minutes.

Remove salmon steaks to serving plate. **Garnish** with lemon slices.

Serve with horseradish sauce.

sauce

In small bowl, **combine** all ingredients. **Mix** well.

Cover and **chill**.

" A healthy recipe that is also simply elegant. "

sauteed soft shell crab

Susan Barsness, IL

serves 4

4	small crabs, soft shell — cleaned
1 1/2	cups milk
3/4	cup flour
	salt and pepper — to taste
2	tablespoons olive oil
2	tablespoons unsalted butter
2	tablespoons parsley — flat leaf, chopped

Per Serving: 586 Calories; 34g Fat (52.0% calories from fat) 17g Protein; 53g Carbohydrate; 1g Dietary Fiber; 73mg Cholesterol; 1165mg Sodium.

Exchanges: 3 Grain(Starch); 1/2 Lean Meat; 0 Vegetable; 1/2 Non-Fat Milk; 6 Fat.

In shallow bowl, **cover** crabs in milk. **Soak** 1 hour. **Drain**. **Discard** milk.

In plastic bag, **combine** flour, salt and pepper. Lightly **dredge** crabs in flour mix.

In skillet, over medium-high heat, **heat** oil and butter. **Place** crabs in skillet, **saute** until golden, about 4 minutes per side.

Add more oil and butter, if necessary.

Sprinkle with parsley before serving.

Serve hot.

shrimp and clam shells

Carol Sukoneck, PA

serves 12

2 1/2	pounds shrimp — peeled and deveined
1/4	pound margarine
1/2	cup oil
3	tablespoons sweet basil
1/2	cup parsley
1	tablespoon oregano
1/2	teaspoon garlic powder
2	tablespoons parmesan cheese — or romano
3	jars marinara sauce
2	cans clams — minced
16	ounces pasta shells — small

Cook shrimp. **Set** aside.

In large pot, **melt** margarine and oil.

Add spices and cheese, then sauce and clams. **Mix** well.

Add cooked shrimp, **stir**. Allow to heat through on low setting on range.

Meanwhile, **cook** shells. **Add** to pot, carefully **mix** through shrimp and sauce.

Serve.

The longer the sauce and shrimp simmer on the range, the more flavorful it becomes.
Stir often to prevent burning on the bottom.

Per Serving: 432 Calories; 20g Fat (43.3% calories from fat) 26g Protein; 35g Carbohydrate; 2g Dietary Fiber; 145mg Cholesterol; 508mg Sodium.

Exchanges: 2 Grain(Starch); 3 Lean Meat; 0 Vegetable; 3 1/2 Fat.

---

shrimp chowder

Shirley Walsh, LA

serves 16

1	small onion — chopped
1	stick margarine
2	tablespoons flour
1	quart milk
1	pint half and half
2	cans (15 ounce) creamed white corn
1	can (15 ounce) corn, white
1	can (10 ounce) cream of potato soup
2	tablespoons worcestershire sauce
2	teaspoons seafood seasoning
1	teaspoon cajun seasoning
2	tablespoons parsley flakes
3	bay leaf
1	bunch green onions — chopped
	salt and pepper to taste
4	chicken bouillon cubes — (optional)
1	pound bay shrimp — peeled and deveined

In large stock pot, **saute** onions in margarine until clear.

Blend in flour. **Stir** until well mixed.

Add remaining ingredients. **Cook** over medium heat, **stirring** occasionally, about 30 minutes.

Serve hot.

Per Serving: 204 Calories; 12g Fat (52.6% calories from fat) 10g Protein; 15g Carbohydrate; 1g Dietary Fiber; 63mg Cholesterol; 524mg Sodium.

Exchanges: 1/2 Grain(Starch); 1 Lean Meat; 1/2 Vegetable 1/2 Non-Fat Milk; 2 1/2 Fat; 0 Other Carbohydrates.

st. simon's shrimp 'n grits

Sarah Looper, GA

serves 4

2 1/2	cups low sodium chicken broth
4	tablespoons butter — divided
3/4	cup quick cooking grits — not instant
6	tablespoons light cream cheese
2	tablespoons fat free half-and-half
1/2	cup green onions — chopped
1	pound medium shrimp, uncooked — peeled and deveined
2 1/2	tablespoons fresh lime juice

Per Serving: 422 Calories; 17g Fat (37.9% calories from fat) 35g Protein; 20g Carbohydrate; trace Dietary Fiber; 215mg Cholesterol; 738mg Sodium.

Exchanges: 1 1/2 Grain(Starch); 4 1/2 Lean Meat; 0 Vegetable; 0 Fruit; 0 Non-Fat Milk 3 Fat; 0 Other Carbohydrates.

In heavy saucepan, **combine** broth and 1 tablespoon butter, **bring** to boil.

Stir in grits, **reduce** heat, **simmer** 5 minutes, **stirring** occasionally.

Add cream cheese and half and half, **cover**. **Simmer**, stirring frequently, until almost all liquid has evaporated and grits are tender, (about 7 minutes).

Stir in green onions, **remove** from heat.

In large skillet, **melt** remaining butter. Over medium heat **add** shrimp, **saute** about 3 minutes, or until shrimp are cooked.

Stir in lime juice, **remove** from heat.

Spoon grits into center of plate. **Top** with shrimp. **Drizzle** with remaining lime butter from skillet. **Serve** immediately.

" I serve this with a green vegetable. Complete the menu with tossed salad, bread and dessert. "

toothbrush replacement

Replace your toothbrush every three or four months — or sooner if the bristles become frayed.

- Children's toothbrushes need replacing more frequently because they can wear out sooner.

- The best way to remove decay-causing plaque is by brushing and cleaning between your teeth at least twice a day, with a soft-bristled brush.

- The size and shape of your brush should fit your mouth, allowing you to reach all areas easily.

- A worn toothbrush will not do a good job of cleaning your teeth.

- When choosing any dental product, look for the ADA Seal of Acceptance, an important symbol of a dental product's safety and effectiveness.

By taking care of your teeth, eating a balanced diet and visiting your dentist regularly, you can have healthy teeth and an attractive smile your entire life.

"brush your teeth twice a day and your teeth will be here to stay"

Ryan, Grade 4

goat

goat

ingredients:

silent service code

In both the American and Continental styles of eating, silverware placement between bites and when you have finished sends a "silent signal" to an experienced server.

- In the **American** style, when you are talking, drinking or resting between bites, place your knife and fork, tines up, parallel to each other with a space in between—resting as if they are the hands of a clock at 10:20. This is called the rest position.

- When you finish a course, place the knife and fork in the 10:20 position, tines up, with the two utensils closer together. This is called the finished position in the American style.

- In **Continental** style, the fork and knife are crossed on the plate, with the fork tines over the knife blade, tines down. This is the rest position.

- When you are finished, place the knife and fork parallel to each other at the 10:20 position, close together, with tines down. This is the finished position in the Continental style.

finished position

amoreart
rosemary goat bbq

Dennise Peterson, CA

serves 8

4	cloves garlic — large, finely chopped
1/2	teaspoon fresh ground pepper
1/2	cup oil
1/2	cup red wine vinegar
1/2	cup grape juice
1/4	cup beef or chicken
1	teaspoon cardamom
1/2	teaspoon garlic salt
3	tablespoons fresh rosemary — minced
4	pack goat — tiny steaks or 2 pack large chops; completely thawed
2	tablespoons fig preserves or fig spread

Per Serving: 273 Calories; 16g Fat (53.8% calories from fat); 24g Protein; 7g Carbohydrate; trace Dietary Fiber; 65mg Cholesterol; 264mg Sodium.

Exchanges: 0 Grain(Starch); 3 1/2 Lean Meat; 0 Vegetable; 0 Fruit; 2 1/2 Fat; 1/2 Other Carbohydrates.

In bowl, **combine** first 9 ingredients. **Mix** to form marinade.

Place goat steaks in shallow pan, **pour** over marinade.

Marinate meat 2 hours or less turning occasionally. **Remove** and reserve marinade.

Heat grill. **Barbeque** 1st side, over medium hot heat, 3 minutes.

Over medium low heat, **barbeque** 2nd side, 4 -7 minutes. (Varies according to desired doneness.)

While meat is cooking, in medium fry pan, **heat** marinade. **Add** fig preserves. **Whisk** on medium high 2 minutes or until reduced.

Add additional 1/4 cup red wine vinegar/grape juice, **whisk** 1 minute.

To serve, **prepare** rice pilaf. **Arrange** rice in circle on plate. **Place** goat in middle of rice circle. **Drizzle** sauce on meat. **Garnish** with sprig of rosemary.

" California Home of the Savanna Goat "

"twinkle, twinkle little star, brush your teeth and you'll go far"

Ruth, Age 7

barbacoa

serves 24

6	pounds goat — deboned, cut in chunks
2	teaspoons salt
3	tablespoons white wine vinegar
5	small hot chili peppers
10	cloves garlic
1	tablespoon mexican oregano
2	teaspoons whole cloves
2	teaspoons cumin seeds
1	teaspoon black pepper
1/2	teaspoon ground cinnamon
8	tomatillos — cooked
1/2	cup toasted almonds, walnuts or pinenuts
2	tablespoons cooking oil
24	flour tortillas

salsa

1	pound ripe tomatoes — chopped
1	cup green onion — minced
1	green bell pepper — chopped
1/2	cup cilantro — minced
1/2	cup fresh tomatillos — chopped
1	teaspoon coriander seeds
1/4	cup fresh basil — minced, (optional)
1	clove garlic — minced
	salt — to taste

Per Serving: 404 Calories; 11g Fat (24.0% calories from fat);
31g Protein; 45g Carbohydrate; 4g Dietary Fiber; 65mg Cholesterol;
620mg Sodium.

Exchanges: 2 1/2 Grain(Starch); 3 1/2 Lean Meat; 1/2 Vegetable;
1 1/2 Fat; 0 Other Carbohydrates.

Place meat in marinade container with 2 teaspoons salt and vinegar. **Cover**. **Chill** overnight or at least couple of hours.

Preheat oven to 350 degrees. **Grease** Dutch oven or baking pan.

In food processor or blender, **put** next 10 ingredients. **Blend** into a paste.

Remove meat from refrigerator. **Smear** paste all over meat. **Place** in prepared Dutch oven. **Cover**.

Roast 350 degrees, 2 1/2 - 3 hours or until tender.

When meat is done, **shred**. **Serve** in warm tortillas topped with salsa.

salsa

In large, greased saucepan, **combine** salsa ingredients. **Cook** over low heat just to simmer. **Remove** from heat.

Spoon over meat in tortillas.

Store salsa left-overs in covered container in refrigerator.

cabrito and vegetable casserole

serves 6

10	ounce package frozen lima beans
1 1/2	cups carrots — thinly sliced
1	cup boiling water
1 1/2	pounds goat — ground
2	tablespoons onion — chopped
1	tablespoon vegetable oil — or bacon fat
1	can cream of mushroom soup, condensed
1/2	cup vegetable juice
1 1/2	teaspoons salt
1/4	teaspoon thyme
6	tomato slices — 3/4" thick
1/2	teaspoon salt
2	tablespoons parmesan cheese — grated

Per Serving: 588 Calories; 11g Fat (16.1% calories from fat); 46g Protein; 78g Carbohydrate; 13g Dietary Fiber; 67mg Cholesterol; 1477mg Sodium.

Exchanges: 5 Grain(Starch); 4 1/2 Lean Meat; 1 Vegetable; 1 1/2 Fat.

Preheat oven to 350 degrees.

In dutch oven, **add** beans and carrots to boiling water. **Cook**, covered, until tender, about 15-20 minutes.

Drain. **Save** vegetable juice.

In skillet, **cook** meat and onion, in oil until Cabrito is lightly brown and onion is done. **Pour** off drippings.

Add soup, vegetable juice, cooked vegetables, 1 1/2 teaspoons salt and thyme. **Mix** well.

Pour into 2 quart casserole. **Arrange** tomato slices on top of goat mix.

Sprinkle with 1/2 teaspoon salt and cheese.

Bake 350 degrees, 35-40 minutes.

Serve.

In Medieval times, eating could be dangerous! Keeping your hands visible reassured others you did not have a weapon in your lap. Resting your wrists on the edge of the table when not in use is still considered polite in all cultures, except American.

tidbits

cabrito stuffed green peppers

serves 4

4	green peppers — cored, seeded
2	tablespoons butter
1/2	pound goat — ground
3	tablespoons onion — minced
1	cup hot cooked rice
2	eggs — well beaten
1/2	teaspoon salt
1/2	teaspoon paprika
1/4	teaspoon celery seed
1/4	teaspoon curry powder
1/4	teaspoon worcestershire sauce

Per Serving: 242 Calories; 10g Fat (36.0% calories from fat); 17g Protein; 22g Carbohydrate; 3g Dietary Fiber; 141mg Cholesterol; 406mg Sodium.

Exchanges: 1 Grain(Starch); 2 Lean Meat; 1 1/2 Vegetable; 1 1/2 Fat; 0 Other Carbohydrates.

Preheat oven to 350 degrees.

In skillet, **melt** butter. **Add** ground meat, onions. **Stir** and **saute** until light in color.

Add remaining ingredients, **mix** well.

Fill pepper shells. **Bake** 350 degrees, 10-15 minutes.

Serve hot.

chevon sausage

serves 2

1	pound goat — ground
1	teaspoon sage
1/4	teaspoon black pepper
1/2	teaspoon red pepper
	salt and pepper — to taste

Per Serving: 249 Calories; 5g Fat (20.1% calories from fat); 47g Protein; trace Carbohydrate; trace Dietary Fiber; 129mg Cholesterol; 186mg Sodium.

Exchanges: 0 Grain(Starch); 7 Lean Meat; 0 Vegetable; 0 Fat.

In mixing bowl, **combine** all ingredients. **Mix** well. **Make** into patties.

In heavy skillet, **fry** patties until brown on both sides and cooked through. Do not overcook.

For a great meal, **serve** with eggs and hash browns.

toothbrush replacement: every 3 or 4 months —and more often for children.

chocolate goat milk fudge

serves 24

2	ounces unsweetened baking chocolate squares
3/4	cup goat milk
2	cups sugar
1	teaspoon light corn syrup
2	tablespoons butter
1	teaspoon vanilla

Per Serving: 92 Calories; 3g Fat (23.9% calories from fat); 1g Protein; 18g Carbohydrate; trace Dietary Fiber; 3mg Cholesterol; 14mg Sodium.

Exchanges: 0 Grain(Starch); 0 Lean Meat; 0 Non-Fat Milk; 1/2 Fat; 1 Other Carbohydrates.

In heavy saucepan, **melt** chocolate in milk.

Add sugar and corn syrup. **Cook** slowly, **stirring** constantly, until sugar dissolves.

Continue **cooking** gently to softball stage (234 degrees), **stirring** frequently.

Remove from heat. **Add** butter, **stirring** until melted.

Cool at room temperature, without stirring, until lukewarm (110 degrees).

Add vanilla. **Beat** vigorously until fudge becomes very thick and looses its gloss.

Quickly **spread** in buttered 11x7 pan.

When firm, **cut** into 24 squares.

Add nuts, if desired, when adding vanilla.

" The richest, smoothest, most melt-in-your-mouth fudge you've ever tasted! "

goat meat and sauerkraut

serves 12

5	pounds goat — rear quarter
2	cans (14 ounces each) sauerkraut
2	medium onions — sliced
2	tablespoons garlic — minced
2	teaspoons salt
1	teaspoon pepper
4	tablespoons worcestershire sauce
3	tablespoons jalapeno pepper sauce (optional)

Per Serving: 228 Calories; 4g Fat (18.4% calories from fat); 40g Protein; 5g Carbohydrate; 1g Dietary Fiber; 108mg Cholesterol; 820mg Sodium.

Exchanges: 0 Grain(Starch); 5 1/2 Lean Meat; 1/2 Vegetable; 0 Fat; 0 Other Carbohydrates.

Preheat oven to 300 degrees.

Place meat in roasting pan. **Spread** 1 can sauerkraut (with juice) around meat.

Spread second can of sauerkraut on top of meat.

Place onions on top sauerkraut.

Sprinkle with remaining ingredients, using jalapeno sauce if desired.

Cover. **Cook** 300 degrees, 4 hours or until meat falls off bone.

Baste with it's own juices several times during cooking.

no bake raspberry cheesecake

serves 8

1	box raspberries, frozen — thawed and drained, reserve liquid
1	packet unflavored gelatin
1/3	cup sugar
1	cup goat milk
2	cups goat cheese — plain
1	pie crust, graham cracker crumb — or pastry shell, baked

In saucepan, **heat** reserved raspberry liquid. **Stir** in gelatin and sugar until sugar dissolves.

Add milk.

In blender, **combine** sugar mix with cheese and raspberries. **Blend** until smooth.

Pour into baked pie shell.

Refrigerate at least 4 hours before serving.

Per Serving: 402 Calories; 19g Fat (41.6% calories from fat); 12g Protein; 48g Carbohydrate; 2g Dietary Fiber; 33mg Cholesterol; 311mg Sodium.

Exchanges: 1 1/2 Lean Meat; 1/2 Fruit; 0 Non-Fat Milk; 3 Fat; 2 1/2 Other Carbohydrates.

northern chevon stir fry

serves 8

3/4	pound goat — cut into 1"x 2" strips
3	tablespoons vinegar
4	tablespoons vegetable oil — divided
1/2	cup chicken broth
1	large onion — chopped
1	bunch broccoli — chopped
3	medium carrots — sliced
2	tart apples — cubed
10	mushrooms — sliced

In self-seal plastic bag, **combine** vinegar, 2 tablespoons oil and chicken broth to form marinade.

Place meat in marinade, **refrigerate** 3-4 hours or overnight.

Heat wok or electric fry pan to very hot. **Add** remaining oil.

Add onion. **Stir fry** 10 seconds.

Remove meat from marinade, **add** to wok. **Cook** 1-2 minutes. **Remove** to serving platter with slotted spoon.

Pour marinade into wok. **Add** broccoli and carrots. **Cover**, steam until tender.

Return meat to wok. **Add** apples and mushrooms. **Toss** until mixture is heated through.

Serve immediately over rice or pasta.

Per Serving: 169 Calories; 8g Fat (42.2% calories from fat); 12g Protein; 13g Carbohydrate; 4g Dietary Fiber; 24mg Cholesterol; 115mg Sodium.

Exchanges: 1 1/2 Lean Meat; 1 1/2 Vegetable; 0 Fruit; 1 1/2 Fat; 0 Other Carbohydrates.

riblets in barbeque sauce

serves 6

4	pounds goat — riblets
8	ounces pineapple chunks in juice — drained, reserve juice
1	lemon — unpeeled, thinly sliced
3/4	cup chili sauce
1/3	cup onion — chopped
2	tablespoons brown sugar
2	tablespoons vinegar
2	tablespoons worcestershire sauce
1	teaspoon salt
1/4	teaspoon ginger
1/8	teaspoon crushed red pepper

In large skillet, **brown** riblets on all sides.

Add pineapple chunks and lemon slices.

In small bowl, **combine** remaining ingredients with reserved pineapple juice. Pour over riblets.

Cover, **simmer** 1 1/2 hours or until meat is tender.

Skim off fat before serving.

Per Serving: 380 Calories; 7g Fat (17.2% calories from fat); 63g Protein; 13g Carbohydrate; 1g Dietary Fiber; 173mg Cholesterol; 662mg Sodium.

Exchanges: 0 Grain(Starch); 9 Lean Meat; 0 Vegetable; 1/2 Fruit; 0 Fat; 1/2 Other Carbohydrates.

white bean chili

serves 12

3	pounds goat — ground
1	tablespoon olive oil
1/4	teaspoon cayenne pepper
1	teaspoon cumin
2	medium onions — chopped
2	cans (4 ounces each) green chiles or jalapenos, diced
1	teaspoon garlic
3	cans chicken broth
1	teaspoon salt
32	ounces navy beans, canned
20	ounces Monterey jack cheese — grated

In large pot, **cook** meat in oil to prevent sticking.

While meat is cooking, **add** next 5 ingredients. **Cook** until meat is done and onions are soft.

Add remaining ingredients.

Simmer a few hours until flavor cooks through, **stirring** occasionally.

Serve hot.

Per Serving: 416 Calories; 19g Fat (41.1% calories from fat); 42g Protein; 18g Carbohydrate; 4g Dietary Fiber; 107mg Cholesterol; 1055mg Sodium.

Exchanges: 1 Grain(Starch); 5 1/2 Lean Meat; 1/2 Vegetable; 2 Fat.

" This can also be done in a slow cooker. "

goat meat and your health

The U.S. Department of Agriculture has reported that goat meat is 50-60% lower in fat than similarly prepared beef and has 40% less saturated fat (1.1 gram) than chicken (even with the skin removed). It contains a similar amount of protein (23 mg.) as beef, pork, lamb and chicken—and even more iron (3.3 gram) than the others.

cooking goat meat

Goat meat will lose moisture and can toughen quickly during cooking since it is low in fat. Two basic rules apply:

    1) Cook it slowly.

    2) Cook it with moisture.

- Tenderness of a meat cut determines the method of cooking. Tender cuts of meat are usually best when cooked by a dry-heat method, such as roasting, broiling or frying. Less tender cuts are tenderized by cooking with moist heat, such as braising and stewing.

- Tender cuts of goat meat are the legs, ribs, portions of the shoulder cut, the loin roast and the breast. Less tender cuts are stew meats, riblets and shanks. In general, it is advisable to cook the meat slowly. Cooking any meat at low temperatures results in a more tender and flavorful product with more juice.

- The French term "Chevon" usually describes meat and dishes prepared with high-quality, young, finished goat meat. Goat meat has been a delicacy in France and Europe for many years. Latin cultures use the terms "Cabrito" and "Cabra" when referring to goat meat. About 60% of the red meat consumed in the world is goat, and approximately 95% of the world's countries are major consumers of goat meat.

"don't eat sweets if you want good teeth"

Shane, Grade 4

desserts

dessert

ingredients:

toasting

Toasting can be done with wine, champagne and water. A toast is a very special honor to the person receiving it. There are two traditional toasts:

- The first toast is at the beginning of the meal: the host or hostess will often remain seated and give a toast to welcome everyone.

- A guest should not take a sip of wine once it is poured until the host or hostess does so.

- The second toast is offered at the time of the dessert course: the host or hostess may propose a toast to the guest of honor.

- The person proposing the toast should stand; *be prepared, be brief, be seated.*

- The recipient of the toast remains seated and does not raise the glass or touch it to the lips. <u>One does not drink a toast to oneself.</u>

- The person who was toasted rises and responds with a toast, to which he/she may drink.

- Other guests may now propose toasts.

"brush your teeth every day so those nasty germs will stay away"

Brooke, Grade 4

bread pudding

Susan Ferry, IL

serves 20

pudding

1	quart heavy cream
1	cup sugar
1	teaspoon cinnamon
2	egg yolks
4	whole eggs
1	tablespoon vanilla
1	loaf cinnamon bread — cut in 1" cubes

caramel sauce

1	cup brown sugar
2	tablespoons cornstarch
4	tablespoons margarine
1	cup boiling water
2	teaspoons vanilla

Per Serving: 276 Calories; 21g Fat (68.5% calories from fat); 2g Protein; 20g Carbohydrate; trace Dietary Fiber; 124mg Cholesterol; 60mg Sodium.

Exchanges: 0 Grain(Starch); 0 Lean Meat; 0 Non-Fat Milk; 4 Fat; 1 Other Carbohydrates.

Preheat oven to 350 degrees.

In saucepan, **bring** heavy cream to boil. **Remove** from heat.

In large bowl, **combine** sugar and cinnamon.

Stir in yolks and whole eggs.

Combine cream, vanilla and egg mixture. **Fold** in bread cubes. **Pour** into 9x13 baking dish.

Place baking dish on cookie sheet with sides. **Pour** 1/2 inch water into cookie sheet.

Bake 350 degrees, 50-55 minutes or until mixture is set.

Remove from oven and immediately **pour** caramel sauce over.

caramel sauce

In saucepan, **mix** together brown sugar and cornstarch.

Add margarine and boiling water.

Cook and **stir**, over low heat, until mixture thickens. **Add** vanilla. **Pour** over pudding.

creme brulee

Diane Obenauer, OH

serves 12

4	cups heavy cream
1/4	cup granulated sugar
8	egg yolks
1/4	teaspoon salt
2	teaspoons vanilla
1	cup light brown sugar — sifted

Per Serving: 377 Calories; 33g Fat (77.0% calories from fat); 3g Protein; 19g Carbohydrate; 0g Dietary Fiber; 251mg Cholesterol; 84mg Sodium.

Exchanges: 0 Lean Meat; 0 Non-Fat Milk; 6 1/2 Fat; 1 Other Carbohydrates.

Preheat oven to 275 degrees.

In a double boiler, **bring** cream just to the boiling point. DO NOT LET BOIL.

Remove from heat, **stir** in sugar until dissolved.

In mixing bowl, **beat** eggs well. **Add** salt and vanilla.

Stir a little hot cream into egg mixture, then gradually **add** the remainder.

Pour mix into 11x7 baking dish. Custard should be about 1 1/2 inches thick.

Place dish in larger baking pan with sides. **Pour** boiling water around custard dish.

Bake 275 degrees, 1 hour, or until set.

Remove from oven, let stand to cool. **Refrigerate** overnight.

Remove from refrigerator. **Layer** 1/2 inch brown sugar over top.

Broil to bubbly then **return** to refrigerator.

Shatter top by tapping with rounded knife handle before serving.

frozen strawberry dessert

Julia N. Boettcher, NE

serves 20

20	ounces crushed pineapple in juice
8	ounces light cream cheese — lightly beaten
12	ounces strawberries — fresh or frozen (no sugar added)
8	ounces whipped topping — light

Per Serving: 84 Calories; 5g Fat (51.3% calories from fat); 2g Protein; 9g Carbohydrate; 1g Dietary Fiber; 6mg Cholesterol; 67mg Sodium.

Exchanges: 0 Lean Meat; 1/2 Fruit; 1 Fat; 0 Other Carbohydrates.

In blender, **combine** pineapple and cream cheese.

Add strawberries. **Blend** well.

Pour strawberry mix into 9x13 dish.

Fold in whipped topping. **Freeze** until firm.

Let **thaw** 10 minutes before serving.

May add 1/2 cup sugar to taste.

grandma manning's famous cheesecake
Linda Manning, IL

serves 20

crust

1	box coconut bars — crushed
1	stick butter — melted and cooled
1/2	cup sugar

filling

24	ounces cream cheese — softened
1	cup granulated sugar
4	large eggs — beaten
1	tablespoon flour
1	pinch salt
1	tablespoon vanilla
1/2	teaspoon lemon juice

Per Serving: 234 Calories; 17g Fat (65.8% calories from fat);
4g Protein; 16g Carbohydrate; trace Dietary Fiber; 87mg
Cholesterol; 165mg Sodium.

Exchanges: 0 Grain(Starch); 1/2 Lean Meat; 0 Fruit; 3 Fat; 1 Other
Carbohydrates.

crust

Preheat oven to 375 degrees. **Grease** and **flour** 9x13 baking pan.

Mix all ingredients until crumbly. **Press** into bottom of prepared pan.

Bake 375 degrees, 7 minutes.

filling

Preheat oven to 325 degrees.

In electric mixer, **beat** softened cream cheese with sugar.

Add beaten eggs, one at a time, **beating** after each addition.

Add flour and salt, **beat** about 1 minute.

Add vanilla and real lemon juice, **beat** another minute.

Pour mix into baked crust and **bake**, 325 degrees, 35-40 minutes.

Refrigerate until serving.

lance's banana delight
Marlene, Lance and Fiona Wascom, LA

serves 2

1	banana
1	tablespoon peanut butter — divided
1/4	cup coconut — divided

Per Serving: 138 Calories; 8g Fat (46.7% calories from fat);
3g Protein; 17g Carbohydrate; 3g Dietary Fiber; 0mg Cholesterol;
40mg Sodium.

Exchanges: 0 Grain(Starch); 0 Lean Meat; 1 Fruit; 1 1/2 Fat.

Slice banana on half, horizontally.

Spread peanut butter on each half.

Sprinkle each half with coconut.

Serve.

> " At age 6, my son made up this recipe for Dental Health Month.
> Now, his 1 1/2-year-old daughter helps me make her Dad's recipe. "

lemon cake custard

Marcy Celino, LA

serves 10

1 1/2	cups sugar
3	tablespoons flour
1/2	teaspoon salt
4	tablespoons butter — softened
1/2	cup lemon juice
4	eggs — separated
2	cups milk

Per Serving: 225 Calories; 8g Fat (31.4% calories from fat); 4g Protein; 35g Carbohydrate; trace Dietary Fiber; 94mg Cholesterol; 200mg Sodium.

Exchanges: 0 Grain(Starch); 1/2 Lean Meat; 0 Fruit; 0 Non-Fat Milk; 1 1/2 Fat; 2 Other Carbohydrates.

Preheat oven to 350 degrees. **Butter** 10 custard cups.

In mixing bowl, **combine** sugar, flour and salt.

Blend in softened butter. **Add** juice and **mix** thoroughly.

Stir in beaten egg yolks.

Add milk gradually.

Fold in beaten egg whites.

Pour equal amounts into 10 prepared custard cups. **Place** custard cups in pan of hot water.

Bake 350 degrees, 45 minutes.

Serve warm or refrigerate until serving.

" This has been a favorite dessert since childhood. It is wonderfully light custard beneath cake. Passed down from my mother, Lillian Coate. "

use only your own toothbrush!

macerated strawberries with balsamic vinegar

Dr. Walter and Gloria Lamacki, IL

serves 8

2	pounds strawberries — cleaned, leaving stem
6	tablespoons granulated sugar
2	tablespoons balsamic vinegar

Per Serving: 69 Calories; trace Fat (4.3% calories from fat); 1g Protein; 17g Carbohydrate; 2g Dietary Fiber; 0mg Cholesterol; 1mg Sodium.

Exchanges: 1/2 Fruit; 1/2 Other Carbohydrates.

When cleaning strawberries leave stem on to prevent water filtering into strawberry.

Then **remove** stems and **cut** the berries that are thicker than 1 inch at their broadest point.

Put all berries into serving bowl.

An hour before serving, **add** sugar, **toss** gently.

The sugar will dissolve and form a thin syrup.

Just before serving, **add** balsamic vinegar, **toss** delicately several times.

Serve immediately.

May use less sugar, depending on ripeness of berries.

"This recipe works well on its own although it goes well with a small sugar cookie."

peach ice cream

Shirley Walsh, LA

serves 20

24	ounces evaporated milk
1	can apricot nectar
3	cups granulated sugar
6	peaches — ripe and mashed
5	cups milk

Per Serving: 219 Calories; 5g Fat (18.5% calories from fat); 5g Protein; 41g Carbohydrate; 1g Dietary Fiber; 18mg Cholesterol; 67mg Sodium.

Exchanges: 1/2 Fruit; 1/2 Non-Fat Milk; 1 Fat; 2 Other Carbohydrates

Ready ice cream maker.

In mixing bowl, **combine** first 3 ingredients. **Mix** until sugar is dissolved.

Add mashed peaches. **Mix** well.

Pour into ice cream maker. **Add** milk to fill can. **Mix** well.

Freeze in ice cream maker.

peaches and cream

Pam Brown, GA

serves 12

crust

1	small instant vanilla pudding and pie filling
3/4	cup self-rising flour
1/2	cup milk
1	egg
3	tablespoons margarine

topping

1	large can peaches — sliced, drained, reserve 3 tablespoons juice
8	ounces cream cheese
1/2	cup sugar — sliced
3	tablespoons peach juice
2	tablespoons cinnamon sugar

Per Serving: 188 Calories; 10g Fat (49.1% calories from fat); 3g Protein; 21g Carbohydrate; 1g Dietary Fiber; 38mg Cholesterol; 232mg Sodium.

Exchanges: 1/2 Grain(Starch); 1/2 Lean Meat; 0 Fruit; 0 Non-Fat Milk; 2 Fat; 1 Other Carbohydrates.

crust

Preheat oven to 350 degrees. **Grease** 9x13 glass casserole dish.

In mixing bowl, **combine** all ingredients. **Spread** in bottom of prepared dish.

topping

After draining sliced peaches, **blot** dry with paper towel. **Place** on crust in two overlapping rows.

In electric mixer, **blend** cream cheese, sugar and reserved 3 tablespoons peach juice. **Dollop** on top of peaches.

Sprinkle with cinnamon sugar.

Bake 350 degrees, 45 minutes.

Cool 30 minutes. **Cut** and **serve.**

" Nice ladies dessert. " quotes

"brush your teeth without delay, and you'll get rid of tooth decay"

Alexis, Grade 4

pumpkin dessert

Julia Boettcher, NE

serves 20

crust

1 3/4	cups graham cracker crumbs
1/4	cup margarine — melted
4	tablespoons brown sugar

filling

60	large marshmallows
1/4	cup milk
2	cups pumpkin
1	teaspoon cinnamon
1/2	teaspoon ground ginger
1/2	teaspoon salt
16	ounces whipped topping, light — divided

Per Serving: 132 Calories; 3g Fat (20.8% calories from fat); 1g Protein; 26g Carbohydrate; trace Dietary Fiber; trace Cholesterol; 137mg Sodium.

Exchanges: 1/2 Grain(Starch); 0 Non-Fat Milk; 1/2 Fat; 1 1/2 Other Carbohydrates.

crust

In mixing bowl, **combine** all ingredients until crumbly. **Press** into 9x13 dish.

Reserve small amount of crumbs for top.

filling

In large saucepan, **melt** marshmallows with milk. (**Butter** pan to prevent sticking.)

Add pumpkin and spices. **Cool** completely.

Fold 8 ounces whipped topping into cooled pumpkin mix. **Pour** onto crust.

Cover with second 8 ounces whipped topping. **Sprinkle** reserved crumb crust on top.

Refrigerate overnight. **Serve** next day.

Toasting dates back into antiquity, maybe even prehistory. It was believed that evil spirits entered the body through alcoholic drinks — but were discouraged by the sound of bells. Thus, the bell-like tone of clinking glasses was thought to ward off evil spirits.

tidbits

195

rainbow
ice cream dessert

Jan Hagedorn, IN

serves 10

1	10-inch angel food cake
3	ounces strawberry gelatin powder
3	ounces lime gelatin powder
3	ounces orange gelatin powder
10	ounces frozen strawberries — sliced, partially thawed
1 1/2	cups fresh or frozen blueberries
10	ounces mandarin oranges — drained
1/2	gallon softened vanilla ice cream

Per Serving: 506 Calories; 12g Fat (20.6% calories from fat); 10g Protein; 94g Carbohydrate; 2g Dietary Fiber; 46mg Cholesterol; 457mg Sodium.

Exchanges: 1/2 Fruit; 2 1/2 Fat; 5 1/2 Other Carbohydrates.

Spray 10 inch tube pan with cooking spray.

Tear cake into pieces dividing equally into 3 bowls.

Sprinkle one bowl of cake pieces with strawberry powder, one with orange powder and one with lime powder.

Toss each until cake pieces are well coated.

Place strawberry pieces on bottom of prepared pan, **spoon** strawberries over cake, **spread** 1/3 ice cream over berries.

Repeat layers with lime-cake pieces, blueberries, ice cream, orange-cake pieces, mandarin oranges, ice cream.

Freeze until firm. **Unmold** on chilled dessert plate. **Serve.**

" My Mom always used to make this for her Euchre club. They loved it. "

"if you brush your teeth
with all your might,
your teeth will be pearly white"

Mike, Age 9

wells kringle

Dottie Hendricksen, VA

serves 8

pastry dough

1	cup flour
1	stick butter
1	tablespoon water

cream puff topping

1	stick butter
1	cup boiling water
1	cup flour
4	eggs — room temperature

icing

1 1/2	cups powdered sugar
2	tablespoons butter — softened
1 1/2	teaspoons almond extract
2	tablespoons milk — warm

Per Serving: 466 Calories; 29g Fat (54.7% calories from fat);
6g Protein; 47g Carbohydrate; 1g Dietary Fiber; 164mg Cholesterol;
295mg Sodium.

Exchanges: 1 1/2 Grain(Starch); 1/2 Lean Meat; 0 Non-Fat Milk;
5 1/2 Fat; 1 1/2 Other Carbohydrates.

pastry dough

Preheat oven to 350 degrees.

With pastry blender, **mix** all ingredients until smooth. **Roll** into two strips on cookie sheet.

cream puff topping

In saucepan, **melt** butter in boiling water. **Mix** in flour until smooth.

Add eggs one at a time, until no egg is showing.

Spread cream puff topping on pastry strips.

Bake 350 degrees, 1 hour or until topping is crisp and golden. **Cool.**

icing

In mixing bowl, **combine** all ingredients until well blended. (May only need 1 tablespoon milk.)

Frost strips. May sprinkle with blanched sliced almonds, if desired

---

yogurt ice pops

Janet G. Styers, NC

serves 16

1/3	cup sugar — or sweetener equivalent
1	cup cold water — divided
1	envelope unflavored gelatin
3	cups frozen strawberries, unsweetened — thawed and drained
16	ounces nonfat yogurt — strawberry or vanilla

Per Serving: 62 Calories; trace Fat (1.1% calories from fat);
2g Protein; 14g Carbohydrate; 1g Dietary Fiber; 1mg Cholesterol;
36mg Sodium.

Exchanges: 0 Fruit; 0 Non-Fat Milk; 1/2 Other Carbohydrates.

In small bowl, **combine** sweetener and 3/4 cup water. **Set** aside.

In saucepan, **combine** gelatin and remaining water, let **stand** 2 minutes. **Heat** until gelatin is dissolved, **remove** from heat.

Place sweetened water, gelatin mix, strawberries and yogurt in blender or food processor. (May have to do in batches.)

Cover, process to smooth.

Fill 16 popsicle molds (3 ounces each), or cups, with strawberry mixture. Insert popsicle sticks. **Freeze.**

Serve when completely frozen.

further facts about
food and dental health

- Food with sugar or starch is safer for teeth if eaten with a meal—not as a snack.

- Snacks should contribute to overall nutrition and health. Examples of healthy snacks are cheese, vegetables, yogurt, peanut butter and chocolate milk.

- A child who licks a piece of hard candy every few minutes or slowly sips a sugared drink is at high risk of developing decay. Long-lasting snacks create an acid attack as long as they are in the mouth.

- If children have poor diets, their teeth may not develop properly—creating problems in speech and appearance. Children need protein, vitamins and minerals (especially calcium and phosphorous) to build strong teeth and resist tooth decay and gum disease.

- Parents are encouraged to select meals and snacks that promote dental health and provide sound nutrition as defined by the USDA food pyramid.

"floss and brush your teeth
well, so your gums
won't swell"

Connor, Grade 4

ingredients:

eating desserts

Dessert is the final course of a meal. Wait until everyone is served before beginning to eat and be attentive to the host or hostess to see if there will be a toast.

- Do not eat dessert until toasting is finished.

- Dessert silverware may be at the top of the plate; if so, bring the spoon to the right and the fork to the left of the plate.

- If silverware is not at the table, it will be brought when dessert is served.

- Dessert may be eaten with the fork in the left hand, tines down, and the spoon in the right. Eat with the spoon and use the fork as a pusher.

- Eat pie or cake with a fork only and ice cream and pudding with a spoon. Leave the unused utensil in place on the table.

- Coffee is usually offered with dessert. It was once thought to aid in digestion.

"i am only 10, but very wise
i eat healthy and exercise
i'd like to keep my teeth in
my head, not in a glass
beside my bed"

Morgan, Grade 5

$100 coconut cake
Patsy Mitchener, IN

serves 20

1	cake mix — yellow
1	cup sour cream
1	cup sugar
2	cups coconut — flaked, divided
1	teaspoon almond extract
1	large whipped topping

Per Serving: 180 Calories; 8g Fat (39.1% calories from fat); 1g Protein; 27g Carbohydrate; 1g Dietary Fiber; 5mg Cholesterol; 128mg Sodium.

Exchanges: 0 Fruit; 0 Non-Fat Milk; 1 1/2 Fat; 1 1/2 Other Carbohydrates.

Bake cake mix as directed on box, in 9x13 pan. **Cool**. **Split** into two layers.

In a small bowl, **beat** sour cream with sugar until smooth.

Add 1 cup coconut and almond extract, **mix** thoroughly.

Spread sour cream mixture between cake layers.

Mix whipped topping and remaining cup coconut. **Ice** top and sides of cake.

Refrigerate until serving.

visit your dentist twice a year for cleanings and oral exams.

best friend cookies

Shari Carter, GA

serves 36 • yields 6 dozen

1	cup butter
1	cup brown sugar
1	cup granulated sugar
1	teaspoon vanilla
2	eggs
2	cups oatmeal
2	1/4 cups all-purpose flour
1	teaspoon baking powder
1	teaspoon baking soda
1/2	teaspoon salt
1/2	cup almonds — chopped
1/2	cup pecans — chopped
1/2	cup walnuts — chopped
1/2	cup cashews — chopped
12	ounces semisweet chocolate chips

Preheat oven to 350 degrees.

In large bowl, **combine** first 10 ingredients, **mixing** well.

Fold in next 5 ingredients, by hand.

Drop no more than 16 rounded tablespoons on ungreased cookie sheet.

Bake 350 degrees, 13 minutes. Do not overbake.

Per Serving: 219 Calories; 12g Fat (48.7% calories from fat); 4g Protein; 26g Carbohydrate; 2g Dietary Fiber; 24mg Cholesterol; 137mg Sodium.

Exchanges: 1/2 Grain(Starch); 0 Lean Meat; 2 1/2 Fat; 1 Other Carbohydrates.

" May have to struggle to incorporate all the nuts and chocolate chips, but remember it is for your best friend! "

"brushing should be a fun adventure, or you might be fitted for a denture"

Mary Patricia, Grade 2

blueberry sour cream pie

Mrs. Jonas L. Miller

serves 8

pie filling

1	cup sour cream
2	tablespoons flour
3/4	cup sugar
1	teaspoon vanilla
1/4	teaspoon salt
1	egg — beaten
2 1/2	cups fresh blueberries
1	pie crust (9 inch)

crumb topping

3	tablespoons flour
1 1/2	tablespoons butter
1/4	cup nuts — chopped

Per Serving: 334 Calories; 18g Fat (46.2% calories from fat); 5g Protein; 41g Carbohydrate; 2g Dietary Fiber; 42mg Cholesterol; 260mg Sodium.

Exchanges: 1 Grain(Starch); 0 Lean Meat; 1/2 Fruit; 0 Non-Fat Milk; 3 1/2 Fat; 1 1/2 Other Carbohydrates.

pie filling

Preheat oven to 400 degrees.

In large bowl, **combine** first 6 ingredients, **beat** until smooth.

Fold in blueberries.

Pour mixture into pie crust. **Bake** 400 degrees, 25 minutes.

Remove from oven, **top** with crumbs. **Return** to oven, bake 10 minutes more.

crumb topping

In small bowl, using pastry cutter, **combine** flour and butter until consistency of small crumbs.

Add nuts. **Mix** well.

A demitasse cup means "half-cup". It is often served in another room following dinner so guests can stretch after a long meal. The cup is half filled and sometimes served with Brandy or liqueur. A second cup is not usually offered.

tidbits

bsf cookies

Linda Lowe, OK

serves 36 • yields 6 dozen

1	cup butter
1	cup granulated sugar
1	cup brown sugar — packed
1	egg — beaten
1	cup vegetable oil
1	teaspoon vanilla
1	cup regular oats
1	cup cornflakes — crushed
1 1/2	cups coconut — flaked
1/2	cup pecans — chopped
3 1/2	cups flour
1	teaspoon baking soda
1	teaspoon salt

Per Serving: 220 Calories; 14g Fat (55.6% calories from fat); 2g Protein; 22g Carbohydrate; 1g Dietary Fiber; 19mg Cholesterol; 150mg Sodium.

Exchanges: 1 Grain(Starch); 0 Lean Meat; 0 Fruit; 2 1/2 Fat; 1/2 Other Carbohydrates.

Preheat oven to 350 degrees. **Grease** cookie sheet.

In mixing bowl, **cream** butter and sugars.

Add egg, **mix.**

Add oil and vanilla, **mix.**

Stir in oats, cornflakes, coconut and nuts, **mix.**

Add flour, baking soda and salt, **mix** thoroughly.

Drop by rounded tablespoons, 2 inches apart, on prepared cookie sheet.

Bake 350 degrees, 12-16 minutes.

Cool on wire rack. **Serve.**

"if you don't brush, you'll have to eat mush"

Chase , Age 9

check bar cookies

Steph Gross, PA

serves 12

1	cup sugar
2	cups flour
2	sticks butter
2	egg yolks
1/2	cup apricot, raspberry or strawberry jam
1	cup pecans — finely chopped

Per Serving: 378 Calories; 22g Fat (52.2% calories from fat);
4g Protein; 43g Carbohydrate; 1g Dietary Fiber; 77mg Cholesterol;
163mg Sodium.

Exchanges: 1 Grain(Starch); 0 Lean Meat; 4 1/2 Fat; 1 1/2 Other
Carbohydrates

Preheat oven to 375 degrees. **Grease** 9x9 inch pan.

Mix first 4 ingredients with pastry cutter until it forms
small crumbs.

Press 1/2 crumb mixture into prepared pan. **Press** to cover
bottom evenly.

Spread jam onto crumb mix. **Top** with remaining crumb mixture.
Press lightly.

Sprinkle with pecans.

Bake 375 degrees, 1 hour or until golden.

Cut into squares.

cherry nut bundt cake

Elizabeth Ferry, IL

serves 20

1	box cake mix — cherry chip
1	box instant pudding mix — vanilla
1 1/4	cups milk
1/2	cup vegetable oil
4	egg whites
1	cup pecans — chopped
1/3	cup frosting mix — chocolate or vanilla

Per Serving: 192 Calories; 12g Fat (53.2% calories from fat);
2g Protein; 20g Carbohydrate; 1g Dietary Fiber; 2mg Cholesterol;
211mg Sodium.

Exchanges: 0 Grain(Starch); 0 Lean Meat; 0 Non-Fat Milk;
2 1/2 Fat; 1 Other Carbohydrates.

Preheat oven to 350 degrees. **Grease** and **flour** bundt pan.

In large bowl, **mix** first 5 ingredients with electric mixer on low,
30 seconds.

Pour mixture into prepared bundt pan.

Bake 350 degrees, 50 - 60 minutes or until toothpick inserted near
middle comes out clean.

Cool in pan 10 minutes. Then turn upside down on plate and
cool completely.

In microwave, **heat** frosting to runny. **Add** pecans and dribble over
top of cake allowing icing to run down sides.

Cover until ready to serve.

coconut custard pie

Jan Miller, IN

serves 8

2	cups milk
4	eggs
3/4	cup sugar
1 1/2	teaspoons vanilla
1	dash salt
1/2	cup baking mix
1/4	cup butter — melted
1	cup coconut

Per Serving: 261 Calories; 14g Fat (48.7% calories from fat); 6g Protein; 28g Carbohydrate; 1g Dietary Fiber; 117mg Cholesterol; 239mg Sodium.

Exchanges: 1/2 Grain(Starch); 1/2 Lean Meat; 0 Fruit; 0 Non-Fat Milk; 2 1/2 Fat; 1 1/2 Other Carbohydrates.

Preheat oven to 350 degrees. **Grease** 9 inch pie pan.

In blender, **combine** all ingredients, except coconut. **Whip** until well blended.

Pour mixture into prepared pie pan.

Top with coconut. Let **set** 5 minutes.

Bake 350 degrees, 40 minutes or until browned and set. Do not overbake.

If not serving warm, **store** in refrigerator until ready to serve.

"If you've got a man in the house that loves coconut as much as my Daddy did, here is a wonderfully fast, easy and healthy pie (that makes its own crust)."

"brush them, floss them make your teeth look like a gem"

Leanne, Age 7

figgy pudding (sugarless cake)

Ele Kammerer, IL

serves 20

2	cups water
2	cups raisins
1	cup applesauce, unsweetened
2	tablespoons sweetener — artificial
2	teaspoons cinnamon
1/2	teaspoon nutmeg
1	teaspoon vanilla
2	eggs
3	cups flour
1 1/2	teaspoons baking soda
3/4	cup corn oil
1	cup walnuts — chopped

Per Serving: 238 Calories; 12g Fat (45.7% calories from fat); 5g Protein; 29g Carbohydrate; 2g Dietary Fiber; 19mg Cholesterol; 106mg Sodium.

Exchanges: 1 Grain(Starch); 1/2 Lean Meat; 1 Fruit; 2 1/2 Fat; 0 Other Carbohydrates.

Preheat oven to 350 degrees. **Grease** and **flour** 9x13 inch baking pan.

In medium saucepan, **boil** water and raisins until water is almost gone. **Cool.**

In large mixing bowl, **combine** all ingredients except nuts. **Mix** thoroughly.

Add nuts, if desired.

Pour into prepared pan. Bake 350 degrees, 25 minutes.

Place dollop of whipped topping on each square just before serving.

Freezes well.

---

fresh fruit pie

Connie Larsen, GA

serves 8

1	pie crust (9 inch) — baked and cooled
2	cups fresh peaches — cleaned and sliced
1	cup granulated sugar or sugar substitute
1	small gelatin powder — flavor to match fruit, may be sugar-free
2 1/2	tablespoons cornstarch
1	cup boiling water

Per Serving: 265 Calories; 6g Fat (20.3% calories from fat); 2g Protein; 52g Carbohydrate; 1g Dietary Fiber; 0mg Cholesterol; 174mg Sodium.

Exchanges: 1 Grain(Starch); 1/2 Fruit; 1 Fat; 2 1/2 Other Carbohydrates.

Place cleaned fruit in baked, cooled, pie crust.

In saucepan, **mix** jello, sugar and cornstarch. **Add** water. **Cook** and **stir** until thickened.

Cool. Pour over fruit in pie crust.

Chill until ready to serve.

Place dollop of whipped topping on each slice before serving.

" Any fresh fruit will do: peach, strawberry, blackberry, etc. "

lemon bars

Jane Edwards, IN

serves 20

bars

1	box angel food cake mix
1 1/2	cans (22 ounces) lemon pie filling

icing

1/4	cup butter — or margarine
3	ounces cream cheese
2	cups powdered sugar
1	teaspoon vanilla

Per Serving: 315 Calories; 7g Fat (19.2% calories from fat); 4g Protein; 61g Carbohydrate; trace Dietary Fiber; 69mg Cholesterol; 226mg Sodium.

Exchanges: 0 Lean Meat; 1 1/2 Fat; 4 Other Carbohydrates.

bars

Preheat oven to 350 degrees. **Grease** sheet cake pan.

In a large bowl, **mix** cake mix and pie filling together.

Pour into prepared pan.

Bake 350 degrees, 20 minutes. **Cool** completely before icing.

After icing, **refrigerate** until serving.

Cut into squares.

icing

In large bowl, **cream** butter and cream cheese.

Stir in powdered sugar until smooth.

Add vanilla. **Mix** thoroughly.

Ice bars and refrigerate.

"i'm the best, because i use Crest"

Jack, Grade 4

orange mandarin cake

Doris Cunningham, NC

serves 15

cake

4	eggs
1	box cake mix — yellow
1/2	cup oil
1	box instant pudding mix — vanilla
1	can mandarin oranges in juice
1	can mandarin oranges in juice — drained

icing

1	large whipped topping
1	small whipped topping
1	small can crushed pineapple — drained
1	box instant vanilla pudding mix
	banana — sliced
	strawberries, sliced

Per Serving: 288 Calories; 14g Fat (42.0% calories from fat); 3g Protein; 40g Carbohydrate; 1g Dietary Fiber; 50mg Cholesterol; 375mg Sodium.

Exchanges: 0 Lean Meat; 1/2 Fruit; 2 1/2 Fat; 2 Other Carbohydrates.

cake

Preheat oven to 325 degrees. **Grease** and **flour** 2 cake pans, 8 or 9 inch.

Combine first 3 ingredients. **Mix** on medium speed 2 minutes.

Fold in UNDRAINED can mandarin oranges, **mix** 2 minutes, medium speed.

Fold in DRAINED mandarin oranges.

Pour equal amounts mixture in both prepared pans.

Bake 325 degrees, 30 minutes.

Cool layers in pans, 10 minutes.

Turn layers out on wire rack and **cool** completely before icing.

icing

In large mixing bowl, **combine** first 4 ingredients, **mix** well.

Frost top of one cake layer, **cover** with thin slices of banana and strawberries.

Lay second layer on top of first and **repeat** frosting and fruit slices.

Frost sides of cake with whipped topping mixture only.

Refrigerate several hours before serving.

May refrigerate several days in cake protector.

" This cake is so easy, yet I have never, and I do mean never, made it that I didn't receive compliments. "

209

pineapple cream pie

Shirley Walsh, LA

serves 8 • yields 1 pie

15	ounces condensed milk, sweetened
9	ounces whipped topping — non-dairy, frozen, softened
20	ounces crushed pineapple — drained
1/3	cup lemon juice
1	teaspoon almond extract
1	graham cracker crumb pie crust

In large bowl, **mix** condensed milk and softened non-dairy topping.

Add drained pineapple, lemon juice and almond extract.

Stir together until smooth.

Pour into pie crust.

Chill several hours before serving.

Per Serving: 465 Calories; 20g Fat (38.1% calories from fat); 6g Protein; 68g Carbohydrate; 1g Dietary Fiber; 18mg Cholesterol; 247mg Sodium.

Exchanges: 0 Lean Meat; 1 Fruit; 4 Fat; 3 1/2 Other Carbohydrates.

" Doubled recipe makes 3 pies. "

pumpkin pie

Marilyn Woerner, MO

serves 8 • yields 1 pie

6	large marshmallows
1	cup milk — heated
2	tablespoons butter — or margarine
3	eggs — beaten
1/3	cup brown sugar
2/3	cup granulated sugar
1/2	teaspoon salt
1/2	teaspoon cinnamon
1/2	teaspoon nutmeg
1	cup pumpkin
1	teaspoon vanilla
1	pie crust (9 inch)

Preheat oven to 425 degrees.

In small saucepan, **melt** marshmallows in hot milk. **Add** butter, cook until melted. **Set aside.**

In large bowl, **beat** eggs well, **add** sugars, salt and spices. **Beat** until mixture is thick.

Add marshmallow mix to egg mixture. **Stir** in pumpkin and vanilla.

Pour pumpkin mixture into unbaked pie crust.

Bake 425 degrees, 10 minutes, **reduce** heat to 325 degrees, continue to bake about 25 more minutes or until tests firm.

Serve warm or cool. **Store** in refrigerator.

Per Serving: 280 Calories; 12g Fat (37.1% calories from fat); 5g Protein; 40g Carbohydrate; 1g Dietary Fiber; 82mg Cholesterol; 349mg Sodium.

Exchanges: 1/2 Grain(Starch); 1/2 Lean Meat; 0 Non-Fat Milk; 2 Fat; 2 Other Carbohydrates.

simple molasses cookies

Eleanora B. Perry, IL

serves 24 • yields 4 dozen

3/4	cup canola oil
1	cup granulated sugar
1/2	cup molasses
1	egg
2	teaspoons baking soda
2	cups flour
1/2	teaspoon cloves
1/2	teaspoon ground ginger
1	teaspoon cinnamon

Per Serving: 152 Calories; 7g Fat (41.6% calories from fat);
1g Protein; 21g Carbohydrate; trace Dietary Fiber; 8mg Cholesterol;
110mg Sodium.

Exchanges: 1/2 Grain(Starch); 0 Lean Meat; 1 1/2 Fat; 1 Other
Carbohydrates

In a large bowl, **combine** all ingredients. **Mix** well.

Chill dough at least one hour to make manageable. May chill
several hours.

Preheat oven to 375 degrees. **Grease** cookie sheets.

Form dough into 1 - 1 1/2 inch balls, **roll** in sugar, place on
prepared cookie sheet, 2 inches apart.

Bake 375 degrees, about 8 minutes. Do not overbake.

Remove from oven immediately, **cool** and **eat**.

sour cream softies

Linda Iczkovitz, IN

serves 30 • yields 5 dozen

3	cups flour — sifted
1	teaspoon salt
1/2	teaspoon baking powder
1/2	teaspoon baking soda
1/2	cup margarine
1 1/2	cups sugar
2	eggs
1	teaspoon vanilla
8	ounces sour cream — or yogurt
1/2	cup cinnamon sugar

Per Serving: 144 Calories; 5g Fat (31.1% calories from fat);
2g Protein; 23g Carbohydrate; 1g Dietary Fiber; 16mg Cholesterol;
144mg Sodium.

Exchanges: 1/2 Grain(Starch); 0 Lean Meat; 0 Non-Fat Milk; 1 Fat;
1 Other Carbohydrates.

Preheat oven to 400 degrees. **Grease** cookie sheets.

In a large bowl, **combine** flour, salt, baking powder and baking
soda. **Set** aside.

In another large bowl, **cream** margarine and sugar.

Beat in eggs and vanilla.

Add flour mix and sour cream alternately, to creamed mixture.

Drop by rounded tablespoons 4 inches apart on cookie sheet.

Bake 400 degrees, 12 minutes. Cookies will be lightly golden
on edges.

Remove from cookie sheets. **Roll** in cinnamon sugar.

Cool on wire racks.

" Very soft, light, cake-like cookie. "

> "brush, brush as best you can try to catch the little green man"
>
> Harrison, Grade 1

strawberry cream pie

Pam Brown, GA

serves 8 • yields 1 pie

1	pie crust (9 inch)
8	ounces cream cheese — softened
1/3	cup granulated sugar
1/2	teaspoon almond extract
1	cup heavy cream — whipped
4	cups strawberries, fresh — halved, washed, hulled
1/3	cup semisweet chocolate chips
1 1/2	teaspoons shortening

Per Serving: 375 Calories; 30g Fat (70.0% calories from fat); 4g Protein; 24g Carbohydrate; 1g Dietary Fiber; 72mg Cholesterol; 242mg Sodium.

Exchanges: 1/2 Grain(Starch); 1/2 Lean Meat; 0 Non-Fat Milk; 6 Fat; 1 Other Carbohydrates.

Bake pie crust as directed on package. **Cool**.

In small bowl, **beat** cream cheese, sugar and almond extract together.

Fold in whipped cream.

Spoon cream mixture into pie crust.

Arrange strawberries on cream mixture. **Chill** at least 3 hours.

In small bowl, **melt** chocolate chips and shortening.

Drizzle chocolate mix over pie.

Chill 3 more hours.

Serve chilled.

" Pretty and Yummy! " quotes

sugarless apple pie

Joan Lawrence, IN

serves 8

pie

6	ounces apple juice, frozen concentrate — divided
2	tablespoons cornstarch
1	tablespoon margarine
1	teaspoon cinnamon
5	large apples — peeled and sliced
2	pastry dough, 9 inch
1	tablespoon margarine — melted

crumb topping

2/3	cup quick-cooking oats
2	tablespoons flour
3	tablespoons margarine — melted
2	tablespoons apple juice, frozen concentrate — thawed

Per Serving: 198 Calories; 8g Fat (34.9% calories from fat); 2g Protein; 32g Carbohydrate; 3g Dietary Fiber; 0mg Cholesterol; 90mg Sodium.

Exchanges: 1/2 Grain(Starch); 1 1/2 Fruit; 1 1/2 Fat.

Preheat oven to 400 degrees.

Peel and **slice** apples. **Place** in bowl and set aside.

In small measuring cup, **mix** 2 tablespoons juice concentrate with cornstarch.

In small saucepan, **heat** remaining juice concentrate. **Blend** in cornstarch mix, **stirring** until smooth.

Stir in margarine and cinnamon. **Pour** mixture over apples, **toss** to **coat**.

Place bottom pastry in pie pan, **cover** with apple mixture, **top** with second pastry.

Brush top with margarine. **Vent** top crust. (Cut holes in top.)

Bake 400 degrees, 30-50 minutes, depending on type of apples used.

Serve warm or cooled.

crumb topping variations

In medium bowl, **combine** oats and flour. **Add** melted margarine and thawed juice concentrate.

Mix until crumbly.

Sprinkle over apples in pie pan.

apple cobbler (bottom pastry only with crumb topping),
apple crisp (no pastry only crumb topping)

wipe your baby's gums with clean gauze or cloth after each feeding. start dental visits by age one or when the first tooth appears.

baby bottle tooth decay

Sometimes parents do not realize that baby teeth can decay soon after they appear in the mouth (around six months). This condition is called Baby Bottle Tooth Decay or Early Childhood Caries. By the time decay is noticed, it may be too late to save the teeth.

- Decay occurs when sweetened liquids are given and left clinging to a child's teeth for long periods.
- Many sweet liquids, including milk, formula and fruit juice, cause problems. Bacteria in the mouth use these sugars as food. They then produce acids that attack the teeth. Each time your child drinks these liquids, acids attack for 20 minutes or longer. After many attacks, the teeth can decay.
- It is not only what you put in your child's bottle that causes decay—but how often and for how long. Giving a child a bottle of sweetened liquid many times a day or allowing a child to fall asleep with a bottle can also weaken the teeth.

"if you brush up and down
and all around,
you will avoid a dentist's frown"

Olivia, Grade 2

chocolate

ingredients:

eating chocolate

Chocolate comes in many forms, including cakes, cookies, pies, puddings, confections, sauces and chocolate indescribables. Whatever the form, chocolate is always delicious!

• Chocolate cake, if non-sticky and served in small portions, may be eaten with the fingers. Otherwise, use a fork.

• Chocolate cookies and chocolate donuts may be eaten with your fingers. Do not dunk cookies or donuts in public.

• Chocolate ice cream and pudding are eaten with a spoon.

• Chocolate sauces can be used over almost any dessert. Sauces are eaten with a spoon.

• When dipping small bites of cake or fruit into chocolate sauce, never double dip.

• Chocolate confections may be eaten with your fingers unless they are unwieldy; in that case, secure them with a fork and cut one bite-size piece at a time.

"good dental health makes pearly wealth"

Catherine, Age 7

aimee's chocolate peanut butter bars

Aimee Mays, AZ

serves 20

first layer

1	cup graham cracker crumbs
2	cups powdered sugar
1	stick butter — melted
1	cup peanut butter, creamy

second layer

2/3	cup peanut butter, creamy
12	ounces semisweet chocolate chips

third layer

1	jar sprinkles

Per Serving: 314 Calories; 21g Fat (56.5% calories from fat); 6g Protein; 30g Carbohydrate; 2g Dietary Fiber; 12mg Cholesterol; 175mg Sodium.

Exchanges: 1/2 Grain(Starch); 1/2 Lean Meat; 4 Fat; 1 1/2 Other Carbohydrates.

first layer

Grease and **flour** 9x13 pan.

In large bowl, **combine** graham cracker crumbs, powdered sugar, melted butter and peanut butter. (Can be mixed with little hands, or if you insist, a spoon.)

Spread graham cracker mixture on bottom of prepared 9x13 pan. **Spread** evenly or not so evenly, with fingers.

second layer

In small microwavable bowl, **combine** 2/3 cup peanut butter and 12 ounces chocolate chips.

Melt in microwave, approximately 1 - 2 minutes, **stirring** after each minute. **Repeat** until mixture is smooth.

Spread melted peanut butter-chocolate mixture on top of graham cracker mixture in pan.

third layer

Decorate mixture in 9x13 pan with sprinkles.

Refrigerate until set. **Cut** into small squares. **Serve.**

" A kid favorite, it tastes like a peanut butter cup.

This recipe is best when Grandma helps. "

"brush your teeth three times a day if you don't your smile will pay"

Lucy, Grade 3

ashley's magic wands

Ashley Mays, AZ

serves 8

16	ounces white or dark chocolate
1	teaspoon paraffin wax
1	pound salted pretzel rods
1	jar sprinkles — multi-colored

Per Serving: 220 Calories; 2g Fat (42.9% calories from fat); 5g Protein; 0g Carbohydrate; 0g Dietary Fiber; 0mg Cholesterol; 732mg Sodium.

In microwave, on high, **melt** chocolate and paraffin about 1 minute. May need to repeat. **Stir** to smooth.

Dip pretzel in melted chocolate until half pretzel is coated.

Sprinkle on sprinkles. **Lay** on wax paper to dry.

Store in sealed container.

Like coffee and tea, chocolate was originally used for medicinal purposes. The taste was unpleasant until sugar was added to make it delicious.

tidbits

chocolate eclair dessert

Sharon B. Wilson, KY

serves 15

pudding

2	small boxes instant French vanilla pudding and pie filling
2	cups milk
9	ounces whipped topping — thawed
1	box graham crackers

frosting

3	tablespoons margarine
2	unsweetened baking chocolate squares
3	tablespoons milk
2	tablespoons light corn syrup
1	teaspoon vanilla
1 1/2	cups powdered sugar

Per Serving: 224 Calories; 10g Fat (38.5% calories from fat); 2g Protein; 34g Carbohydrate; 1g Dietary Fiber; 5mg Cholesterol; 158mg Sodium.

Exchanges: 0 Grain(Starch); 0 Lean Meat; 0 Non-Fat Milk; 2 Fat; 2 Other Carbohydrates.

pudding

In small bowl **mix** pudding and milk. Let **stand** in refrigerator 15 minutes.

Add whipped topping. **Mix** well.

Layer graham crackers in bottom of buttered 9x13 pan.

Spread with 1/2 pudding mixture.

Repeat graham cracker and pudding layers.

Top with frosting. **Refrigerate** overnight.

Cut into squares and **serve**.

frosting

In large saucepan, **melt** margarine and chocolate.

Add other frosting ingredients. **Beat** until smooth.

"The light and creamy texture has guests asking for seconds every time. Best prepared one day in advance."

chocolate mound cake

Pam Sullivan, TN

serves 20

cake

1	box German chocolate cake mix
4	eggs
1/2	cup sugar
1/2	cup oil
1	cup water

frosting

1	cup milk
1/2	cup sugar
23	large marshmallows
7	ounces coconut — flaked
2	cups sugar
1/2	cup milk
3	tablespoons cocoa
3	tablespoons light corn syrup
1	stick butter

Per Serving: 371 Calories; 17g Fat (38.8% calories from fat); 3g Protein; 56g Carbohydrate; 2g Dietary Fiber; 52mg Cholesterol; 189mg Sodium.

Exchanges: 0 Grain(Starch); 0 Lean Meat; 0 Fruit; 0 Non-Fat Milk; 3 Fat; 3 1/2 Other Carbohydrates.

cake

Preheat oven to 350 degrees. **Grease** two, 8 inch round cake pans.

In large mixing bowl, **combine** first 5 ingredients. **Mix** well.

Pour equal amounts into each prepared cake pan.

Bake 350 degrees, until toothpick inserted in center comes out clean.

Cool completely before frosting.

frosting

In large saucepan, **combine** milk and sugar. **Boil** 1 minute.

Add marshmallows and coconut. **Stir** until marshmallows are melted. **Spread** between cake layers.

In large saucepan, **combine** 2 cups sugar, 1/2 cup milk, cocoa and corn syrup. **Boil** 1 minute.

Remove from heat, add butter. **Beat** until butter is melted and mixture is cool.

Frost top and sides of cake.

"This most marvelous cake brings back childhood memories."

"i brush my teeth every day to keep them clean in every way"

Todd, Grade 1

chocolate nests

Suzanne Bowden, TX

serves 10 • yields 20 cookies

1	small can shoestring potatoes
6	ounces chocolate chips or caramel
2	tablespoons crunchy peanut butter

Per Serving: 118 Calories; 8g Fat (54.2% calories from fat); 2g Protein; 13g Carbohydrate; 1g Dietary Fiber; 0mg Cholesterol; 28mg Sodium.

Exchanges: 0 Grain(Starch); 0 Lean Meat; 1 1/2 Fat; 1/2 Other Carbohydrates.

In heavy saucepan, over low heat, **melt** peanut butter.

Add chocolate (or caramel) chips. **Stir** until melted.

Remove from heat and **stir** in shoestring potatoes.

Drop by teaspoon on waxed paper.

Refrigerate to cool.

" *Prize winning recipe became a favorite at family gatherings.* "

chocolate shake

Jacob Catey, Rylee Catey and Cavan Williams, IN

serves 5

4	cups skim milk — cold
1	small box chocolate pudding mix — instant or sugar-free instant
3	drops vanilla
1/2	cup ice cubes

Per Serving: 143 Calories; 1g Fat (4.8% calories from fat); 7g Protein; 28g Carbohydrate; trace Dietary Fiber; 4mg Cholesterol; 174mg Sodium.

Exchanges: 1 Non-Fat Milk; 0 Fat; 1 Other Carbohydrates.

In blender, **combine** first 3 ingredients. **Cover. Blend** to smooth.

Add ice cubes. **Cover. Blend** until combined.

Let **stand** 3 minutes to thicken slightly.

Serve in 8 ounce glasses.

chocolate shots

Kimberly Lamacki McGuire, IL

serves 12 • yields 2 dozen

1	cup butter
1	cup powdered sugar
2	tablespoons vanilla
1 1/2	cups flour
1/2	teaspoon baking soda
1	cup oatmeal — not instant
5 3/4	ounces chocolate flavored sprinkles

Per Serving: 263 Calories; 16g Fat (54.5% calories from fat); 3g Protein; 27g Carbohydrate; 1g Dietary Fiber; 41mg Cholesterol; 209mg Sodium.

Exchanges: 1 Grain(Starch); 3 Fat; 1/2 Other Carbohydrates.

With electric mixer, **cream** butter at medium speed until soft. **Add** sugar and vanilla. **Beat** until blended.

Add flour, baking soda and oatmeal. **Mix** well.

Refrigerate dough in mixing bowl 10 minutes.

Remove dough from refrigerator and **form** into sausage-like rolls, about 2 inches in diameter.

Place chocolate sprinkles in pie plate or shallow pan. **Roll** the "sausages" in chocolate to coat completely.

Wrap in plastic wrap, refrigerate overnight. (Will keep several days if well wrapped.)

Remove "sausages" from refrigerator. **Cut** into cookie slices 1/2 inch thick. **Place** on greased cookie sheet.

Bake 325 degrees, 20 minutes or until lightly browned and somewhat firm to touch.

"With a recipe passed down by Kim's grandmother, Kim was a 1996 Chicago Tribune Holiday Cookie contest winner. Grandma has passed on but her recipe lives."

x-rays detect dental problems early—
saving you time, money
and unnecessary discomfort.

"brush your teeth and you will see you will be cavity free with me"

Rebekah, Grade 4

chocolate tower

Nash Binkley, TN

serves 15

1	box fudge brownie mix
2	packages instant chocolate mousse
6	one ounce chocolate covered toffee bars
16	ounces whipped topping

Per Serving: 368 Calories; 24g Fat (55.2% calories from fat); 4g Protein; 39g Carbohydrate; 1g Dietary Fiber; 78mg Cholesterol; 99mg Sodium.

Exchanges: 4 1/2 Fat; 2 1/2 Other Carbohydrates.

Prepare brownie mix as directed on package. **Cool** completely and break into small pieces.

Prepare the chocolate mousse according to the directions on the package.

Using a food processor, **crush** chocolate covered toffee bars into small pieces. **Reserve** approximately 1 tablespoon.

Layer one-half the broken brownies, chocolate mousse, toffee bars and whipped topping in a trifle dish. **Repeat** ending with whipped topping.

Sprinkle reserved candy on top as garnish.

Serve immediately or chill, covered, until ready to serve.

" From the grandson of Trish Nash. "

crunchy chocolate bars

Nate Williams, IN

serves 20

1	package fudge brownie mix
10 1/2	ounces miniature marshmallows
2	cups semisweet chocolate chips
1	cup peanut butter
1	tablespoon butter
1	1/2 cups crispy rice cereal

Per Serving: 289 Calories; 15g Fat (42.6% calories from fat);
5g Protein; 40g Carbohydrate; 2g Dietary Fiber; 2mg Cholesterol;
140mg Sodium.

Exchanges: 1/2 Grain(Starch); 1/2 Lean Meat; 2 1/2 Fat; 2 Other
Carbohydrates..

Preheat oven to 350 degrees. **Grease** 9x13 baking pan.

Prepare brownie mix as directed on package. **Bake** 350 degrees,
28 minutes (don't over bake). **Remove** from oven.

Top brownies with marshmallows, return to oven and **bake**
3 minutes longer. **Cool.**

In saucepan, **mix** chocolate chips, peanut butter and butter.
Cook and **stir** over low heat until smooth.

Remove from heat, **stir** in cereal. **Spread** cereal mix
over brownies.

Refrigerate 1- 2 hours before cutting into squares.

" This is very good, easy to make and looks great. Too bad it has so many calories ! "

hot cocoa mix in a jar

Kelly Ann Christensen, IL

serves 12

6	cups instant non-fat dry milk
1 1/2	cups sugar
1	cup cocoa
2	tablespoons cocoa
1 1/2	cups miniature marshmallows — optional

Per Serving: 346 Calories; 2g Fat (3.9% calories from fat);
23g Protein; 64g Carbohydrate; 3g Dietary Fiber; 11mg
Cholesterol; 325mg Sodium.

Exchanges: 1/2 Grain(Starch); 0 Lean Meat; 2 1/2 Non-Fat Milk;
0 Fat; 2 Other Carbohydrates.

In 2 quart jar or container, **mix** all ingredients.

Seal with a lid.

" Put these instructions on the jar: Measure 1/2 cup cocoa mix into a mug.

Stir in 1 cup boiling water. "

mocha oatmeal cake

Anna Marie Hartzell, PA

serves 12

2	tablespoons instant coffee powder
1/3	cup boiling water
1	cup rolled oats
1/2	cup butter or margarine — softened
1	cup granulated sugar
1	cup packed brown sugar
1	teaspoon vanilla
2	eggs
1 1/2	cups sifted all purpose flour
1	teaspoon baking soda
1/2	teaspoon salt
2	tablespoons cocoa

frosting

3	tablespoons butter or margarine
2	cups granulated sugar
	salt to taste
1	teaspoon vanilla
2	tablespoons instant coffee (reserved from above)

Per Serving: 451 Calories; 12g Fat (23.4% calories from fat); 4g Protein; 84g Carbohydrate; 1g Dietary Fiber; 60mg Cholesterol; 319mg Sodium.

Exchanges: 1 Grain(Starch); 0 Lean Meat; 2 1/2 Fat; 4 1/2 Other Carbohydrates.

Preheat oven to 350 degrees. **Grease** 9x9 baking pan.

In small bowl **combine** coffee and boiling water. **Reserve** 2 tablespoons for frosting.

In mixing bowl, **pour** coffee mix over oats. **Stir. Cover.** Let **stand** 20 minutes.

In mixer, **cream** butter and sugars until fluffy. **Blend** in vanilla and eggs. **Add** to oatmeal mix.

In medium bowl, **sift** dry ingredients. **Add** to oatmeal mix.

Bake 350 degrees, 50-55 minutes in prepared pan.

frosting

In electric mixer, **combine** all ingredients until smooth.

Frost cake when cooled.

Variation: Use 3 - 9 inch round cake pans. Spread any flavor jam between layers. Frost only top and sides of cake.

" This is my husband's favorite cake. I make it every year for his birthday. "

225

noelle's champion chocolate torte

Nancy Steele, IN

serves 16

cake

3	eggs
1 1/4	cups sugar
1	cup melted butter
1	teaspoon vanilla
1	dash salt
1/2	cup cocoa
1/3	cup flour
3/4	cup finely chopped pecans

chocolate glaze

3	tablespoons butter
3	tablespoons light corn syrup
1	tablespoon water
1	cup semisweet chocolate chips

Per Serving: 305 Calories; 21g Fat (59.7% calories from fat); 3g Protein; 30g Carbohydrate; 2g Dietary Fiber; 72mg Cholesterol; 173mg Sodium.

Exchanges: 1/2 Grain(Starch); 0 Lean Meat; 4 Fat; 1 1/2 Other Carbohydrates.

Preheat oven to 350 degrees. **Butter** bottom only of 8 inch cake pan. **Line** with "release" foil.

In large bowl, **beat** first 5 ingredients on high speed of electric mixer for 3 minutes, until smooth and thick, scraping bowl often.

Add cocoa and flour, blending well.

Stir in pecans.

Spread batter in prepared pan. **Bake** 350 degrees, 35 minutes.

Cool 15 minutes on wire rack. Turn out of pan, peel off foil, cool completely before glazing and garnishing.

chocolate glaze

In saucepan, over medium heat, **combine** and cook butter, syrup and water. **Stir** constantly until mixture boils.

Remove from heat, **stir** in chocolate chips until melted. **Cool** mix to room temperature, then **pour** glaze over cake.

Garnish is optional. Try white chocolate curls, fruit, or whatever you like.

" My daughter, Noelle, won Champion at the County Fair with this recipe. Not healthy or "low" anything, but so rich and delicious you'll only need a tiny slice ! "

super delicious popcorn snack

Fran Schmidt

serves 8

8	cups popcorn — popped
3	cups puffed corn cereal — unsweetened
2	cups corn chips — crushed
1	pound white chocolate — chips or discs

Per Serving: 395 Calories; 26g Fat (53.9% calories from fat); 4g Protein; 46g Carbohydrate; 5g Dietary Fiber; 0mg Cholesterol; 169mg Sodium.

Exchanges: 1 Grain(Starch); 5 Fat; 2 1/2 Other Carbohydrates

In microwave, on 50% power, **melt** chocolate. Takes about 4 minutes. **Stir** once.

In large bowl, **combine** other ingredients. **Add** melted chocolate. **Stir** to coat evenly.

Spread on 2 large sheets waxed paper to dry (until chocolate is no longer shiny).

To serve, **break** into pieces. **Store** left-overs in sealed container.

ultimate chocolate dessert

Connie Slyby, IN

serves 12

crust

7	tablespoons butter
1/2	cup graham cracker crumbs
1	cup chopped pecans
1	teaspoon cinnamon

filling

1	cup butter — softened
1/2	box powdered sugar
1	tablespoon vanilla
1	tablespoon cornstarch
18	ounces semisweet chocolate chips — melted
6	eggs
1/4	cup whipping cream

Per Serving: 549 Calories; 45g Fat (70.0% calories from fat); 6g Protein; 38g Carbohydrate; 3g Dietary Fiber; 160mg Cholesterol; 280mg Sodium.

Exchanges: 1/2 Grain(Starch); 1/2 Lean Meat; 0 Non-Fat Milk; 9 Fat; 2 Other Carbohydrates.

crust

Preheat oven to 325 degrees.

In small bowl, **mix** all ingredients well. **Press** in bottom of 9 inch springform pan.

Bake, 325 degrees, 8 minutes. **Cool**.

filling

Preheat oven to 350 degrees.

With electric mixer, **beat** butter, powdered sugar, vanilla and cornstarch until blended.

Add melted chocolate chips. **Mix** well.

Add 3 eggs at a time.

Add whipping cream, **mix** well.

Pour over crust in springform pan, bake 350 degrees, 10 minutes.

Cool in refrigerator 6 hours before cutting and removing from pan.

chocolate and dental health

Chocolate lovers take heart! Chocolate does not cause tooth decay. In fact, it actually contains ingredients that help inhibit tooth decay.

Recent research shows:

- Chocolate changes the cavity-causing potential of its sugar. The cocoa bean, its main ingredient, stops the production of bacteria and decay.
- Cocoa butter in chocolate melts quickly and helps to clear the mouth, thereby reducing the potential to cause cavities.
- Chocolate is one of the snack foods that is *least* likely to contribute to tooth decay since it contains phosphate and other minerals.
- Chocolate promotes less tooth decay than many other carbohydrate foods, such as crackers, raisins and granola bars.

To promote healthy teeth and gums and prevent decay:

- Brush twice a day with fluoride toothpaste.
- Floss daily to remove decay—causing bacteria between teeth where toothbrush bristles can't reach.
- Eat a balanced diet from the five major food groups, following the USDA Food Pyramid.
- Limit between-meal snacks and give preference to nutritious foods.

"white and bright your teeth will stay, as long as you brush them twice a day"

Destiny, Age 7

stop the pop!

ingredients:

drinking from bottles and cans

As in everything else, drinking out of bottles and cans has certain etiquette. However, in today's world, safety may be an issue—and safety overrides etiquette.

• Casual situations allow drinking out of bottles or cans.

• In some public places, it is important to be in charge of your drink at all times. In those cases, individuals should get a bottle or can that is closed and be in charge of opening it.

• Avoid open glasses at large parties or concerts where the possibility of having something dropped into it is greater.

• Ideally, canned or bottled beverages should be poured into a glass.

• Hang onto your drink at all times. If you lose sight of it, get a new one.

• Some restaurants will open a bottle or can in front of you and pour the beverage into your glass at the table.

blueberry shake

Ruth Alsobrook, TN

serves 2

1/8	teaspoon ground nutmeg
3/4	cup half and half — or skim milk
1	cup vanilla ice cream — or reduced fat ice cream
1	cup fresh blueberries — or frozen
2	tablespoons sugar — or substitute
1/2	teaspoon vanilla

Per Serving: 344 Calories; 18g Fat (45.8% calories from fat); 5g Protein; 43g Carbohydrate; 2g Dietary Fiber; 63mg Cholesterol; 94mg Sodium.

Exchanges: 0 Grain(Starch); 1/2 Fruit; 1/2 Non-Fat Milk; 3 1/2 Fat; 2 Other Carbohydrates.

Frost 2 glasses.

In blender, **combine** all ingredients. **Blend** until frothy. **Scrape** sides of blender occasionally.

Pour into frosted glasses.

May **garnish** with whipped cream or blueberries.

> " A refreshing fruit milkshake that is just as delicious in the low fat version.
> My husband doesn't like blueberries but he enjoys this shake! "

"look at my smile so you can see what brushing and flossing has done for me"

Joel, Grade 1

cantaloupe shake

Lori Daby, CA

serves 1

1/3	cantaloupe — ripe, diced
3/4	cup vanilla ice cream
1/4	cup milk
1/4	teaspoon vanilla

Place ingredients in blender, in order listed.

Blend. Serve.

May substitute 2 ripe peaches for cantaloupe

Per Serving: 304 Calories; 13g Fat (38.2% calories from fat); 7g Protein; 42g Carbohydrate; 1g Dietary Fiber; 52mg Cholesterol; 126mg Sodium.

Exchanges: 1 Fruit; 0 Non-Fat Milk; 2 1/2 Fat; 1 1/2 Other Carbohydrates.

" My older sister made this for me after I had my wisdom teeth out. I have since made it for my children. Delicious and nutritious! "

double peach slush

Tammi Catey, IN

serves 3

8	ounces peach yogurt
8 3/4	ounces canned peaches — drained
6	ice cubes — or more if needed

In blender, **mix** yogurt and peaches to smooth.

With blender running, **add** ice cubes one at a time, to form slush.

Serve immediately.

Per Serving: 138 Calories; 3g Fat (16.8% calories from fat); 3g Protein; 28g Carbohydrate; 1g Dietary Fiber; 10mg Cholesterol; 39mg Sodium.

Exchanges: 1 Fruit; 1/2 Non-Fat Milk; 1/2 Fat; 1/2 Other Carbohydrates.

"go to the dentist twice a year so you will have no dental fear"

Alyssa, Grade 3

"brush and floss, you'll be the boss"

Glenn, *Age 9*

frosted cider cup

Karen Simonsen, UT

serves 1

1/4	cup sherbet — lemon
12	ounces apple cider — chilled

Per Serving: 227 Calories; 1g Fat (5.1% calories from fat); 1g Protein; 54g Carbohydrate; trace Dietary Fiber; 25mg Cholesterol; 25mg Sodium.

Exchanges: 2 1/2 Fruit; 0 Fat; 1 Other Carbohydrates.

Drop lemon sherbet into large glass.

Pour apple cider over sherbet.

Serve at once.

" Easy and Fast "

fruit smoothie

Eleanora B. Perry, IL

serves 4

14	ounces sweetened condensed milk
8	ounces yogurt — low fat, plain or vanilla
1	small banana — cut
8	ounces crushed pineapple
2	tablespoons lemon juice
1	cup fresh strawberries

Per Serving: 427 Calories; 11g Fat (21.9% calories from fat); 11g Protein; 76g Carbohydrate; 2g Dietary Fiber; 41mg Cholesterol; 154mg Sodium.

Exchanges: 1 Fruit; 0 Non-Fat Milk; 2 Fat; 3 1/2 Other Carbohydrates.

Place all ingredients in blender.

Blend on high to smooth.

Serve immediately.

hot percolator punch

DebraAnn Grimes, TN

serves 12

3	cups pineapple juice
3	cups cranberry juice cocktail
1 1/2	cups water
2	lemon slices
1 1/2	teaspoons whole cloves
2/3	cup firmly packed brown sugar
2	cinnamon sticks — broken

Per Serving: 124 Calories; trace Fat (1.7% calories from fat); trace Protein; 32g Carbohydrate; 1g Dietary Fiber; 0mg Cholesterol; 9mg Sodium.

Exchanges: 0 Grain(Starch); 1 Fruit; 0 Fat; 1 Other Carbohydrates.

Mix juices and water in a 12-cup percolator.

Place remaining ingredients in percolator basket.

Percolate through entire cycle.

Serve hot.

"This recipe fills your kitchen with a wonderful aroma few can resist." quotes

In warm weather, bees are attracted to sweet beverages and may fly into an open container. Examine any liquid before drinking it to help prevent being stung in the mouth or throat.

tidbits

your teeth will last a lifetime—
if you take care of them!

peanut butter banana smoothie
Patsy Dumas, IN

serves 4

2	bananas — sliced
1/3	cup peanut butter
1/2	cup plain yogurt
1	cup half and half — or 2% milk
12	ice cubes

In a blender, **mix** all ingredients on high, until smooth.

Serve immediately.

Per Serving: 279 Calories; 19g Fat (58.3% calories from fat); 9g Protein; 22g Carbohydrate; 3g Dietary Fiber; 26mg Cholesterol; 142mg Sodium.

Exchanges: 1/2 Grain(Starch); 1/2 Lean Meat; 1 Fruit; 1/2 Non-Fat Milk; 3 1/2 Fat; 0 Other Carbohydrates.

strawberry ice
Shelly Geddes, UT

serves 8

16	ounces frozen strawberries
12	ounces apple juice, frozen concentrate
1	cup water
1/8	cup fresh lime juice
2	tablespoons lime zest — grated

In blender, **mix** all ingredients. **Blend** well.

Serve as smoothie or **freeze** to desired consistency.

Per Serving: 117 Calories; trace Fat (1.8% calories from fat); 1g Protein; 30g Carbohydrate; 1g Dietary Fiber; 0mg Cholesterol; 12mg Sodium.

Exchanges: 2 Fruit.

" A favorite family recipe. It is low on sugar, big on taste.

Quick and easy to make, it is perfect for a hot summer night. "

"brush your teeth every day
to keep cavities away
then you'll have a great day"

Nathan, Age 9

strawberry smoothie

Eleanora B. Perry, IL

serves 2

8	ounces yogurt — low fat, strawberry
1	banana — cut up
1/2	cup skim milk
1	cup fresh strawberries — or frozen

Per Serving: 167 Calories; 4g Fat (22.1% calories from fat); 7g Protein; 27g Carbohydrate; 3g Dietary Fiber; 16mg Cholesterol; 85mg Sodium.

Exchanges: 1 1/2 Fruit; 1/2 Non-Fat Milk; 1/2 Fat; 1/2 Other Carbohydrates.

Place all ingredients in blender.

Blend on high to smooth.

Serve immediately.

tea smoothy

Patsy Dumas, IN

serves 2

1	cup tea — unsweetened, iced (your favorite)
1	mango — chopped, or other fruit like peaches, strawberries, etc.
1/4	cup orange juice — or juice of 1 lemon
1	tablespoon honey
	ice cubes

Per Serving: 156 Calories; trace Fat (1.8% calories from fat); 3g Protein; 39g Carbohydrate; 3g Dietary Fiber; 0mg Cholesterol; 24mg Sodium.

Exchanges: 1 1/2 Fruit; 1 Other Carbohydrates.

In blender **mix** all ingredients. **Blend** to thick and smooth.

Add more ice as needed.

Serve immediately.

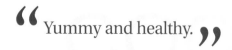

" Yummy and healthy. "

quotes

victorian tea

Janet G. Styers, NC

serves 10 • yields 10 cups

4	tea bags — individual
4	cups boiling water
11 1/2	ounces cranberry-raspberry juice — frozen, thawed
4	cups water — cold
	ice cubes
	fresh mint — as garnish

Place tea bags in teapot. **Add** boiling water. **Cover**. **Steep** 5 minutes.

Remove and discard tea bags.

Refrigerate tea in covered container.

Just before serving, in 2 1/2 quart pitcher, **combine** juice concentrate and water. **Stir** in tea.

Serve over ice. **Garnish** with fresh mint.

\er Serving: 23 Calories; 0g Fat (0.0% calories from fat); trace Protein; 6g Carbohydrate; trace Dietary Fiber; 0mg Cholesterol; 8mg Sodium.

Exchanges: 1/2 Fruit; 0 Other Carbohydrates.

> " Pretty and refreshing, this flavored iced tea was well received at a bridal shower. Try it any time for a different iced tea taste. "

winter warm-up

Dr. Phil Catey, IN

serves 16

1	quart apple cider
1	pint cranberry juice
1	cup orange juice
3/4	cup lemon juice
1	cup sugar — or substitute
1	teaspoon whole cloves
1	teaspoon whole allspice
3	sticks cinnamon — broken

In percolator, **mix** all ingredients. **Perk** through entire cycle.

Serve hot.

Per Serving: 109 Calories; trace Fat (1.5% calories from fat); trace Protein; 28g Carbohydrate; 1g Dietary Fiber; 0mg Cholesterol; 4mg Sodium.

Exchanges: 0 Grain(Starch); 1 Fruit; 0 Fat; 1 Other Carbohydrates.

> 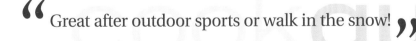 " Great after outdoor sports or walk in the snow! "

stop the pop!

Children of all ages need strong, healthy teeth to chew food easily, pronounce words properly and speak clearly, smile with confidence—and provide space for their developing adult teeth.

There is a growing concern among America's dentists that children and teens are consuming record numbers of sugar-filled sodas and sweetened fruit drinks that can lead to cavities—and destroy teeth.

- A nationwide "Stop the Pop" campaign is being spearheaded by the Missouri Dental Association to inform children and teens of the perils of drinking too much soda pop and sweetened fruit drinks. Over indulgence can be harmful—not only to teeth but to overall health. In addition to cavities, heavy pop consumption has been linked to diabetes, obesity, kidney stones, heart disease and osteoporosis.

how decay starts

- Sugar in pop combines with bacteria in the mouth to form acid.
- The acid attacks teeth.
- Each acid attack lasts about 20 minutes, and acid attacks start over again with every sip.
- Ongoing acid attacks weaken tooth enamel.
- Cavities begin when tooth enamel is damaged.

how to reduce decay:

- Drink pop in moderation.
- Don't sip on soda or sweetened drinks for extended periods of time.
- Use a straw to keep the sugar away from your teeth.
- After drinking, rinse your mouth with water to dilute the sugar.
- Never drink pop or juice before sleeping without brushing first.
- Read labels. Regular pop is high in sugar and acid, and diet pop contains acid too.
- Drink water instead of pop.
- Get regular dental checkups and cleanings to remove bacteria buildup (plaque).
- Floss regularly and use a fluoride toothpaste.

The Foundation for Dental Health Education supports the campaign to Stop the Pop as part of its mission to enhance the public's dental health awareness.

zzzz: grind when you sleep?
    see a dentist for a nightguard.

dining check-up

host, hostess duties

Being prepared and considerate of guests can reduce anxiety and stress when entertaining.

- A considerate host or hostess should ask for food preferences (strong dislikes or philosophical influences) and/or allergies.

- When introducing guests who are not well acquainted, tell a little about each one — thus providing a starting point for conversation.

- A guest of honor is seated to the right of the host.

- Mixing people up at the table provides for interesting conversation.

- Using place cards avoids confusion about where your guests should sit.

taking your place at the table

Whether you sit at a table for a seven-course meal or a four-course luncheon, some basic rules apply for navigating a meal gracefully.

- Do not touch anything on the table until everyone is seated.
- Be prepared for the custom of saying grace. If the custom differs from yours, sit quietly and do not touch anything until grace is finished.
- Wait for the host, hostess or senior person at the table to pick up his or her napkin.
- Napkins should be unfolded on your lap. Large napkins should remain folded in half with the fold toward your waist. Smaller napkins can be unfolded completely. Paper napkins are treated the same as cloth.
- Assess the table before you pick up any silverware. If in doubt about what to use first, watch someone in the know. The amount of flatware corresponds to the number of courses being served. Start from the outside and work in.
- Flatware placed above the plate is for dessert. Sometimes, it is brought with the dessert course.
- Glasses are at the right of the dinner plate. Bread and butter plates are to the left. The acronym BMW (Bread-Meal-Water) is a way to keep the order straight.
- When you leave the table briefly, place your napkin on the seat of the chair and push it under the table. In some upscale restaurants, the wait staff may refold your napkin and place it on the table or on the arm of your chair.
- At the end of a meal, pick up the napkin by the center and place it loosely to the left of the place setting.

essentials for a savvy diner

The following guidelines provide a quick review of some of the essential "Table Manners" used in *DISHING UP SMILES*. Manners specific to eating certain foods are included within those sections.

- Assess the table and pause before picking up any dining utensils. Wait for your host, hostess or senior person to start. Once you have started eating, never put the utensils back on the table.

- Place napkin on your lap to unfold. When leaving the table temporarily, place the napkin on the chair. At the end of the meal, place it to the left of plate.

- When encountering a multi-course meal with multiple utensils, start from the outside and work in toward the plate.

- Cut one bite at a time.

- Solids, such as bread and butter, are on the left of the dinner plate, and liquids are on the right.

- Break bread in bite size pieces and butter one bite at a time over the bread and butter plate.

- When someone asks for the salt, pass both the salt and pepper in anticipation of their need.

- Keep personal items, such as purses, glasses and cell phones, off the table. Purses should stay on your lap or under the chair.

- Refrain from putting on make-up, combing hair, picking teeth or blowing your nose vigorously at the table. "If you do it in the bathroom, don't do it at the table."

- If someone offers a toast to you—do not drink to yourself!

- If in doubt about what to do, watch someone at the table who knows.

- When leaving the table temporarily, do not announce where you are going. Say simply, "Excuse me."

- Chew with your mouth closed. Take small bites to avoid talking with food in your mouth.

- Try a little of everything presented unless you are allergic to a certain food.

- Don't talk about food likes and dislikes at the table.

- Maintain good posture. Keep arms and elbows off the table.

- Don't push your plate away from you when you have finished eating. Wait until everyone is finished before plates are cleared.

- Don't gesture with your knife and fork.

THE MAP OF A FORMAL PLACE SETTING

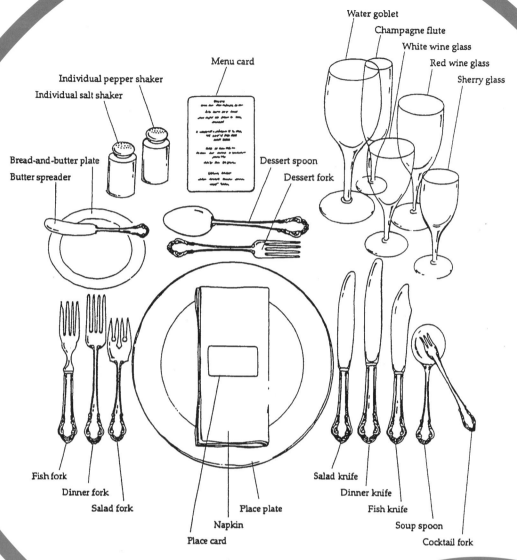

Individual pepper shaker
Individual salt shaker
Menu card
Bread-and-butter plate
Butter spreader
Dessert spoon
Dessert fork
Water goblet
Champagne flute
White wine glass
Red wine glass
Sherry glass

Fish fork
Dinner fork
Salad fork
Place plate
Napkin
Place card
Salad knife
Dinner knife
Fish knife
Soup spoon
Cocktail fork

THE MAP OF A SIMPLE PLACE SETTING

Butter spreader
Bread-and-butter plate
Dessert spoon
Dessert fork
Water Goblet
Wine Glass

Napkin
Salad fork
Dinner fork
Place plate
Dinner knife
Soup spoon

Illustrations provided by
Protocol School of Washington®

242

Professional Courtesy

Karen Hickman and Nancy Sweet of Professional Courtesy have long held an interest in etiquette and protocol.

After completing their training and certification at the esteemed Protocol School of Washington®—a major resource for The Joint Military Attaché School of Washington, D.C.—their energies have been directed toward developing programs that bring the most current and universally accepted etiquette to the business community and contemporary society.

Seminars for business include *Business Etiquette, Dining Skills, How to Succeed in the International Arena* and *Dine Like a Diplomat*. As graduates of The Tea School, they also offer *Etiquette and Protocol of Tea*, which combines the latest in social and business etiquette with an appreciation for the cultural and historical significance of tea. Three courses are designed specifically for children and young adults, and two special programs on *Medical Office Etiquette* and *New Employee Training* round out their extensive curriculum.

Their contribution to *DISHING UP SMILES* adds a special dimension that AADA knows readers will enjoy and appreciate.

contact information:

Professional Courtesy, P.O. Box 15353, Fort Wayne, IN 46885-5353
Karen Hickman: 260/486-7758 • karhic@aol.com
Nancy Sweet: 260/432-8581 • nksweet01@aol.com

Napkins were often the size of bath towels before people used silverware when dining. Table linens were a sign of wealth and passed along in estates. Some of the finest linens came from Damascus, hence the name "damask."

finger bowls

A finger bowl is usually served at very formal dinners. One may never encounter a finger bowl, but if you do, there are some guidelines to avoid making a faux pas. The bowl contains tepid water and a lemon slice or rose petals. These help cut any grease left on fingers and provide a refreshing scent to ones fingers.

- The finger bowl may be presented on the dessert plate (1) before the dessert, with a doily underneath. If it arrives before dessert, place it (with the doily) where the bread and butter plate had been. (2)

- If this is the case, after dessert bring the bowl and doily (3) down in front of you.

- Often, the finger bowl is served after the dessert and put in front of each guest.

- Whatever the timing of presentation, when it is time to use it, dip your finger tips in the bowl, one hand at a time and dry them on a napkin.

- A key point is to not drink out of your finger bowl! This is not a weak soup.

"brush and floss equals gloss"

Lenora, Age 8

thankful helpings

connie slyby

dinah catey

jan miller

norine bertagni

meet the
AADA
dishing
up
smiles
committee

susan ferry

patsy dumas

jan hagedorn

jean weathers

susan martindale

dishing up smiles chairman patsy dumas

has been the spark behind numerous successful fundraising projects — both in her community and in dentistry. When she was asked in October 2002 to develop and lead an AADA project to help fund dental health education in the United States, she responded with her characteristic leadership ability, creative energy and contagious enthusiasm. *DISHING UP SMILES* is the culmination of two years of daily volunteer effort and the involvement of many individuals who she invited to help her move the project from conception to reality. A recipient of the coveted *AADA Thelma J. Neff Distinguished Service Award*, Patsy has endeared herself to numerous friends and colleagues. She is a past president of the Alliance of the Indiana Dental Association, having also served as treasurer, parliamentarian, DHE chair and Ways & Means chair. She has also served the Alliance of the Isaac Knapp District Dental Society for 35 years in many capacities, including president. A seasoned international traveler who has led a dozen porcelain and crystal-buying trips in France, Germany, and Italy, Patsy is married to Dr. James E. Dumas, an oral and maxillofacial surgeon from Fort Wayne, Indiana. Three of their six children have chosen careers in dentistry.

dishing up smiles co-chairman connie slyby

has been a dynamic member of the Alliance of the American Dental Association for 35 years and a relentless champion for *DISHING UP SMILES* in asking over 400 dental businesses and organizations for financial support. For her, the book has been a dawn-to-dusk cooking venture—along with her many other volunteer responsibilities in the Alliance of the Indiana Dental Association and the AADA. Currently, Connie is the newly elected AADA secretary—having previously been comptroller, DHE chair, PR chair, and treasurer of the Foundation for Dental Health Education. A past president of the Alliance of both the IDA and the Isaac Knapp District Dental Society, she is a recipient of the *IDA Special Service Award*, the *AIDA Golden Heart Award* and the *AADA Thelma J. Neff Distinguished Service Award*. Connie continues to practice dental hygiene parttime in her husband's family dental office in Fort Wayne, Indiana, where she and Dr. Roland Slyby reside. They are parents of Dr. David Slyby, a general dentist and fiancé of the book's photographer, Colette Simon.

dishing up smiles editor dinah catey

is a founding member and charter president of the Alliance of the Wabash Valley Dental Society, organized in 1987. Since then, she has served the local, state and national alliances in numerous capacities, including chairing AADA Conference 2000—a six-day event that brought hundreds of alliance volunteers from across the country to Indiana's capitol city for intensive leadership training. As editor of *DISHING UP SMILES*, she has planned and organized the book's contents, kneaded the recipes, researched their nutritional content, and served as primary liaison with the printer, Modern Graphics. Dinah is a past president of the Alliance of the Indiana Dental Association and a recipient of the *AIDA Golden Heart Award* and the *Wabash Valley Alliance MVP Award*. An R.N. employed parttime in an oral, maxillofacial and cosmetic operating room, she and her husband, Dr. Philip Catey, reside in Gas City, Indiana, where he practices general dentistry with their daughter, Dr. Mara Catey Williams, and dental technician son, Cameron Catey.

dishing up smiles co-editor jan miller

has spent 17 years in association management—first as executive director of the Isaac Knapp District Dental Society and currently as director of development for the Indiana Dental Association Foundation for Dental Health. Her volunteer involvement in *DISHING UP SMILES* has brought professional writing and editing expertise to the book—and a cutting editor's eye to solicitations and correspondence of the committee. Jan is a founding member and editor of the American Society of Dental Foundation Executives and a past president of the Association of Component Society Executives of the ADA. She was named an Honorary Member of the Indiana University School of Dentistry Alumni Association in 2002 and is a recipient of the *IDA Special Service Award*, the *IDA President's Citation* and three journalism awards from the International College of Dentists. She and her husband Bob, a teacher and coach, reside in Bloomington, Indiana.

recipe coordinator norine bertagni

became involved in the Alliance of the Illinois State Dental Society in 1995 when she was asked to co-chair the Ways & Means Committee and then develop and co-edit the Illinois Alliance cookbook, *Tastebuds— A Collection of Family Treasures*. That "preparation" placed her in a perfect position to be tapped as recipe coordinator for *DISHING UP SMILES*— a job that included organizing taste-testers for the more-than 600 recipes submitted to her Wauconda, Illinois, doorstep. Besides that huge undertaking, she has served in many executive positions in the alliance, including president of both the Alliance of the Illinois State Dental Society and the Alliance of the Chicago Dental Society, and as a delegate and alternate to several AADA conventions. Norine is married to Palatine family dentist and cook, Dr. Hugo F. Bertagni.

business manager susan ferry

served as co-chair of the 2000 Alliance of the American Dental Association Annual Convention in Chicago and as editor of KEY, the AADA newsletter, when it was recognized in 2001 by the International College of Dentists for its attractive redesign. Her participation in *DISHING UP SMILES* has been fundamental, as she chaired the Dental Health Slogan Contest, selected winning slogans from the children of America and continues to "keep the books"—and direct book sales. Susan serves on the board of the Foundation for Dental Health Education and is immediate past president of the Alliance of the Illinois State Dental Society, having gone through the chairs as president, president-elect, vice president and treasurer. She and Dr. John Ferry, a general dentist, reside in Taylorville, Illinois, where she has a home-based association consulting and meeting-planning business, SDF Management Services.

publicity chairman jean weathers

is immediate past president of the Alliance of the Georgia Dental Association and an alliance member of 29 years. As publicity chair for *DISHING UP SMILES*, she has been responsible for communicating the importance of the project to alliance members nationally through *KEY* and state alliance publications. With release of the book, she turns her attention to the national media to reach the eating and buying public and heighten their dental health awareness. Jean has served as alliance legislative chair at the state, local and national levels and received the prestigious *ADA ADPAC Award*—the first Alliance member ever to be so honored. She belongs to the Alliance of the Northern District Dental Society and is a recipient of their *Meritorious Service Award*, as well as the *AADA Thelma J. Neff Distinguished Service Award*. Her husband, Dr. Dwight R. Weathers, is vice chairman of Pathology, Oral, Head & Neck Division at the Emory University School of Medicine in Atlanta.

marketing chairman susan martindale

is immediate past chair of the Foundation for Dental Health Education— the charitable arm of the Alliance of the American Dental Association. An alliance member of 25 years, she has also served as president of AADA and president of the Alliance of the Mississippi Dental Association. With a reputation for noteworthy achievements *(She spearheaded the Mark McGwire baseball card program that raised over $100,000 for the AADA Foundation.)*, she will now stir up interest in *DISHING UP SMILES* as she develops plans to market the book throughout the United States. Susan's service to dentistry includes membership on the Samuel Harris Grant Review Committee of the ADA Foundation. She is a recipient of the AADA's highest honor, the *Thelma J. Neff Distinguished Service Award*, and resides in Monticello, Mississippi, with her husband, Dr. Daniel G. Martindale, a family dentist.

ex-officio member jan hagedorn is the newly

inducted AADA president—an honor received following 35 years of service to the local, state and national alliances. As AADA president-elect, she was the primary liaison between *DISHING UP SMILES* and ADA headquarters. Jan knows the staff well at 211 E. Chicago Ave. —having served as AADA vice president, treasurer, District 4 trustee, editor and reference committee chair. She is a founding member of the Foundation for Dental Health Education; past president of both the Alliance of the Indiana Dental Association and Isaac Knapp District Dental Society, and recipient of the *IDA Special Service Award*, the *AIDA Golden Heart Award* and the *AADA Thelma J. Neff Distinguished Service Award*. She is married to Dr. Lloyd Hagedorn, a periodontist and 7th District ADA trustee. They reside in Fort Wayne, Indiana, where they are esteemed by their dental colleagues for their leadership, generosity and friendship.

photographer colette simon
is a 2001 graduate of the Rochester Institute of Technology, with a Bachelor of Arts degree in professional photographic illustration. Since entering the world of professional photography, her work has been included in the Professional Photographers of America General Exhibit Book and the International Loan Collection. Working from her southwest Fort Wayne studio, Captured Moments — and on location, Colette's photographic artistry has enhanced *DISHING UP SMILES*. She is a member of the Professional Photographers of America and the Professional Photographers of Indiana.

We gratefully acknowledge all of the contributors to *DISHING UP SMILES*.

Educational Grant from Pfizer — Makers of Listerine

section sponsors

AADA District V (Illinois, Missouri, Tennessee)

Alliance of the Brevard County Dental Society

Alliance of the California Dental Association

Alliance of the Florida Dental Association

Alliance of the Georgia Dental Association

Alliance of the Indiana Dental Association

Alliance of the Isaac Knapp District Dental Society

Alliance of the Mississippi Dental Association

Amore Art Goats

Belmont

Dupont Oral & Maxillofacial Surgery, PC

Dr. & Mrs. Gerald Bird

Dr. & Mrs. James E. Dumas

Florida Dental Association

GE Medical Protective

IMG/Relyaid

Massachusetts Dental Society

North Carolina Dental Society

Oral Health Products

Pennsylvania Dental Association

Pizza Hut of Fort Wayne

Procter & Gamble

Helen J. Tiedge Family

financial patrons

Alliance of the Chicago Dental Society

Alliance of the Richmond Dental Society

Hugo Bertagni, D.D.S

Philip L. Catey, D.D.S.

James E. Dumas, D.D.S.

John Ferry, D.D.S.

Foundation for Dental Health Education

Lloyd Hagedorn, D.D.S., M.S.D.

Indiana Dental Association

Daniel G. Martindale, D.D.S.

Robert C. Miller

Mississippi Dental Association

Oral B

Ron Slyby, D.D.S.

Dwight R. Weathers, D.D.S., M.S.D.

information & publication contributors

John Bertagni

Boer Goats (Jack and Anita Mauldin)

Jacqueline J. Davis

Sheila Duda

James E. Dumas, D.D.S.

Jean Ferrone

Delaine Hall

Richard Haught, D.D.S.

Laffin K Goats

Gloria Lamacki

Trish Rubik-Rothstein

Douglas Torbush, D.D.S.

Shirley Walsh

Baron Whateley, D.D.S.

photographic models

Robert S. Bechert

David Bleeke, D.D.S.

Anastasia M. Buchholz

Antonio Cardenas

Rylee Catey

George Cooper

Grant Crawford

Austin Dellinger

Ethan Dellinger

Marissa Dellinger

Austin Dumas

Chelsea Dumas

Amanda Frey

Jared Frey

Brooke Gabrek

Rachel Hoagburg

David Lewright

Hope Lewright

Jane H. Martin

Journey Masters

David Peters

Coltonn Peterson

Kay Peterson

Samantha Rahrig

Amanda Simon

Andrea Simon

Denise Simon

Jessica Simon

Rachel Simon

Jill Stetzel

Leah Stetzel

Charlie Stoner

Freddie Stoner

Haley Stronczek

Michel R. Sturm, D.D.S.

Caroline Sweet

Aurelius D.Todd

Ryan Tom

Ellie Vollmer

Karlie Walker

Cavan Williams

Jordan Young

Dennis J. Zent, D.D.S.

Wendy J. Zent

recipe taste testers

Jonathan Barsness

Sarah Barsness

Susan Barsness

Debbie Brown

Kendell Christensen

Nancy Colantino

Sammie DuVal

Judy Ecklund

Gretchen Frydrchowicz

Beth Gavzer

Nadine Gerling

DebraAnn Grimes

Mary Higgins

Christine Maggio

Dennis Manning, D.D.S.

Linda Manning

Lori Maurer

Victor Michet

Celeste Nicholas

Eleanora Perry

Steven Preusker

Elizabeth Thornton

Jessica Thornton

Mary Beth Thornton

Dorothy Unger

slogan contest organizers & judges

Lee Ann Beane

Marcy Celino

Elizabeth Ferry

Chrissy Foxworth

DebraAnn Grimes

Linda Manning

Lori Maurer

Marianne Moss

Julene Newland-Pyfer

Rose Pendleton

Eleanora Perry

Dennise Peterson

Sherry Pippen, D.M.D.

Rosemary Seago

Elizabeth Stormo

Becky Sullivan

Ellen Tom

Sandra Turner

Jennifer Walker

Crunchy Wells, D.M.D.

Karen Williams

Lisa Wilson

making recipes healthy

In choosing from the recipes in *DISHING UP SMILES*, readers are encouraged to make the necessary modifications to meet their own dietary needs—especially in the areas of reducing fat, cholesterol, sodium/salt and sugar. With a few simple modifications, recipes can be made healthier—while keeping their delicious taste. The following tips may be used as a guideline:

to reduce fat and cholesterol:

In Recipes with Dairy Products, Choose:

- Skim milk, 1% or 2% low-fat milk, evaporated skim milk and low-fat buttermilk
- Low-fat or non-fat, sweetened condensed milk
- Light or fat-free sour cream
- Fat-free Half & Half *(not suitable for making candy)*
- Fat-free or low-fat whipped topping
- Low-fat cottage cheese
- 2% low-fat or fat-free cheese
- Skim Ricotta cheese
- Farmer's cheese
- Neufchatel or fat-free cream cheese

In Recipes with Meat, Poultry and Fish, Choose:

- MEAT—
  Lean cuts of meat, such as beef round, eye of round, rump, flank, sirloin, goat meat, pork tenderloin, lean ground meat or lean ground turkey or chicken.
  Trim all visible fat before cooking and drain off fat during cooking.
  Cook stews and soups in advance; refrigerate and then remove solidified fat.
- POULTRY—
  White meat over dark and remove skin before cooking.
  Use a rack in a roasting pan so fat drains off.
  Use low-fat or fat-free smoked turkey sausage.
- FISH—
  Fresh fish, fresh frozen fish and frozen fish.
  Canned tuna and canned salmon packed in water.

In Recipes with Eggs, Fats and Oils, Choose:

- EGGS—
  Two egg whites for one egg or use egg substitutes, found in the freezer section or dairy case.
  Egg substitutes are made from real eggs and are fat free, cholesterol free and pasteurized.
  They can be used in cooking and baking recipes that call for uncooked eggs by following package directions.
- FAT AND OILS—
  Low-fat mayonnaise and salad dressings.
  Light margarine or light butter for spreading and for flavor in cooking
  (but regular margarine or butter for baking).
  Use butter substitutes or fat-free butter-flavored sprays for flavor on vegetables.

Use non-stick pots and pans to prepare foods, like pancakes and omelets that require some fat, and for browning meats and sautéing or reheating vegetables.

Use non-fat cooking sprays or the end of a stick of margarine or a pastry brush dipped in oil to give a light coating of fat for sautéing.

Use vegetable oils for salad or cooking. Choose canola, olive or peanut oil.

- **OTHER—**
    Use bacon bits or Canadian bacon.
    Use reduced-fat peanut butter.
    Use fat-free canned cream soups.

to reduce sugar:

- Sugar in recipes can be reduced by one-third to one-half.
- Use canned fruit packed in its own juice or light syrup.
- Use reduced-calorie pancake and waffle syrup.
- Use low-sugar or sugar-free fruit spreads.
- Use sugar substitutes. There are many different brands to choose from. Follow package directions for making substitutions, as the intensity of sweetness varies greatly, and not all sugar substitutes are appropriate for baking and/or cooking.

to reduce salt/sodium in seasoning:

- Salt in recipes can be reduced by one-half.
- Choose sodium-reduced salt or salt-free seasonings and seasoning blends.
- Use herbs and spices like basil, thyme, sage, oregano, poultry seasoning, curry powder, celery seed, rosemary, seasoned pepper, chives, dill and cayenne pepper.
- Substitute garlic powder and onion powder for "salt" versions.
- Choose condiments that are reduced in calories or lower in sodium, like "lite" soy sauce.
- Omit salt in recipes that call for processed canned foods, which already contain salt.
- Select canned vegetables, vegetable juices and soups marked "no salt added."

recipe measurement conversions:

cup	fluid ounce	tablespoon	teaspoon	milliliter
1 c	8 oz	16 T	48 t	237 ml
3/4 c	6 oz	12 T	36 t	177 ml
2/3 c	5 oz	11 T	32 t	158 ml
1/2 c	4 oz	8 T	24 t	118 ml
1/3 c	3 oz	5 T	16 t	79 ml
1/4 c	2 oz	4 T	12 t	59 ml
1/8 c	1 oz	2 T	6 t	30 ml
1/16 c	1/2 oz	1 T	3 t	15 ml

tidbits

guide to recipes

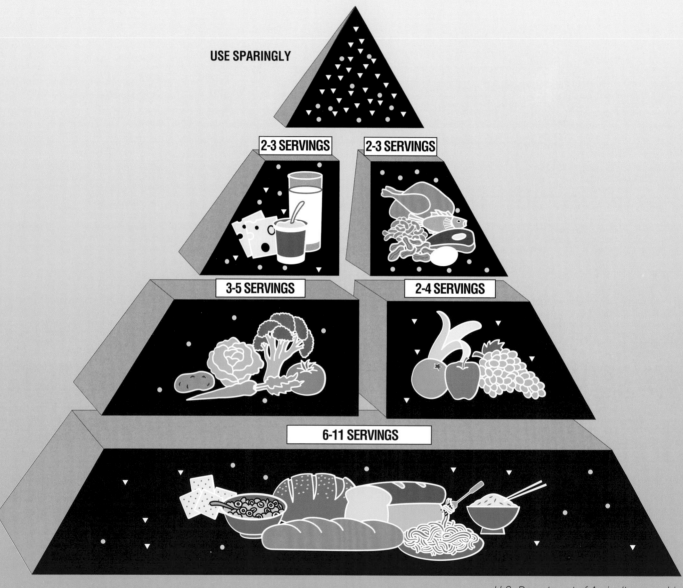

USE SPARINGLY

2-3 SERVINGS **2-3 SERVINGS**

3-5 SERVINGS **2-4 SERVINGS**

6-11 SERVINGS

U.S. Department of Agriculture graphic

this guide is based on the usda food guide pyramid

The Food Pyramid illustrates the research-based food guidance system developed by the U.S. Department of Agriculture (USDA) and supported by the U.S. Department of Health and Human Services (HHS). This dietary guideline for children and adults is not a rigid prescription but a general guide to assist consumers in choosing a healthful diet that provides the nutrients and calories needed to maintain healthy weight. Complete information is available from the USDA. The illustration of the food pyramid is courtesy of the USDA and the HHS.

listing by food group

"even if you're in a rush, you must take some time to brush"

Camille, Age 7

254

fruit group

(2-4 servings per day)
A Serving = 1 medium apple, banana, orange, pear;
1/2 cup chopped, cooked or canned fruit;
3/4 cup fruit juice

index by section

"brush your very best, so you can get in the treasure chest"

Dezaray, Grade 1

Dishing up s

Tooth-Friendly Recipes, Table Manners and Tips for Dental Health
from the Alliance of the American Dental Association

to purchase
additional copies of
DISHING UP SMILES, contact:

**Alliance of the
American Dental Association**
211 East Chicago Ave.,
Ste. 730
Chicago, IL 60611-2616

telephone:
800/621-8099, Ext. 2865

Visa and MasterCard
accepted.

to obtain an order form for *DISHING UP SMILES*, contact:
Alliance of the American Dental Association online at: www.AllianceADA.org
Direct purchase is not available online.

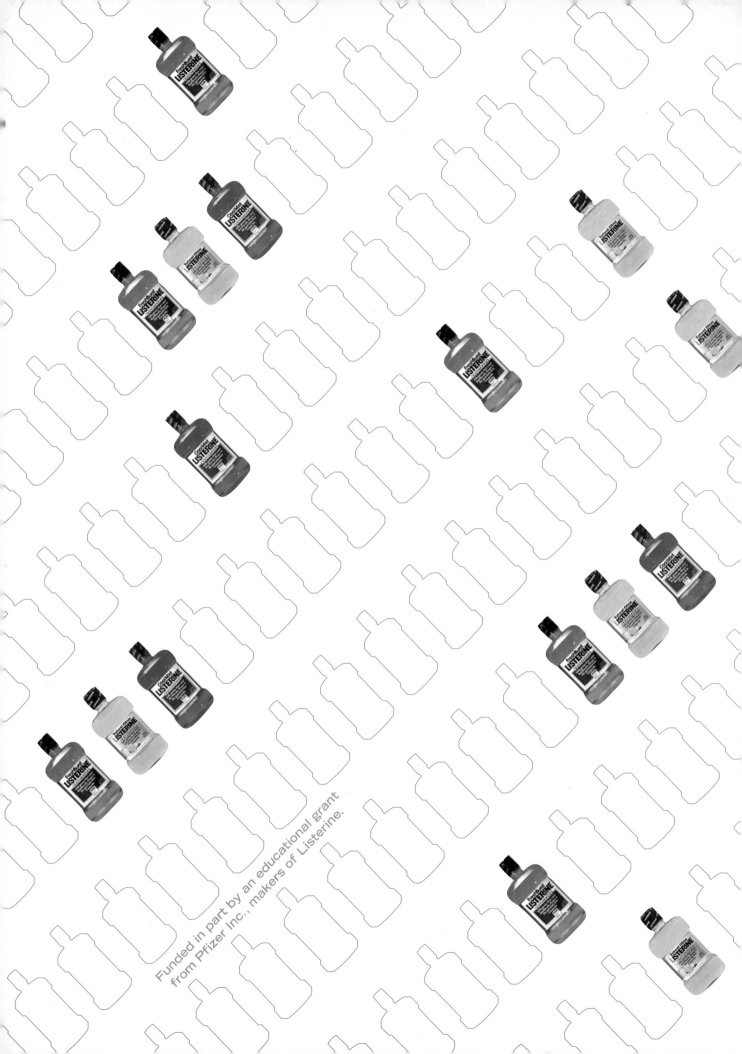

Funded in part by an educational grant from Pfizer Inc., makers of Listerine.